# Dorothy Heathcote:
## collected writings on education and drama

# Dorothy Heathcote

*collected writings on education and drama*

Edited by Liz Johnson and Cecily O'Neill

## Hutchinson

London   Melbourne   Sydney   Auckland   Johannesburg

Hutchinson & Co. (Publishers) Ltd

An imprint of the Hutchinson Publishing Group
17–21 Conway Street, London W1P 6JD

Hutchinson Publishing Group (Australia) Pty Ltd
16–22 Church Street, Hawthorn, Melbourne, Victoria 3122

Hutchinson Group (NZ) Ltd
32–34 View Road, PO Box 40–086, Glenfield, Auckland 10

Hutchinson Group (SA) (Pty) Ltd
PO Box 337, Bergvlei 2012, South Africa

First published 1984
Reprinted 1985
© Liz Johnson and Cecily O'Neill 1984
Set in 11 on 12pt VIP Ehrhardt by
D. P. Media Limited, Hitchin, Hertfordshire
Printed and bound in Great Britain by
Anchor Brendon Ltd, Tiptree, Essex

**British Library Cataloguing in Publication Data**
Heathcote, Dorothy
  Dorothy Heathcote: collected writings on
  education and drama.
  1. Drama in education
  I. Title      II. Johnson, Liz      III. O'Neill, Cecily
  792'07        PN3171

ISBN 0 09 149261 0

# Contents

5

# Foreword

A few years ago when Dorothy Heathcote was asked by the BBC to take part in a series of programmes where each contributor was to be asked to talk about his or her heroes from the past and present, one of the people she considered including was an English village schoolmistress, Miss Harriet Finlay-Johnson, who was developing a progressive approach to drama teaching at the turn of the century. Miss Finlay-Johnson, who published a fascinating account of her work in *The Dramatic Method of Teaching* anticipated Dorothy's approach to drama in a number of respects. Indeed, if the intervening drama pioneers had taken more notice of Harriet Finlay-Johnson's dramatic method the story of drama teaching in this century might have taken a different turn. (It is curious how drama innovators tend to ignore each other – I do not expect to find in the Heathcote writings in this volume any reference to any drama enthusiast other than herself – it is perhaps something to do with a necessary independence of mind.)

When Dorothy Heathcote began her professional life at Durham University in the early 1950s, she brought to her drama teaching what had been absent for nearly forty years: a high degree of respect for knowledge. Both she and Miss Finlay-Johnson used drama to increase children's respect for science and the humanities as well as the arts. Previous pioneers had given quite different emphases: Caldwell Cook believed in the importance of the artist's craftsmanship; Peter Slade preferred the 'play' approach to dramatic expression; and Brian Way trained children in life skills of intuition, sensitivity, etc. Dorothy Heathcote brought back drama to the track of pursuing knowledge.

Her philosophy is of course superior to Miss Finlay-Johnson's and indeed, to that of many of our educationalists today. Her assumptions about the integrated relationship between art and science are in advance of many of our educational leaders whose understanding does not go beyond little divisions of knowledge competing with each other for space in the curriculum.

It has taken teachers a long time to grasp Dorothy's view of drama and learning (perhaps, in all fairness, one should concede it has taken her a long time to articulate it, but it is not easy to find the new language when new ground is being broken), but one innovatory aspect of her work which 'hit' people straightaway because it presented itself so obviously in her practice was that for her, drama was a large group experience. This represented much more than a new methodology; it was a fundamental challenge to all those practitioners in drama who were pursuing Brian Way's much quoted dictum that drama teachers are concerned with 'the individuality of the individual'. Dorothy intuitively knew that the very essence of drama is its commonality. As a gifted and committed teacher she of course respects the importance of each individual, but she also knows that drama is a means of uniting their differences in a communal expression.

It is interesting to note that in introducing 'whole group' drama she was also reviving a respect for the group which was emerging from some writing early in the century – before the cult of the individual took hold. Joseph Lee, for example, in his book *Play in Education* published in 1915 talks about the symbolic meaning of the circle – a shared bond among a group of people. Peter Slade, however, some forty years later although using similar terminology to Lee, gives a contrasted interpretation to a circle's symbolism. For Slade the circle is what each child is at the centre of: each child has his or her own personal circle. It took Dorothy Heathcote to swing the emphasis away from this psychological symbolism to an anthropological one.

Dorothy was a 'first' in so many things connected with drama education it is difficult to know what to select. But perhaps her risk-taking methodology with its special use of teacher-in-role is the technique for which she is most well known. I am among the few people who in the early 1960s was close enough to her to watch her develop and refine this most dynamic of teacher strategies. Like many others I resisted its usage at first, not because it was not effective, but because the idea of a *teacher* actually *joining in*, was more than my traditional teacher-training and attitude to professionalism could stomach!

Which brings me to the final and perhaps the most remarkable innovation. Dorothy Heathcote has challenged what a teacher *is*. It is easy for someone like me, who only works in schools as a visitor, to assimilate her code of what a teacher stands for, but for many teachers who are trapped by the system what she is offering must seem like the Holy Grail – forever out of reach. But she demands that teachers are bigger than any system. So, as she might put it: 'What's keeping you? Go on. Get Cracking . . . read the rest of this book for a start!'

And I promise you . . . it is a book that will stir you to 'think big'.

GAVIN BOLTON
University of Durham

# Introduction

It would be a sad waste if, in the foreword to a book on Drama in Education published in AD 2050, Dorothy Heathcote's enormous contribution to the educational development of teachers and children was summarized in a couple of lines, in the same way that Harriet Finlay-Johnson's work has been mentioned in the foreword to this volume, although, to be fair, Finlay-Johnson's achievements cannot really compare with those of the author of the papers in this book. Informed observers of both women have testified to their remarkable teaching styles and to the fact that both seek excellence in the quality of the response drawn from the children lucky enough to have been taught by them. We know from their writings that both regard dramatic activity as a valuable tool for learning across the curriculum, but at this point the comparison must end.

In a fascinating article entitled 'Lessons Made Easy' published in the magazine *Home Chat* in 1908, Harriet Finlay-Johnson's pupils' traversing of the North Pole in their Sussex playground is described enthusiastically by the journalist, who also comments on the fact that the teacher did not seem to be required and spent the lesson watching them from the sidelines. This comment could not possibly be made of Dorothy Heathcote, who throughout this book, and more particularly in B J Wagner's *Dorothy Heathcote: Drama as a Learning Medium* appears at the centre of the activity. It is this which is most strikingly visible in her teaching and which sets her apart from other pioneers of drama in education. Her view of herself as an 'intervening' teacher, struggling to set up shared experiences with her pupils through the subtlety, power and challenge of her negotiations can provoke adulatory, bewildered and, at times, hostile reactions from onlookers.

Dorothy Heathcote was born in Yorkshire in 1926, where her formal schooling ended at fourteen, and where she worked for a time in a mill. In 1945 she became a theatre student at the Bradford Civic Playhouse School where she was taught by Esme Church and Rudolph Laban. After several years in theatre in the provinces, in 1950 she was appointed by Professor Brian Stanley to the Institute of Education at Newcastle University. She never trained as a teacher or taught as a full-time member of staff in a school, and accounts for what she calls her 'innocence' of vision and expression by the lack of early exposure to intellectual and academic models. It is partly this which gives her work its unique flavour, as her language and ideas have been shaped by intuitive modes of thought, a powerful sense of community, and exposure to biblical texts, poetry and the theatre.

Harriet Finlay-Johnson, at the turn of the century, was forced to retire after her marriage. Dorothy Heathcote, in a more liberal age and married to a supportive husband, has spent more than thirty years working with children, students in training in Newcastle and teachers throughout the world. Those who watch her at work are sometimes daunted by her unique gifts and the magical quality of her personality and fail to see the powerful educational principles which lie behind her practice. There are many dedicated 'Dorothy Watchers' in this country and abroad, who have attempted through recordings, transcripts, interviews and articles to understand and explain the nature of her teaching. One of the most sensitive and experienced is Dr John Fines, of Bishop Otter College, Chichester. His own work as an historian and a teacher has been deeply influenced by his awareness of the essential elements in Dorothy Heathcote's approach to teaching and learning. This is how he describes her at work in the classroom:

> She is a maker in every sense of the word. There is a struggle for quality – that power to demand what children have not yet the courage or organisation to ask on their own. She takes enormous risks herself and presses children harder than anyone else dares to, with miraculous results. She is hard, but hard with the knowledge that making is hard but also wondrous and a delight to all concerned (the art is to make all concerned, of course). She elicits tiny fragments from everyone and builds with these a magic mountain – but it is still their mountain, not hers, because all the pieces were once theirs before they gave them up in the communal co-operative act of drama. She is also candid in her questioning – she really wants desperately to know. Children are so used to teachers who know already that Dorothy comes as an astounding shock to them: here is someone who doesn't just listen, like some old counsellor, but actually wants to listen. But the most important thing is that she transmits it all back again at double power – making each hesitant offering of a mite seem like a generous donation of a millionaire. And she adds a little something herself. These moments when Dorothy gives (especially, I feel, when she sings) are particularly moving. She arranges, orchestrates the offerings, making tentative whistles turn into symphonies. The time Dorothy spends at a blackboard is most important to her teaching. Whatever one does in the mind, it begins with making a list and ends with an arrangement of that list that focusses on to the significant.
>
> Dorothy focusses quickly, for she knows the great truth that no-one can cope with more than about four things at any one time, and one of them has got to win, to gain primacy in the mind. This is why at this stage she spends time in her mind moving towards big questions, challenging questions

which say primarily 'Which of these is going to be your winner today?' Her questions focus down and lay the responsibility for choice. The question that shocks into deep thought, that searches for powerful symbols, that asks for action, that evokes greater eloquence, this is the Dorothy question. But even with the immense drive for depth, for focus, she is still not determining things, it is the children who do that. She knows with a kind of deep inner conviction that makes the knowledge very special indeed, that all the drama, all the knowledge, all the skills, everything is there in the children already, before she enters the room.

The approach to teaching which John Fines describes has sometimes been misunderstood and misapplied. Non-specialist teachers and those working with the handicapped seem to recognize more readily the validity of Dorothy Heathcote's work, but some specialist drama teachers are suspicious or critical of what they see as teacher domination or manipulation, or the non-transferable skills of one charismatic practitioner. It is ironic that excellent practice should have this effect. This collection of her writings will help to provide a much needed balance in the response to this gifted woman, and help teachers to see behind the dazzling surface of her work. Like her writing, the real Dorothy Heathcote is complex, diverse, practical, poetic, inspirational and demanding. She herself does not see this collection as the final exposition of a doctrine to be handed on to others. She regards her writings as attempts to clarify her immediate concerns, using the ideas, experience and language which is available to her at that moment. She happily borrows ideas and terminology from other writers and disciplines, and transforms them for her own use. These papers indicate her achievements but do not sum them up – they are 'pause buttons' in John Fines' phrase. Readers will not find here a magic formula which will enable then to teach in Heathcote's style, nor will they read endless narrative and description of past successes. This is not what occupies her thinking time. Her concerns lie not with her own skills but with the need to develop the skills of others. She does not hope for or work towards a race of drama teachers who are merely mass-produced replicas of herself.

> No one teaches a teacher how to teach. Teachers are made in the classroom during confrontations with their classes, and the product they become is a result of their need to survive and the ways they devise to do this.

Primarily Dorothy Heathcote sees herself as a teacher, and only secondarily as a teacher of drama. In her struggle to use this powerful tool for learning, a number of central concerns remain constant. Above all, she recognizes the validity of the knowledge and experience which her pupils already possess. She is dedicated to helping her pupils discover what they already know – to bringing this knowledge into consciousness in order to build a path for change. In other words, she is truly child-centred in her approach. But unlike the kind of 'progressive' teacher who abandons the child to its own resources, she accepts that teaching is an act of benign interference in the lives of the children. For Dorothy Heathcote, as for John Dewey, whose doctrines of education through experience are often distorted, the teacher, as the most mature member of the group, has not merely a right but a responsibility to intervene, since learning is the product of intervention.

It is this which sets Heathcote apart from other pioneers of drama in education. In fact, her stance as enabler and challenger within the action is more subtle and effective than that of teacher/instructor or teacher/director which is typical of the kind of drama based on exercise and small group improvisation. In the last ten years, the power of this approach is beginning to be understood. As early as 1972, Robert Witkin, in the *Intelligence of Feeling*, insisted that for the arts to operate successfully in education the teacher must be part of the creative process. Gavin Bolton, in his recent writings, has done much to clarify the teacher's function in structuring experience and reflection for learning.

The chief method by which Dorothy Heathcote intervenes, and the one most closely identified with her teaching, is by taking a role in the drama. In her hands this becomes an extraordinarily subtle, flexible and effective means of promoting learning. It allows her to refrain from burdening her pupils with her own knowledge, to pay attention to their needs but to withhold judgement, and through the role to negotiate an exchange of power with the class. The work operates at the level of subjective meaning, but serves the development of intellect as well as emotion, and enables her to raise ordinary experience to significance. The encounter with the role may be intense and absorbing for her pupils, but it will also be objective and reflective, since experience alone without reflection will not lead to learning.

Heathcote goes far beyond the objectives of personal development and social adjustment which satisfied drama teachers in the past. Her aim is to build on her pupils' past experience and give them a deeper knowledge not just of themselves but of what it is to be human, as well as an understanding of the society they live in and its past, present and future.

In these papers, she offers teachers the means of creating security for themselves and their pupils in the encounter which is classroom drama. She outlines the kind of knowledge which will support them in their task of creating and sharing significant learning experiences – not just the academic subject knowledge contained in most teacher training courses, but a more important kind of knowing. This will include a deep understanding of the basic elements which drama and theatre share, a grasp of how time, tension, sign and symbol operate in drama, an ability to find focus, to distort productively, and to negotiate with honesty and subtlety. She urges teachers to have the courage to come to terms with themselves and to rely on what they are in their struggle for authenticity. She releases teachers from the burden of being instructors – people who must know everything – and allows them to become something much more complex: sharers in learning experiences with their children, enablers, and seekers after excellence. Underlying all her writing, whether she is discussing method, curriculum or teachers' training, she displays a deep, urgent, political concern that society should value and reward good teaching.

Dorothy Heathcote's work has been described as magical, but really Dorothy is far too earthy and practical a person to be thought of as a witch. Her approach has all the appearance and characteristics of a midwife, and this is an image of drama and the drama teacher with which she seems comfortable. The patient – teacher, student or child – struggles to produce the infant – creative knowing. Dorothy is there, sleeves rolled up in charge of the event, alternately urging, cajoling and comforting the patient. When the moment of knowing is born, Dorothy weighs and measures it, pronounces it fit, and then, most difficult and important of all, gives it back to the person who made and fought for it. The product is not the property of the teacher/midwife but of the student/mother. How the prized possession survives and thrives from that point on is the concern of the person to whom the treasure belongs while the midwife moves on to the next case. Such skilled women are being replaced by larger organizations, impersonal machine-orientated hospitals, and the midwife is no longer a valued member of the community. It is possible that the teacher/technician threatens to replace the teacher/artist and that society, which already undervalues good teachers and creativity in teaching will allow the pursuit of excellence and high quality endeavour in teaching to become extinct.

Such a possibility leads us to the main purpose of Dorothy Heathcote's writing, which like her teaching should 'challenge, shatter and reform ideas'. It may not be possible to imitate with the same success her style of teaching, but it is possible to learn from her skills and experience and to join her in the demand for better and more rigorous and relevant teacher training, which will produce committed young teachers capable of pursuing excellence and authenticity in our schools.

# Part One

# Teachers and Teaching

# Introduction

Although Dorothy Heathcote is invariably seen in action teaching children, much of her time and energy is spent in teaching teachers and proposing alternative ideas for College of Education courses. This is because she has become dissatisfied with conventional programmes of teacher training which are devised to widen the students' own understanding, without always giving the same high-level priority to the translation of their academic learning into classroom practice.

Dorothy Heathcote's paper 'Training Teachers' first published in 1970 and again in a shortened form in 1972 by Pitman in *Drama in Education I*, edited by John Hodgson and Martin Banham, appeared after ten years' rapid expansion in teacher training and a proliferation in courses offered by Colleges of Education and Universities. Expansion was necessary due to the post-war 'bulge' in the birth rate, and also because teacher training courses were extended from two to three years. Following the James Report the trend was to offer students a course consisting of education and one main subject, to be studied in greater depth than was possible before. A Bachelor of Education degree was introduced, requiring a fourth year of study. Universities also offered to the large post-war generation of theatre and drama courses for the first time.

As the concept of an 'all graduate' profession was realized, the consequences for prospective teachers of drama became apparent – the higher educational standard required for acceptance together with an emphasis on an academic approach to these new courses pared away time spent on practical classroom work and the degree moved closer to an 'Eng. Lit.' concept of the subject.

The expansion attracted tutors with a wide background of drama experience; from the classroom, through amateur dramatics to the professional theatre. Students were offered courses which concentrated on their personal development, with particular emphasis on the theatre arts, much of which bore little resemblance to the work suggested as possible in the classroom. This division between theory and practice and between main subject courses and education studies fragmented the approach to using drama in the classroom. Newly trained teachers emerged with academic competence in their subject but without that same competence in their teaching skill.

Five years after Dorothy Heathcote's paper, it was evident that little had changed. The Schools Council Drama Teaching Project (10–16), 1975,[1] comments that their investigations pointed to a 'Considerable need for more highly competent teachers ... that few teachers in their initial training received adequate preparation for teaching drama in schools'. One of the reasons given for this situation by the Working Party was that there appears to be some difficulty in validating practical work as part of degree qualification, and that courses submitted for approval containing a large practical element might be rejected by the examining body.

In 1978, still concerned with teacher development, Dorothy Heathcote's paper 'Excellence in teaching' addresses teachers themselves rather than college tutors, and touches on the invisible qualities which make for good teaching. These invisible qualities provide a springboard for the final paper of this book: 'The authentic teacher and the future' in which the notions touched on in 'Excellence in teaching' are examined in detail.

---

[1] *Learning through Drama*, McGregor, Tate and Robinson, Heinemann, 1976.

# Excellence in teaching

*An abridged version of a lecture given in Christchurch, New Zealand in 1978, and published in the New Zealand journal* Education.

## Relating to people

What do we mean when we say, 'That is an excellent teacher'?

For me, an excellent teacher is one who knows the difference between relating to things and relating to people. Both need great skill, but the greatest skill lies in how we relate to people.

If I am to aspire to excellence as a teacher, I must be able to see my pupils as they really are. I mustn't discourage them – I must accept them. This means adjusting myself to my pupils, and seeing things from another standpoint.

I must also preserve an interest in my students and, in this way, grasp something of their potential. I must see what they are in the process of becoming. When children come to us with labels – this is a slow learner, this is a non-reader – we tend to shut our minds to change: but the ability to preserve an interest in children prevents teachers from stereotyping them in all sorts of ways.

As an excellent teacher, I must not be afraid to move out of my centre, and meet the children where *they* are. The ability to go forward to meet people gives me the opportunity to vary my approach and my responses. If I do this, I shall not be afraid to try unfamiliar things, because I'm not afraid of being rejected. Rejection is not part of trying to meet someone. Even if some rejection must take place, let that be of the idea and not of the person. I think we – the teachers and the pupils – often feel rejected in the school when it's really our ideas that are being rejected.

I must also have the ability to see the world through my students, and not my students through it. This ability can give a teacher a new perception, a renewal of energy and teaching style; there is a sort of regeneration when suddenly a class shows you a whole new way of looking at something.

As an example of this, I might describe what happened recently when I was working with some young men in a Borstal institution. I was in the tricky position of making the Borstal boys take the role of prison officers whilst their prison officers sat watching us. I hoped that the boys would treat my prisoner just as their prison officers had been treating them. So I became an official from the Bureau of American Indian Affairs, and I

18

put them in charge of Ishi, the last surviving member of his tribe. Ishi really had been found earlier this century on a railway station, and the bureau had decreed that this man – ill, sick, forlorn, speaking tongues nobody had ever heard – was to be put in the local jail until such time 'as he should be made city-like, and civilized'. Of course, the boys defied all my desires to get Ishi put in the jail. They said, 'You're not putting him in jail. We'll build him a house.' And they built him one – without any windows. I protested at this, but they insisted, and I realized we were looking at the house from two different points of view: for them it gave privacy, and for me it was a prison. I'm still pondering why they did it. Perhaps it was something to do with the fact that I couldn't look in and peer at Ishi. The fact that he couldn't see out either made no difference. It was what I might do to him that mattered. To understand this, I had to look at their house through their eyes, not through mine.

But, as a teacher who seeks excellence, I must also have the ability not to be lessened by my students, to withstand them, to use my own eyes sometimes, and be myself.

One of the ways of avoiding being lessened is to refuse to give back what the pupils give you, especially if they are unco-operative. So often, it is easier to play tit-for-tat, and be lessened.

I must have the ability to withstand certain pressures. I must be able to say, 'I respect how it looks from your point of view but I'm not giving in, because I can explain why I want it my way.' It's often easier to let the children get away with it, because it's too tiring to keep battling on. But the real battle is for a higher quality of response. I feel this ability to withstand is to know something of the chastity of one's purposes.

The ability to resist is a little like the ability to withstand. While withstanding may be to hold the status quo, resisting is to demonstrate, 'No further! That's it!' I've had to spend a lot of energy in my teaching to create circumstances in which I can resist without pain, either to me or to the class. All my strategies enable me to create a disciplined world, and to find ways of using power without its being my power. Frequently I use the power of the subject to discipline a group. I say, 'It demands this of us' – not 'I demand this of you.' By resisting people, you help them to find guidelines and boundaries which can begin to function for all of us. Sometimes these boundaries are painfully constraining, and sometimes these moments when one says, 'No further!' are very risky. There are times when I know a group of children could just laugh me out of the room because, from where they stand, I am an idiot in an idiotic system. But then it's necessary to stand there saying, 'Why do you laugh and tear your own work down?' when it would be so much simpler to laugh with them, and get out of the room safely.

If I wish to be an excellent teacher, I must also have the ability to dominate the scene for my students when it is necessary, and in the guise of one thing, do another, so that the pupils can grow. This is where you take risks in order to gain, where you approach the work by guile, by the delicate use of lures, and use oblique approaches to attain your goals. I'll give you an example of how domination worked with delinquent boys. I once went to my class in a school, taking my three-month-old daughter with me. I walked in and, for some crazy reason, I expected the class to be doing *Julius Caesar* because that's what the timetable said. So I wheeled the pram gaily in, and was met by a line of black-browed, beady-eyed morons. There was anger all over that room! So of course I said, 'Oh, I thought we were doing *Julius Caesar*', and they glowered in return.

This was one day when I dominated – I was very tired at the end of it! I looked one of the boys in the eye and said, 'There *are* days like today. Why don't you have a pint on me?' And I offered him one. The lad took it (thank God he *did* take it!) and I drew pints all round and dominated the situation. The clouds did not lift, but the pints were not thrown back in my face.

So then I had to find a way of showing that I valued what they had done in just letting me be in the room with them. I said, 'You think *you've* got troubles? Have you seen my brat? I'm not going to see *her* father again. You think you've got troubles? Not one of you signs that notice saying you don't want my pub to close. It's going to shut next month. You've come in here and drunk my beer, but you'll let me lose my job, won't you?'

And they said, '*We* didn't know it was going to shut. We didn't even know it was going to open.'

'Ah, well it is, and not one of you've signed the notice, have you?'

'Well, we *would* have signed it, if we'd seen it.'

'I've heard *that* before.'

And then I stopped and said, 'There must be somebody worse off than us. Somewhere in the world there must be somebody worse off than me and this brat, and you with all your troubles. Tell you what, come to the bar, and don't tell the fellow next to you what's up with you, but see if you can find out what's up with him.'

And the crowd of black gloom drifted over to the bar (the teacher's table), and I stood there pulling pints, sloshing them down, and groaning about my brat. And I asked if they had found out anything about each other, and I heard incredible things. 'I've had a row with the wife this morning,' and, 'I've drunk all me wages,' and so on. And so the moaning and groaning went on. (They should have been doing *Julius Caesar* but I didn't dare draw their attention to that fact, because the gloom would have come down again.)

I said, 'I wonder if anybody *could* come in here who was worse off than us?'

And one lad thought a bit and said, 'Yes, a tramp could come in here; a tramp that's got nowt could come in here.'

'Do you want to be a tramp that's got nowt?'

And he said, 'Ay.'

And he put on a sacking coat, and walked up to the counter that didn't exist, and I reached up and gave him a pint in one of the better glasses. He took the pint and had just begun to drink it, when I looked at one of the other lads and asked, 'Now what made him come in here, into this gloomy hole? I mean, we're all standing here like cheese at fourpence and yet he comes in here. There's nowt to cheer him up in here.'

And the tramp said something that was really to open all our eyes: 'All the other pubs have music.'

An amazing new view – it was quiet in here! And at that point I said, 'Well, the reason it's quiet in here is because we're doing *Julius Caesar*. We are, you know! And what's more tomorrow one of these silly devils is going to fight at Philippi. And the bloody generals are arguing over eighty bloody drachmas. And it's you and me that's going to be fighting at Philippi.'

And at that point, we became drunken soldiers just before Philippi. And, from there, we got on to the way ordinary private soldiers carry the responsibility for the generals who never come into the front line.

You know, that's as good an introduction to *Julius Caesar* as I've ever found. It took about an hour, but I think it's a good example of dominating people.

As an excellent teacher, I must be able to bring power to my students and to draw on their power. This negotiation, this exchange of power is a realignment of relating. If children are damaged too much in school, they won't let you exchange power with them. They want you to keep it because that way they can continue saying, 'See, nobody likes school with her about. I can't do it the way she wants it done.' It's quite difficult, I find, to get children to take power, and then give you back a bit, and then keep on taking more. I really think it's a shame that we've set up our schools so that children don't feel they can take power.

But all this can be achieved only when we recognize that we must pay constant attention to others, and be slow to make judgements. This isn't just a matter of survival, but a matter of respect.

Paying attention starts when I begin working with a class. I notice how they walk in, how they look at each other. Do I see elements of self-neglect, or do they neglect each other? This boy is tired-looking, that girl looks as if she's had a bad knock. I can't judge whether I'm right, but I can pay attention and, in so doing, recognize a little of the conditions of people.

The ability to withhold judgement is often seen as ambivalence in a teacher. We all know a teacher who never makes up her mind whether some student is good or bad. Why can't she? She *must* know! And often a lack of rigour is the reason why such teachers fail to make judgements. They have no proper standards by which to measure people. But one can be desperately wrong if one moves too soon. I remember once working with a highly skilled colleague who told me that he was going to fail a student. I found myself thinking, 'Haven't you realized she's forty-eight and she's plain, and that's the reason you're going to fail her?' I imagined that he had missed a centre to her teaching that, to me, was sticking out like a sore thumb. She was carrying a burden, and I reckoned it was her plainness. We both went into the classroom to watch her teach, and she gave quite a scintillating teaching performance. My colleague was astonished, and so was I. Talking with her afterwards, I asked her if she had put on a special performance that day. She replied, 'Well, you see, today my mother was calm when I left for school.' She was able to teach that day because her mother had been calm. So much for my guesses about the burden she was carrying!

Being slow to make judgements allows me constantly to renew my view of each pupil and to update it. I think this is one of the hardest things we must train ourselves to do if we aspire to excellence in teaching. We should stop believing things other people tell us about children, stop taking things for granted, stop saying that because we once knew nasty Jimmy Jones, and *his* eyes were close together as well, *this* lad's going to be the same. One of the most rejuvenating things is to give everyone a fresh start each morning. The ability to do this is part of the condition of innocence. I think innocence has a chance of bringing with it enormous gaiety and trust, so that you walk into the classroom clean every morning, however mucky you are at the end of the day.

## Relating to self

Before we can relate to people successfully, we must first come to terms with ourselves.

To keep my teaching in trim, I must first be able to look straight at myself, and take my own measure. I must be almost obsessed with myself. This isn't as selfish as it sounds because, if I know what I am, then I know what is needed to renew myself. Otherwise, I go into the classroom tired, and I'm not paid to go into a classroom tired. Some people seem born tired, and some people seem to become tired, but in the long run, nobody's going to make you tired except yourself.

The ability to be obsessed by ourselves seems to me to be a marvellous gift. We are constantly concerned and interested in ourselves – 'How funny! I wonder why I feel like *that* today?'

I don't think this is a bad thing. It leads towards interest in the outcome of how we feel, and what we see ourselves to be. We can use this interest in the classroom to see ourselves through children's eyes. I remember that lovely story in Laurie Lee's *Cider with Rosie*, where he says that he was furious with the teacher the first day he went to school because she told him to 'stand there for the present', and he never got the present!

Being obsessed with ourselves enables us to see what renews us, and so be able to renew ourselves, and to accept the palliatives we need. Some people need the palliative of a long gin at four o'clock. I think we have to learn which palliatives regenerate energy, and forgive ourselves, and use them with temperance. One palliative I require is just five minutes to cook in peace. I also need to see that I am prepared for my work. But I don't need the palliative of a long sleep – I can get up ever so early, as long as I have a few minutes at the end of the day to take some sort of action in another direction: my palliative is to change action. Another of my palliatives is my sewing. I think if we took more heed, very consciously, of the kind of things that give us long holidays (because I don't think it's necessarily long holidays that give us long holidays), we could experience a great gulf of rest. Just the lifting of the pressures then makes us ready for something else.

Then we have the energy to work at ourselves. This, to me, is very important. My mother used to say, 'Nay, I'd rather work out than rust out.' I believe the same.

I see working at myself as the ability to examine the journey of my life, to constantly review it, and to perceive where I'm at in it. I foresee my death and I look forward to it, not in a morbid sort of way, but by constantly recognizing my humanity. I seem to get a certain amount of restoration when I look at the many parts of me, and wonder what ancestor each came from. I find it infinitely exciting to look at children in this way too, even if one hasn't known their fathers and mothers, and to realize that they are the product of so many forerunners.

Teaching demands that we give ourselves fully to the task in hand. To do this means that we must be complete and completely self-knowing. This demand is one of the gifts of teaching which isn't necessarily talked of by the unions. It is a repayment to a teacher which no one mentions. And being forced to concentrate on the task in hand means that we can often temporarily forget all the other things that are bothering us. There aren't a lot of jobs like that.

We need, too, to allow ourselves to be restless spirits – to be in the process of becoming. I don't mean darting about like a gadfly, trying first this innovation and then that. I'm talking about the spirit that says, 'I can see where they're at – I'll show them the next hill.' It's the restlessness that, while confirming what is understood, leads on to the next mystery. I find that very exciting.

But, in all this, we must have the ability to be ourselves and not a facade of ourselves. If we are ourselves, then we have the ability to accept the limitations of our situation. We don't have to agree to these limitations, but we can accept them until we can do something about them. This is why I'm a pain in the neck to people when I come to lecture for them. They say, 'What sort of a room would you like to use?' and I say, 'I don't mind. As long as it has a roof over it, it'll do.'

'Would you like a blackboard?'

'Well, I must have a blackboard.' (All other limitations can disappear, as long as I've got something I can write on and rub out on!)

'How big a class would you like?'

'Well, I don't mind.'

'What age of class?'

'Well, I don't really mind.'

'What would you like to do with them?'

'I don't really mind.'

You see, if we don't ask for a special set-up, then we have to be ourselves for we have nothing else to draw on. Then we see what drives us, what kinds of teaching space and noise and discipline we can and cannot stand; and what our concerns in the classroom really are.

By being ourselves in this way we are able to affect others and to be affected by them.

On days when all my skills function happily, I am in a condition of excellence. I am all right with myself.

But is achieving excellence in teaching a realistic aim? It seems to me that the reality is in aspiration, and that aspiration to excellence is a reality. Excellence still exists, and it always did. But the conditions that promote excellence rarely exist, and they rarely have. So we have a choice whether, in conditions which often scarcely contribute to excellence, to choose to aspire to it. We can practise choosing; we can renew and review our choice. We make our choices on excellence daily, minute by minute, each choice dictating the next. You can't reach excellence for a whole day; you can only reach it minute by minute. And this is one of the excitements of teaching – the constant exhilaration of recognizing the choice we have made at any moment. When we stop choosing, things go radically wrong with us.

In this work, drama, what we are trying to do is to make 'ordinary experiences significant, and that's a hard thing. That is the excellence we strive for. To distort experience into significance means that we have to get children to pay attention, and they may not have the vocabulary for it. I don't mean spoken vocabulary – they may not have practised the ability to pay attention. They do practise it privately, because they pay attention to the things that concern their survival, such as the mood their parents are in, or what'll happen if they hit the cat, or read that book that they shouldn't, or go out with their mates when they're supposed to be doing their homework.

All these things *make* them pay attention. But there's something a bit odd about saying to children, 'I'll create this depicted world so that you can pay attention to it.' Children often don't have experiences to make that work. And so we need the skill of high-level negotiation to help the classes we work with pay attention when we try to distort matters into significance for them. To do this we have to be able to create significance, and we cannot do this if we teach casually. We can only create moments when children stumble upon an authentic experience if we teach with attention to detail and its relation to the whole. This is the root of excellence. We sold our young teachers down the river when we told them to be nice and easy with the kids, and casual and friendly. We sold our profession down the river. In trying to get rid of distance and formality, we got rid of significance.

If I could give young teachers anything, I would give them the ability to negotiate with significance. This, to me, is what high quality endeavour means.

# Training Teachers to use drama as education

*Part of this paper was published as 'Training needs for the future' in* Drama in Education 1: The Annual Survey, *edited by John Hodgson and Martin Banham, published by Pitman, 1972.*

When we discuss the training of teachers to use drama as education, we have to ask these questions:

1  Can we train people to use the arts? Or is good use of them 'natural talent'?
2  What is special about drama as a tool in education?
3  What can be taught to the would-be teacher in the comparative seclusion of college?
4  Which experiences are of most lasting value?
5  Which areas can be left for the teacher to find out for herself or himself?

In the light of decisions taken on these matters, we can then plan a realistic course and isolate the task of the tutors in expediting such a course.

## All people can learn to teach well

I believe that all people can learn to teach well, if they are not put into defensive areas during their training. Teaching is creative work, and creative work has five features:
the drive to want to do it;
the feed-back to satisfy the having done it;
content of the doing of it – the level of function within the topic area;
signals to communicate during the doing; and
the rituals of going about it.
These areas apply to all creative work, to the teacher, the student and the tutor. The tutor has to create the method for the would-be teacher, the teacher for the pupil. When we are in the role of pupil in a situation, we do not have to be responsible for the same aspects as when we are in the role of the teacher. It is essential therefore that in training teachers we make certain that they are given experience in committing others to work. I believe that this area of training is grossly ignored in training schemes. Much energy goes into planning for keeping the would-be teacher in the 'pupil' role, and hardly any in the 'teacher-instigator'

26

role. If you accept this, then the tutor's task takes on quite a different aspect, and college experience has a very different emphasis.

As a tutor to teachers, I believe that the following are my functions, but as I learn more by practice of my job, they must be constantly subject to review by me, aided by the teachers I teach, who are in the best position to help me to review my thinking. I believe that:

1 I should aim to preserve the students' personality, not erode it to fit a pattern conceived by me.
2 That I should be seen to be more at risk than the students in our work together.
3 That in considering our work, I should identify with the students in that I want them to 'win'; which means structuring so that they have to work to win, not giving in to them easily.
4 That students shall discover for themselves whether or not they are prepared to put in the necessary effort to learn to teach but this has to be structured for and not left to chance.
5 That I shall be seen to fail in front of students, and be seen to recover, then that this be open to discussion.

I pledge myself to:

1 Avoid withholding information in order to 'spin out' my knowledge.
2 Allow students to take decisions and to test them in action.
3 Allow students to prove to themselves that they understand the nature of their own functioning as teachers, thus starting a lifelong process.
4 Allow the students to prove to me and themselves that they will still be, however experienced, student of teaching.
5 Constantly review my own priorities in teaching.
6 Prove that my ideas are open to review *by the students*.
7 Give evidence of my ability and readiness to listen.
8 Give evidence of having patience, positive and unfailing, so long as students give evidence of working.
9 Be honest at all levels of praising and criticizing work – my own and others.
10 Be a 'restless spirit', understanding when to move forward, press for more effort, or be content with present achievement, yet give each moment of achievement its due.
11 Be interesting.
12 To be professional always. By this I mean to remember why I am doing the job; to be task-orientated, not coming between the student and the task in false self-interested ways.

27

13  Never to permit myself to be bored.
14  Ensure that the students understand that I am concerned with
    training to teach in school – with realistic knowledge of the
    problems of teaching in ordinary school circumstances.

## A vulnerable state

It can readily be seen that in my work I am constantly seeking to be a
working companion with my teachers, rather than someone who has all
the answers. I do this in order to try to avoid putting my students into
the defensive areas during their training. I believe that more damage is
done by this than almost anything in the training of teachers. The
teacher is doomed to function in a very vulnerable state. He or she often
works alone and yet there is constant pressure to appear 'to be able to
do the job', in the eyes of colleagues who will rarely witness them
actually at work. The teacher often finds that it is almost impossible to
communicate to other teachers the things which are causing trouble, as
it often appears that no one else seems to have the same difficulties; and
staff room talk seems to avoid the issues of 'how do we really manage
our teaching?' All too often the new teacher must find that staff room
talk suggests that the nitty gritty of teaching lies in results, rather than
the 'how and why' of classroom practice. I think that if any revolution is
to come in our methods of teaching in schools, it must come through
the new generations of the teachers we train. Train so that they are
capable themselves of looking at their work and supporting each other
in that work, so that the real issues of methods of achieving are
discussed rather than only their results. This means a generation of
teachers in whom honest appraisal rather than value judgements about
work comes into action, and 'results' reporting is replaced by sharing
approaches, thinking and planning together to help one another to
function well and with security. It means allowing one's work to be open
to scrutiny knowing it will not be torn apart, but valued for what it
did achieve and built on by examination. This can only be achieved
by a new approach to the training of teachers, and we trainers have to
decide first whether we are in the 'teaching of young adults' field or
in the 'teacher training' field. At present we seem not quite to be in
either.

## Creating a learning situation

One of the problems is that we still train through a 'body of knowledge'
approach. Can we really accept that the body of knowledge type of
learning is what the future generations need? Growing people will,

provided they stay in the growing business, always go on to absorb and acquire for themselves new knowledge; the knowledge left for them as well as that which they acquire for themselves. What is required in order for this to happen? The lively interest of the 'stirred' individual, education for 'being involved in knowing' rather than just knowing by memory alone. It also means being involved in taking and testing decisions rather than accepting the decisions of others; being research-orientated rather than learners about the researches of others; using their own 'expertise' however limited so that they test their thinking and then consult other's researches to compare their thinking; and then to behave with the responsibility of experts instead of only hearing about experts. I do not suggest that the already known body of knowledge is unimportant; only that it comes best after the trial of one's own thinking so that the learner is turned on to the problem in a way which makes for receptive acquisition of that which has gone before.

So we need to train our teachers to structure for a learning situation to happen rather than a sharing of information in a 'final' way to take place. We have to train them to withhold their expertise to give their students opportunitity for struggling with problems, before they come to the teacher's knowledge, and to reach an answer because of the work they do rather than the listening they have done. This will not lower standards, nor will it deny that which others have struggled painfully to achieve, nor will it 'waste' more time. What it will do is keep knowing at first hand alive, and thus encourage the desire for knowledge from those who went before.

Of course it will demand that teachers must cease to rely on their memories, and their information, as the main tools of their trade, and instead to rely on what they are, where they are in their thinking and how they communicate their ideas rather than what they say to their students via the traditional verbal interchanges which form so large a part of our school and college systems. This method has been used for years in those arts and sciences which can only be 'got at' through doing and participating. These subjects (and drama is one of them) have tended to develop around them a kind of mystique and this has blocked real research into how some teachers get their results. We hear of 'personality' rather than teaching techniques, and teaching systems, which is a great pity.

## The master/apprentice relationship

Training people to structure learning situations places great stress upon the relationship of teacher and student, and we cannot ignore this in planning future training schemes. It contains elements of the 'master/apprentice' relationship and demands that the work of students in schools shall be related to real problem solving rather than theory problem solving. It means great upheavals in approach to programme planning and curriculum content and examination. Where it is happening it is soon obvious that the students have a new dynamic in their learning, and that the quality of their commitment immediately improves, closely followed by improved self-discipline, a desire to work harder, for longer spells of time, and a greater sense of responsibility. But the biggest revolution in the world will not provide our schools with teachers of greater calibre unless we trainers of teachers start the revolution ourselves. Already classes are harder to handle, more and more students are making their feelings felt about the content of their course. The ones I meet are not asking for less work, or easier work, they are asking for meaningful work.

## Present courses

Present courses in drama in colleges of education tend to deal with the following matters. There are exceptions of course, but the emphasis is generally as follows. Teachers in training will probably cover:

A study of texts, and approach to text. Some of their experience will be practical and they will interpret plays.
They will be encouraged to go to the theatre, make their own productions, for children, their peers and for public audiences.
They will work on theatre skills such as lighting, sound, make-up, interpretation, design, costuming and production skills and architecture and characterization.
They will be students of theatre history, theatre architecture, written style, the acting styles of other ages and plays of other periods.
They will study children's theatre at practical and theory levels.
A small time will be given over to child drama and the changing needs of children.
They also study something called 'education', which will probably cover play, processes of learning, skills of teaching, history of education and educational systems of other times and places.

The usual results are that during their course, they acquire a basic knowledge of the above areas and some discover a flair in themselves for teaching. Many acquire an interest in the classroom application of drama. But they have hardly understood how to set about structuring courses for the uncommitted classes they will teach for most of their lives.

30

## Theatre understanding

Drama has become accepted but many headteachers still think of it as watered down theatricals, not because they are stupid, but because they themselves have only seen theatricals, or done theatricals in their own time in school.

Theatre understanding is most necessary in classroom practice, but not the elaborate game element of showing which professional theatre must employ. Teachers need to understand it at the deeper level of cause and effect upon individuals and groups. Its primitive heart and driving power rather than its 'slave' areas of architecture, lights and make-up. Among teachers there is, for example, a dearth of knowledge about how theatrical tension is created, of understanding about the differences in the experiences of, on one hand, dramatizing for others and, on the other, making drama serve the needs of those who create it whilst they are creating it. Teachers need to understand and come to terms with their unique position of 'witch doctor, guru and restless spirit' when they are leading a class into work. To obtain progression in their work they must not only understand *how* to obtain progression in the work but also the differences between *linear* development in play-making, the flow of the story line, the unfolding of events in true dramatic form, and the *volume* development of the work so that the events are personally meaningful to the children.

From our colleges many teachers emerge with the skills to teach about 5 per cent of the school population, the ones committed to learning, but I believe they could emerge able to teach most of the students they meet, for it is not their youth or their inexperience which holds them back. It is the bias we give to their training. Many teachers of drama emerge with too little academic background to their work and also too little experience of thinking and talking about their job. The neglected area is that which deals with the 'cause and effect' aspect of teaching, the way in which teachers affect and are affected by their classes.

## The rules of drama

What is special about teaching drama? What does a teacher of drama have to do? First, understand the 'rules' of the medium, not the narrow ones of stage effects but the deeper ones. The study of how meanings are revealed and made explicit in a moment by moment experience of life which nevertheless has been selected so that form is at the centre of the creation, and all that is extraneous to that form has been pared away, leaving only the meaningful for examination. In the theatre this is revealed by the six elements:

31

Sound – all that which can be heard, from voices to thunder.
Silence, in contrast, so that it makes its impact.
Movement, all types from a single gesture to that of massed crowds.
The contrast of the meaningful stillness of individuals and groups.
That which is not seen as in darkness, or absence while we wait.
All the most brilliant light which leaves nothing to shadowy form, and
either cruelly or kindly allows us to perceive each and every person and
thing before us.

It is not enough to hope that by giving teachers practice in theatrical
presentations, they somehow will learn this, for that is not how they
must employ it in their classes. They have to learn how to employ this
magic, to make the experience a real one at the moment of its happening, so that those who actually make it, learn the magic of it and get the
experience themselves, not give it to the onlookers. This must be
broken down for the teachers in their training so that they can become
skilled in using it in the day-to-day classroom situations they have
to work in. The kinship with the storyteller under the tree, of the saga
told and retold to those unable to read, can easily be seen here. So
the teacher has to be able to make explicit with very limited means
that which is implicit in relationships. I believe that teachers who
consider that they have little or no 'talent' for drama can learn very
quickly to understand and master this if their training takes it into
consideration.

## Significant selection

Next the teacher has to be able to compact the detail of events into a
selective form so that action is representative of an event but does not
necessarily reveal all of that event. You cannot reveal all war upon a
stage or in a classroom, but by significant selection of a portion of a
circumstance, the reflection of aspects of war, and how it affects people,
can be revealed and give opportunity for reflection to take place. Surely
the getting of an 'education' is really the widening of our areas of
reference in meaningful ways, so that our reflective powers and our
attitudes become more and more significant to us, and to those concerned with us? The theatre, by compacting the area we see, makes it
possible for us to believe we can at least get a hold of it to grapple with it
successfully for a while. The teacher then must be able to take a
significant view from a general one, and make it happen with meaning
to those who bring it into focus. In this the teacher functions as a
playwright. This can be taught. It involves the training of the selectivity
of a person, and the disciplines of understatement.

32

## Seeing with significance

A further area which is relevant is the special perception of the teacher. The way in which the eye sees with significance that which underlies the creations of painters, architects, sculptors, natural lines of land-scape, forms of artifacts. The training in the natural seeking to go beneath the outer form to the inner meanings so that the apparently dissimilar are revealed to have common areas of meaning. The great universals. This leads to the understanding of the significance of rituals, to the seeking for the nature of objects as well as the shapes of objects. It gives unity to experiences. It finds form everywhere, from the momentous form in buildings towering in space to the movements of a child in play. Given this sense no meaningless or 'cheap' artifact will be introduced into the classroom, and form will be an integral part of the experiences in that classroom. This is not effete or artfully artistic. It is strong, matter-of-fact, ordinary experience which can shape new think-ing. It leaves pupils free to be selective in their own ways, and does not trammel them with value judgements, for it gives opportunity for many forms to be 'experienced' rather than taught about or intellectually 'looked' at.

## Handling language

A further skill the drama teacher needs is to put words and spoken language to efficient use, to open feeling and understanding through language, to select language so that it comes as close as it may to being a vehicle of experience. The poetic, selective handling of language is necessary, again not the effete 'smoothness' of accent and delivery, but the economical, selective, powerful choice of words where 'fitness for purpose' is paramount. This also means a good ear, and tonal control above the normal used or expected to be used in everyday commerce. All teachers need this skill of course, but the teachers using drama need it especially because their material is so much more than the outward form, and it can only be fully revealed by the richest range of tone, volume pitch and all the immense variety of a well controlled choice of modulation and vocabulary. Of all these related skills perhaps the most important of all is the choice of vocabulary employed by the teacher, and this must demand the utmost sensitivity from the teacher so that it is constantly and meaningfully employed in the classroom. It seems that it is possible to commit teachers to start to find out how to develop the necessary skills. To commit teachers to trying, to valuing, is all that training can do – life has to do the rest, life and all the classes they ever teach who slowly reveal to them the values and truths they personally hold to be important enough to keep on working to perfect. All teaching skills are constantly honed in use and practice, giving pleasure in their use to teachers and inspiration to classes.

## Worthwhile tension

Drama needs moments of tension to be felt, seen and experienced, and the ability to create tension of this kind, out of the air almost, is necessary. Whenever human behaviour is examined it has to be related to where, when, and who with. The multitude of circumstances available to the teacher arising out of these factors in a variety of combinations make it necessary for the teacher to learn the ability to select what will be worthwhile tension for each particular group to experience. Teachers have to be able to classify life itself very swiftly and put it into action immediately. Tension is not a matter of huge terrifying events such as earthquakes, mutinies, armies and so on; it is more a matter of finding a lever from within the situation which is capable of laying on pressure, in the way that sore places can develop on the skin as a result of abrasion. This has the effect of making the most hackneyed situations spring into new focus and create new awarenesses.

A few examples might help here. The class of children who are gathered round a teacher saying they need to have a new baby christened, can have a tense experience in just agreeing on the name if the teacher has noticed that one child has not liked a name offered for consideration. That tension was not seen to be present by the children till the teacher began to put pressure on the area of 'It appears that we're going to have trouble in agreeing on the best name for this baby'. The tension of having to move rocks in a valley before they can even find a place to sit down after a long and dangerous journey, the final straw type of tension. The tension when a class say 'We want a bit of peace', and the teacher says 'Do you want the peace of before birth, or after death?' Most dramas, like most things of value, often start very ordinarily and grow into experiences of value. A class does not need to be histrionically inclined to produce experiences of great beauty and value, but it can't get there in the face of a mediocre teacher who doesn't understand the homespun of tension-making.

## Non-verbal signals

Control of and projection of non-verbal signals in the classroom are also of paramount importance. This is common sense, for the main source of our reactions throughout our lives is first through the meanings we read into the non-verbal signals we receive and codify. Children in the beginning have to rely on 'true' interpretation of these in their parents, and in school this is one of their skills. If they do not develop this ability how can they 'read' adults and predict safely? All too often the teacher's words bely the deeper signal, and the child then starts – and rightly so – to mistrust the teacher's words; the meaningless praise, the automatic non-listening comment; the empty phrases all add up to apathy and mistrust, which lead gradually to cynicism if not recovered in time.

## Interpretation of material

The skill to take anecdotal material such as stories, accounts of experiences, discourse, letters, objects, pictures of various kinds, artifacts, ideas, enquiries, comments, news items; all the attempts to hold on to experiences known to us, and turn them into moment-by-moment discovering through dramatic experimentation is also required. Without this skill not only does the original material become ill used, denied its own truth, but the drama achieved as a result is of mediocre value. This means the sensitive understanding of the nature of other art forms has to be achieved.

## The particular to the universal

Learning to codify many 'particulars' which seem different and finding common universals so that the particular aspects of the materials used gain deeper significance for participants is essential. It is not enough to say that teachers have to know the difference between story and theme. The universals bring the thematic experience into the conscious use of concepts; into the head as well as the heart type of experience. An example of this might be seen in these seemingly different particular soldiers: Romans guarding the Roman Wall in northern England; Trojans fending off the Argonauts; Americans in the wars between the states. The common theme may be 'A few people can hold many at bay'. But that is not a universal in the sense meant here. A universal might be 'There always seems to have to be wars'. 'These are all licensed to kill'. Drama ideas usually begin with a general area of interest, narrowed to a particular, then, if the experience is to be related to the person's own experience universalized to draw in the unique experience of the group at work on the idea. This dropping of the particular into the universal is the digestion process of the arts, which creates the opportunity for reflection which is what education is all about. The centralizing in oneself of all the different experiences one meets so that they can come into direct (though not necessarily recognizable) use for each person.

35

## Recall

A strong sense of recall – visual and sensory, is required, for the images used in drama, often not previously experienced, cannot be projected without selection. To visualize 'a horse' is useless for drama. For that is not dramatic material. A horse with a damaged foot may be what is needed for one situation, a huge beast of uncertain temper for another, a well armed horse for a third. The selection of the significant again. But not the significant for the theme only, or for the facts or for the period. The significant for the particular class is a factor also.

A sense of identification with and relating to people, not just being in the same room with them is a further necessity for the teacher, not only for drama of course, but especially relevant in drama. It is this sense which enables the teacher to select from the range of images of horse which is available.

Also needed are patience, toleration of trial and error, absence of meaningless value judgements, and the ability to take people just where they are, give them credit for it and start off from there, in a reality not a dream world, and the ability to make a situation really meaningful from within for the participants rather than just outwardly *seeming* to be of meaning.

## Personal commitment

What I am really saying is that in teaching, no matter what the discipline we actually work through, be it a language, mathematics, history or any of the other subject areas, the factor which makes it illuminated from within, and therefore incapable of being either arid or limited is that the teacher is really operating from deep wells of personal commitment related to the fundamental concepts by which he or she lives. If we attempt to train without unfolding, an understanding and knowledge of these concepts to the teacher, then we are doing a dis-service not only to that person but we are actually blocking the development of the teacher in that person. In my own experience as soon as this aspect of themselves is under review (by them not me) young teachers achieve a totally different approach to the task. They are 'inside' their training as it were, and not seeking to find meaning in it. Suddenly they know how to make all the new information coming towards them relevant, and above all there is true commitment to teaching, and a wholeness in their grasp of techniques.

The fundamental concepts in my own teaching would read something like this:

All things must die, having had a time of living, of being born and growing.

36

There is all that has been before my life, to be tapped and learned about.
I hold a measure of responsibility for how I function, so that those who will come are not cheated by anything I do.
Form in all things is a constant delight.
People are always interesting.
Value judgements teach us nothing.
The thoughts of others can lead us to our own.
Keep fresh the ability to receive.
'cast bread . . . it returns.'
Awareness always alert to environment, shapes, colours, line, sounds.
Use all things as symbols to guide to deeper reflection.
Codify experience.
Taking nothing for granted keeps respect alive.
Restraint keeps appreciation fresh.

Strange though it may appear as a foundation for a teacher of, say, French, I know it to be the true start of the mastery of teaching, and I do *not* say that the teacher of French need not also study his or her discipline. That, I take for granted, will be part of the college course. But without the central concepts there is no true base from which to operate, and to keep on operating for all the years to come.

One glance at the above list, and the special problems facing the teacher of drama, suggests the need to be superhuman – and certainly to be mature – when we all know that the teacher in training is usually not very old or experienced. And it can be argued that we will find it impossible to train for these concepts anyway, as the teacher in training is too young to be able to learn them yet, that it is only with the passing of time and much teaching that these things can become available to the teacher. I suggest that to take up this attitude is to bring defeat to training before we have even started. I suggest that young teachers in training are secretly aware that there is no heart to their training. I hear more than anything the statement that they feel there is no real standard being demanded of them in their work; that 'anything goes', and that they feel an apathy relating to values during their courses in college. I cannot believe when I see young teachers at work on a project, with all the energy they are capable of at this time, that it is impossible to train them in the teaching skills as well as their 'subject' skills.

I would also suggest that they have all their lives in which to become more and more absorbed in and delighted by the amount of information available on this earth, but that if it is filtered through failure to commit their classes to wanting to work with them, they lose heart and gradually begin the process of 'getting through the day' rather than keeping the enthusiasm alive for learning more and more how to create learning situations for others. Children will respect a teacher who doesn't know everything – and even one who seems to know very little about something, so long as they see that person trying alongside them in learning endeavour. But children do not respect the teacher they can see perfectly well is covering shabbiness in a cloud of spurious status-seeking ploys because that teacher has never understood the difference between status and stature. The latter grows out of real care for the people and the task, the former out of self-seeking to preserve the hierarchy in the work. Master and slave get us nowhere; master and apprentice with both learning together seem to give both a chance to progress. But of course it can be argued that 'some people have it and some people don't'. I would argue that the very people to best learn this relationship are those young people, often idealistic, once one gets below the outer sometimes cynical cover, who enter the colleges of education. They cannot learn it if they are put in the position of being sent into the lion's den on their teaching practices, so that to survive at all costs begins to be their code.

One good lesson where the tutor is seen to fail and recover whilst actually in the teaching situation, or where the tutor has worked alongside as a colleague, followed by discussion on why the session went as it did, does not teach any better about teaching, but it sets up a mutually respectful relationship, which is often lacking from the tutor-student relationship. Given the mutual respect we are in a position to start learning together. We need not spend all our time in schools for this respect and communication to take place. It can happen anywhere of course, but if we are training teachers we must remember that the relevant area is in training for the ability to structure and follow through, and progress in, learning situations for others. This requires class contact, with the student-teacher as instigator.


## A proposal

Finally, which experiences have to be fashioned for the teacher who uses drama as the medium of giving learning experiences to classes? I propose that something on these lines might take the place of the training we are giving now:

*The academic aspects.* The birth and origins of saga, myth, legend, folk-lore and the varying attitudes to and the uses made of it in different societies – past and present.
Differences in dramatic form, that is tragic, comic, didactic, absurd, and the forms of dramatic play.
Group dynamics.

Anthropological study of the place of theatre and drama in the human condition.

Understanding of play – its origins, elaboration procedures and purposes.

Child development and the stages of drama need in individuals and groups.

Motivations in learning.

Analysis of the types of confrontation which create dramatic tension.

History of educational drama not only in western education but in, say, Aborigine hunting training.

Mental health.

Sociology of groups.

Modes of communications.

The understanding of the universals and how they are revealed via experience in many 'particulars'.

With regard to the above what needs to be done is to give a thorough and exciting introduction to all these, trying to awaken the teacher's own learning concepts to give them a centre to relate to, then the teacher can go through life adding to the truthful centre which has been begun in college.

*Practical experiences*. Understanding the techniques of how to make language meaningful, the ability to relate written, spoken, and heard in a meaningful way.

To 'produce' (without the dull and formal) plays and novels into real experiences.

Self-discovery of teaching skills and strengths and weaknesses.

Harnessing the instinct for drama in classes of children to the classroom tasks.

Handling groups of all types, sizes and sorts in all sorts of spaces.

The collecting of sources and resources, with integrity in their usage.

Understanding of how and when drama may aid other disciplines in the curriculum.

Learning how to focus material for groups so that they work productively and share in work and decision-taking.

Experience in watching, analysing themselves and others, and in communicating their analysis.

Controlling for effect and affect their signalling in the teaching situation.

Skills of verbalizing. Varying styles, vocabulary, pitch modulation and projection.

Skills in making productive tension and confrontation with their classes.

Learning to listen with care and imagination.
Learning to recover and rehabilitate in the teaching situation.
Classifying in the ongoing teaching situation.

I believe that all these can be broken down and 'taught', or rather learnt. Of course the studies will look very different from those at present being taught, and the timing will be different. There will be little time for play productions, visits to plays and the amassing of play lists and programmes, and those long and short essays written at term end. The pace will seem very 'loose' at first, slower too in the beginning and the teacher will need help to find the relevance and relatedness of all the work to a centre. The course will demand patience and commitment to *teaching*.

The difference may be that we create a race of teachers who are unafraid to make relationships with classes, who are unafraid to admit that they do not know, who never stop seeking to learn more about the dynamics of teaching; who bring all of themselves to school and demand that their classes do the same; who can actually change their modes of work to suit the needs of their classes at any time so that learning is kept meaningful, who like to get on with the people they teach because they are unafraid of the dull, the aggressive, the unacademic, the 'naughty'; who are able to admit that they are tired today, so that their classes can take some responsibility. It is surely worth trying a different way. I have seen 'old' teachers begin to live in their teaching again, and I have seen 'new' teachers suddenly believing they are going to be able to teach after all. I wonder when it can receive a thorough testing?

# PART TWO

# The nature of
# educational drama

# Introduction

Drama in education has altered greatly during the last twenty-five years, and it is still changing. There has been a shift in direction from an interest in the personal development of the individual pupil, through the acquiring of theatrical and improvisational skills to the recognition of drama as a precise teaching instrument, which works best when it is part of the learning process. Drama is no longer considered simply as another branch of art education, but as a unique teaching tool, vital for language development and invaluable as a method in the exploration of other subject areas.

Dorothy Heathcote's papers in this section reflect this shift in emphasis, and the consequent significance in the changing role of the teacher and changing teaching style. Her first paper 'Improvisation' was published only two years after Brian Way's *Development in Drama* – a book which stemmed from the Peter Slade 'Child Drama' movement of the 1950s, and which was responsible for separating drama in education from theatre activities. Slade and Way considered Child Drama to have its roots in play and that its function was to develop the child from within through creative self expression. In this book *Child Drama* Slade writes: 'It is the great activity, it never ceases where there is life; it is eternally bound up with mental health. It is the Art of Living.' In his view the teacher's function was not to teach the skills and arts of performance but to encourage self realization – hence the teacher's role was to be that of a 'loving ally' creating an environment which would foster children in their natural growth.

Gavin Bolton and Dorothy Heathcote hold that this child-centred approach to teaching drama appears not only to reduce the function of the teacher, but also to reduce the status of the subject since the emphasis on personal growth ignores the importance of content and the pursuit of knowledge, and as Gavin has already pointed out in the foreword, Dorothy has been a major force in the pulling back of drama to the track of pursuing knowledge.

In her teaching and writing she considers herself primarily as a teacher and only secondarily as a teacher of drama, using the powerful tool of drama for her purposes as an educator. Instead of being an onlooker and supporter, the teacher works within the group, and has a

42

positive and leading share in the direction of the group's activities and a peculiar responsibility for the interactions which are the life of the group. Dorothy Heathcote has always recognized that she has these responsibilities as the most mature member of the group she works with. In setting up and sharing learning experiences with children, she operates from within the creative and educative process. It is this basic teacher attitude, more than any other, which sets Heathcote apart from her predecessors in drama in education.

# Improvisation

*From a pamphlet 'Drama in Education', produced by the National Association for the Teaching of English, and published by Bodley Head, 1967.*

Drama is becoming 'respectable' in our schools. Many timetables now take cognisance of this activity and the word is being introduced into our staff rooms and conferences, but to many teachers it still remains a great mystery better left alone, and not the least mysterious facet of it is the activity called 'improvisation'. Why should this be? One reason lies in the fact that there are as many definitions of it as there are practitioners. So let us try to define it simply and clearly. Throughout this essay I am assuming certain attitudes in the reader and define them as follows:

1   A respect for children and what they bring to the learning situation.
2   A will to accept and use what they offer in class situations.
3   Self identification as a member of a team – older, more experienced, as a rule, able to keep the team together, work them to capacity, forwarding their projects efficiently, using their strengths and helping them to know and overcome their weaknesses, stretching their potential all the time and keeping their 'sights' true for the task in hand.

Improvisation in my view means 'discovering by trial, error and testing; using available materials with respect for their nature, and being guided by this appreciation of their potential'. The *'end-product'* of improvisation is the *experience* of it. *Any* artist in *any* field will tell you this. What then is improvisation in drama? Dramatic improvisaton is concerned with what we discover for ourselves and the group when we place ourselves in a human situation containing some element of desperation. Very simply it means putting yourself into other people's shoes and, by using personal experience to help you to understand their point of view, you may discover more than you knew when you started. What this 'more' is depends upon the purpose of the exercise in the first place, that is what the motivation was. More of this later.

We use this system of discovery, naturally, all the time – it seems inborn in us, as natural as breathing – in our first playing, in our reading for pleasure where we share the lives of others, thus stretching our experience; when we seek to understand another person as in friendship and caring; in the worlds offered by cinema, TV, radio and the

44

theatre. This of course is always a *personal* role-playing, *personally* motivated, whereas the class is a group which requires motivating at specified times during the school day. The mystery has arisen partly because of this, and because the real issues have been clouded by theatre and 'showing' issues both laudable in themselves and to be desired in their place.

It can now be seen, I hope, that improvisation is not a subject area (though it may be so sometimes), it is really a tool for the teacher, to be used flexibly at times when 'personal identity' role-playing is the most efficient way of crystallizing what the teacher wishes to make clear. It is available to teachers of science as well as of the arts, though it will possibly be employed by the former in a somewhat more limited form. Possibly because we have not yet done sufficient research into matters like this, but wherever understanding of human behaviour, feelings, hopes and attitudes is required it will function speedily and efficiently. It must be understood at this stage that I am not writing of the improvisation used by children in their own play, or of the improvisation used in class when the teacher takes up the position of onlooker in order to enable the children to have child drama opportunities. I am concerned, here, solely with the use of improvisation to aid a learning/teaching situation, and many child drama elements will be present in a well-conducted one – it cannot really succeed if they are not. An example used recently with a fourth form in a secondary school will serve to illustrate what I mean. The main purpose of the work was to try to break down the verbal shyness of the form. So the teacher began with the question, 'If we had a million pounds to spend for the good of humanity, on what would we spend it?' The debate ranged over Oxfam, 'The Pill' for India, research into cultivation of deserts, Cheshire Homes, Geriatric and Maternity Wards, and for a time remained polite and uninspired. But as soon as the class were asked to explain Oxfam and, in this case, the use of a modern highly efficient plough, to the teacher, who became an Indian peasant anxious only to work the land of his ancestors in the way his father before him had done, then the real and deeper issues were thrown in their faces. Once the deep issues were raised, the class worked in a different dimension of communication and no longer could it remain at a polite level, it became a series of personal committals, highly demanding and equally satisfying.

This class of children were astonished at their ability to become involved in the problems of an Indian farmer and even more astonished at their ability to *express* their involvement. Because the teacher's aim was to help the children to enjoy verbal communication via argument, role-playing, debate and discussion he did not allow the situation to be developed as a play, but kept the verbal challenge as the first priority. How the various officials portrayed character, etc., he did not interfere with; timing and all the theatrical aspects were not his concern, only their means of achieving verbal understanding did he press, though of course he realized that many other facets of this situation were available to him should he wish to press them, for as soon as we place someone in their own environment, with their prejudices, attitudes and hopes, the world is our oyster in study terms. This is why dramatic improvisation is of such value to us, and yet so confusing, for selectivity must be used and this is a great difficulty for many teachers.

Can this be made easier? A class is a series of individuals who bring not only their individual points of view but their individual experiences, visions and interpretations to the situation. This often causes teachers to fail when they first try this way of working. Let us see if there is a recipe for built-in success. In my experience the following factors must be present for improvisation to succeed:

*Individuality should be celebrated*

1    A genuine desire by the teacher to bring relevant class experience and information to the fore and make it available to all the group. (This of course can be uncomfortable for some teachers, for part of this they may find hard to accept, e.g. moral attitudes they do not approve of, expressed in terms they find disagreeable.) This cannot happen unless there is a good working atmosphere promoted by permissiveness and mutual respect between teacher and class.

2    The core of entry to the situation must be tailored to fit the experiences and attitudes the class will generally hold. For example a group of rather tough youths recently were challenged to examine their moral code regarding work. The situation started in a pub, this being acceptable to them; it ended (if it will ever be ended – for who knows what reflections will continue in their minds after the initial class experience is over?) after two hours, in their examining *how* they were different because one tramp had braved the bright lights of the pub and caused them to measure their world of day-to-day work and events against his. The teacher in this case was interested to press for 'moral code at work' to be examined, but many more issues could have been taken up. I consider it to be the teacher's task to ease the way into the situation for the class. This means a sensitive examination of and willingness to understand what will be the 'kicks' for the class. If a 'pint of bitter' start does it, then it's worth using. There must be withdrawal of moral judgement on the part of the teacher but this does not mean that he or she may not take a moral stand on any issue, just that it must not be set it up as the 'right' one. There are none that are 'right' for all people in all circumstances.

3    The teacher must understand the way in which dramatic improvisation functions. As pictures need pigment and surface, drama uses

the six elements of stillness, movement, silence, sound, darkness, light; in every possible combination and graduation. These six elements are the only means of communication in this medium. I will try to clarify this by example. Let us take a situation often used by teachers in primary schools – the capture of Persephone and the ultimate agreement reached between the earth mother and Pluto. Persephone is often playing with her friends when the God of the underworld takes her to his kingdom. Here we may have the *sounds* of children's voices at play, their *movements* at play. Suddenly this may be frozen into *silence* and *stillness* as the God emerges with *sounds* unlike those previously heard and the *movements* unlike those previously seen. They (Pluto and Persephone) may then depart with *movement* of a quite different intensity and accompanied not by *sound*, but *silence*. The friends may then depart in *movement* totally unlike their first play and the place be left in complete emptiness and *silence* or there may be the *sound* of Persephone's weeping. Likewise all these situations will be richer if *light changes* occur as well, and musical sound may be used effectively too. This theme is capable of being explored by a hundred different combinations of the above, depending on: what the children feel at their stage of development to be 'true'; and the purpose the teacher has in mind in choosing (or allowing the children to choose) this theme. The theatre with all its resources can only employ these six elements and drama must do exactly the same. Of course, in the classroom, teachers often lack the resources of light and darkness and musical sound but the children are adept at imagining or 'making do' and an unlit lantern used by a child 'creates' darkness. Try it if you don't believe me, but you must *believe* the children if you do try it!

4   The teacher must be prepared to enter the children's world once they begin to work in the medium. It is easy to 'believe' if you encourage in yourself two attitudes: a 'willing suspension of disbelief'; and a 'serious' approach to their work. I do not mean here an absence of humour of course. Drama and gaiety go hand in hand as do drama and tears. The latter situation is often easier for the tentative teacher.

5   The teacher must know the *basic* purpose of the exercise and in the development of the situation keep this to the fore. He or she must continually be selective as the work is helped along. There may be many different possibilities for development within any improvisation situation. For example:

(a)   children showing what they know factually about, say, a period in history so that the teacher can learn where to clarify or develop in this field;

(b)   children revealing how they function in small groups. Who are the natural leaders?

(c)   children revealing ability to concentrate;

(d)   children being challenged to listen to each other;

(e)   children's response to verbal ideas, and so on. These are obviously only a few of the vast field open to the teacher via this medium.

6   The thing to be taught must be discovered via human beings in action – that is, 'living through' the situation (the Greek meaning of drama). If this kind of discovery cannot be made, then improvisation is the wrong medium, and the teacher should look about for a more efficient way of bringing understanding to the class.

When these elements of permissiveness, belief, sympathetic entrance to the theme, guidance to teaching point, understanding of the medium and the things it can and cannot achieve, are present, then improvisation will succeed in the task of stimulating personal discovery for children and teacher alike.

You may feel none the wiser for having read this. All I can suggest to you is that you try it with your classes for just five minutes the first time; openly discuss with them your difficulties as far as you are able to clarify them and gain their co-operation to help this method of work to succeed by discussion and trial and error. No written help can give you as much as that given to you by experience gained with your classes. Remember to keep in the forefront of your mind this maxim. Drama is not stories retold in action. Drama is human beings confronted by situations which change them because of what they must face in dealing with those challenges. An 'open-ended' situation is easier for teachers who feel themselves to be novices than a story where the beginning and end are pre-known.

# Role-taking

*These notes were prepared for a paper given at a conference in the USA in 1968 and which appear in the booklet* Drama in the Education of Teachers, *published by the Institute of Education, the University of Newcastle upon Tyne.*

Educational Drama can be defined as having two significant aspects and aims. One of these we can define as 'creative work', the other as 'coping-work'. Both are significant areas of experience in the developing person. A broad definition of educational drama is 'role-taking', either to understand a social situation more thoroughly or to experience imaginatively via identification in social situations. How does role-taking help in these processes of coping and creating, and how may schools best structure these learning situations?

Dramatic activity is the direct result of the ability to role-play – to want to know how it feels to be in someone else's shoes. Throughout a life-time each person possesses the gift to a greater or lesser degree to identify with others and to re-live or pre-live situations of importance. It is one of the most efficient ways of gleaning information in the area of emotional experience without having the actual experience. Each person will tend to employ the following system of clarification at these times:

1  When it is essential to look forward because of unease and insecurity about the outcome. For example, before worrying situations like interviews, driving tests, health anxieties entailing hospital visits or interviews with doctors, meetings with authority figures. All persons will, however fleetingly and tentatively, attempt to pre-live these experiences in imagination, if only in order to plan them. Sometimes this planning takes the form only of fleeting images, verbal phrases leaping to mind, but sometimes it may become elaborated into conversations with others about the problem, or even to an acting out in private the sequence of events. It surely is directly akin to the ancient magic employed by primitive tribes when they danced the hunt and the rain when in need of food and water.

2  When an experience has been of extreme importance and too big to understand immediately. An accident, an operation, a quarrel, a telling-off or criticism from authority or one's friends, an emotional break with a person important to one's life are times when a re-living via role-taking may become necessary. The adult joke about my operation is an excellent example of this. The first

account of the operation will be concerned with seeking to put the experience into perspective by communication but later accounts will take on order, style, selection, so that later, the account will be not a re-living of the actual event (which is now in perspective) but a re-experience of the effectiveness of the previous tellings, with one eye upon the recipient. Again we can compare this with the ancient magic of the warriors who, returning from a successful hunt, sought a channel for their joyful emotion as well as recognition of their power by tribe-members and later this became formed and stylized.

3    At times of extreme receptivity, for example when taking up a book to read a story, watching a play, hearing radio or viewing TV.

These processes of identification are not only valuable for the amount of 'easement' they bring to the individual but they make certain valuable demands upon the individual, and these are of relevance to our first question 'How does role-taking help in the processes of coping and creating?'

Teachers are creators of learning situations for others. They are therefore concerned in arranging their 'material' in such a way that by meeting the material the pupils are changed or modified in some way. This 'modification' process would appear to be related to these aspects:

It must arrest attention.

It must employ that which is already known and understood in some positive way.

It must demand decision taking.

It must promote awareness and understanding of the areas newly acquired.

Let us therefore examine which demands role-taking makes upon the individual. We may be then in a position to employ it efficiently and relevantly in our schools. The process of role-taking requires of the persons these things:

1    A 'taking-in', from the situation under consideration (by observation of persons or recalling of significant facts).
2    A harnessing of all relevant information known from previous experiences.
3    The realignment of the relevant information to be applied to the situation under consideration so that old experience becomes useful when applied to the newer problem, thus enabling us to see new and deeper meanings.

So far we have been considering the individual and their own intuitive use of role-taking. What of the group situation in schools? It would appear that an important element in personal development is this acquiring of skill in empathy to apply in our dealings with others. It smooths the paths of understanding, awareness and communication. When applied in groups it seems to have certain additional bonuses for the teacher and class alike in that it allows group pressure to be applied in two ways; to produce differing attitudes and experiences to be available to the group and to demand adequate communication of these attitudes by the individuals in the group, to the group. To quote an example, a group of adolescent boys elected to do a play about a protection gang. This gang therefore must be composed of all the attitudes the individuals have available at the present time. These attitudes are the sum total of the soundings they are able to take of the situation based upon all their previous experiences, real-life, fictional, absorbed from TV, radio, and their reading. As soon as the gang begins to live as they think these people live these attitudes begin to be revealed to the group itself. All the decisions, choice of language, behaviour thrown up by individuals begins to affect all the others by a sort of rubbing-off process. Some attitudes will be new to certain individuals (like the idea one of this particular class had that you could lead a good moral private life, yet still function professionally as a gang-member) other attitudes will be taken for granted (like 'everyone is fair game to a protection gang', it is a matter of business not of feeling). Once all these available attitudes are floating, they are liable to this process of modification by group interaction and values. Because the individuals function via their prejudices, because this is their first contribution, there is a heightened sensitivity to others' points of view. Not to be open to them but to take cognizance of them in order to defend oneself! This seems to be good ground for teachers to till, not through moral judgements and value judgements but by exposure of what has been thrown up so far in order that it may be examined.

The most important aspect of role-taking is that it is unpremeditated, unplanned and therefore constantly can surprise the individual into new awareness. It is therefore important that teachers do not plan surprise out of the class work they may structure.

## The teacher's role in employing drama in education

This can be summed up as follows:

1   To create a climate in which value-judgements do not apply, but where honesty of individual contributions is valued and respect is shown to individuals' ideas and methods of contribution.
2   To employ children's ideas and make them 'work' positively employing the natural laws of the medium.

51

3   To create a working situation of integrity employing the adult world within the situation but allowing the children their own world of concepts and values.

4   To understand thoroughly the way drama functions in promoting the release of varying and conflicting attitudes within the group.

5   To be able to 'forward' the work towards teaching ends without destroying the children's contribution.

6   To be able to prepare and plan, yet retain for the children the necessary 'surprise-confrontation' element.

7   To understand that drama is not stories re-told, but confrontations between individuals, lived at life-rate.

## Thresholds of security

Most communication with regard to drama is related to giving information about needs of children, types of work and techniques of application. The most fundamental area is left unexplored yet it contains the key which could unlock all the other relevant thinking. This area is that of the teacher's own personality and classroom functioning in relation to her or his 'thresholds' of security in order to work successfully. These can be identified as follows:

*Noise threshold*. The quality in noise which first causes discomfort to the teacher.
*Space threshold*. This refers not to emptiness but to the distance between the class and the teacher which the latter feels happy with.
*Group-size threshold*. The sizes of groups most comfortably and efficiently dealt with in the teacher's subjective view.
*The decision-threshold*. The way in which decisions are taken in the teaching situation.
*The subject interests* of the teacher.
*The evaluation resources* of the teacher.
*The variety of teaching registers* the teacher may use in the day-to-day confrontations which are made.

Before examining children's needs, dramatic themes and techniques teachers must understand their behaviour as teachers and the resources they have. Role-taking is so flexible in its application in education that it will work for all personalities and under all teaching circumstances. So first the inflexible must be understood. Teachers are not taught how to teach. They become able to function in the role through a series of class confrontations which they must be able to survive. So they acquire techniques because of their need to survive and those are related to how they need to survive. This is the most important aspect of understanding drama in education and one not properly analysed or trapped by our training schemes.

# Dramatic activity

*This paper was reprinted as a pamphlet entitled 'Drama', from an article in the journal* English in Education, *Vol. 3, No. 2, Summer 1969, published by NATE in association with OUP.*

Dramatic activity is concerned with the ability of humans to 'become somebody else', to 'see how it feels', and the process is a very simple and efficient way of crystallizing certain kinds of information. Humans employ it naturally and intuitively all their lives. 'Put yourself in my shoes' is a readily understood request, and one easily complied with, though some are more capable than others of achieving deep insight by this means. It has been turned into a complicated and therefore often misunderstood subject in school, by teachers (perhaps those who see childhood as merely the time spent waiting to become an adult, and deny the value of a child's experiencing being a child?) who have replaced the real experience with 'exercises for' the real experience. The underlying assumption is that children are not capable of experiencing 'the real thing', so substitutes in the form of watered-down exercises are employed instead. This, together with a lack of understanding of the relationship between so-called 'improvisation' and 'theatre' experiences, and a paucity of adequate generally accepted vocabulary to order the thinking, has caused much confusion. A further complicating factor is that a good drama experience cannot either be preserved or transferred easily, so that those using drama intuitively in the classroom or club find it difficult to communicate what they do to achieve their ends, or the means they employ to learn which ends are relevant at that time and in that particular circumstance. Most good infant teachers are able to judge when they may venture to join children at play, especially wendy-house play, but many would be at a loss to explain how they judge.

Like many human learning experiences, drama is at once a subject area for research opportunity – for example theatre skills, and a tool for personal development – in personal role-playing. Because drama is concerned with the kinds of associations and conflicts which people in their public, personal and religious lives enter into, it offers two unique opportunities to the teacher:

1 The fact that for its expression it always demands crystallization of ideas in groups,
2 It can employ the individuals, working as a group, to conceive the ideas, area, and level of interest in the first place.

Therefore, even as the group – because such is the nature of groups – constantly modifies and gives form to its ideas, expression and sentiment, employing the natural laws of drama, it is also a direct result and expression of the inter-personal relationships of the group, and the individual strengths and weaknesses of those in it. A team-game or class project will also reflect these. The factor special to drama is that it achieves these in 'heated' not 'cold' circumstances, for it draws directly upon the individual's life and subjective experiences as its basic material, and achieves this in circumstances which are unique – that is when 'a willing suspension of disbelief' applies, and when those concerned are using their subjective world to illuminate and understand the motivations of others through role-playing.

Dramatic activity is concerned with the crises, the turning points of life, large and small, which cause people to reflect and take note, and it functions within the following disciplines:

1   It must use women and men in their total environment. That is, employing their experiences *before* the event in question, all their knowledge factual and subjective, their abilities, failings, blindspots, skills, *together with what is not known*, their particular character and personality to assist in revealing their ability to face the crisis chosen to confront them at the present time.

2   Humans (or animals or creatures possessing human qualities, or attributes) must in action and situation be placed in some kind of emotional relationship with others, even if the topic and reason for their meeting is an intellectual one, for example, two doctors discussing the technique of a brain operation is not dramatic, but the same two doctors, both in love with the patient whose brain is damaged, is dramatic.

3   The statement achieved must be achieved *in the present* and must be seen to occur (drama means 'living through'), so that the personalities must behave at a 'life-rate', performing those acts and saying those words which would be relevant to the situation and period in time, and, as in life, show no future or advance knowledge of what will occur as a result of their actions – unless they are Gods or superhuman beings.

4   The achieved final statement must have 'form'. That is, everything irrelevant to the main issues must be lacking, and the relevant material must achieve order and style, so that what is revealed is a refined distillation of all the ideas embodied in the chosen material and *considered by the group to be relevant*. So form in this case is conceived as a sliding scale and related to the standards the group are able set themselves and perceive as required in the first place. The infant child, the ESN child and the sixth-former will all

require to 'in-build' rules for their work as they develop it, though these rules will be vastly different in each case.

5  Drama must in its most refined condition be capable of being shared by others who participate in a different way – the audience, which may consist of only one person carefully chosen for some quality such as sensitivity to the actors' needs (for example teacher or headmistress), or the mixed mass of persons who pay to have the experience in the theatre.

Often the child's drama and that of the theatre are seen as being in opposition. The terms 'informal' and 'formal' drama suggest this. They do in fact spring from the same roots – the need of people to role-play, to enable them to measure themselves and their own experiences and viewpoints against those of others, not only in order to see where they are *different*, but also to discover wherein they are alike, so that they can achieve a sense of belonging, especially in those areas of living which are not capable of being communicated by words alone. Theatre in its most complex form (say a highly skilful presentation of 'Lear') is related to the child's first groping attempts to improvise upon an idea in that there is a natural progression from the tentative meeting of the group's ideas, through the group's achieving with those ideas a statement with form, to a theatrical presentation of a group's ideas.

## Drama and education

Let us look now at some of the opportunities, and some of the demands, of drama. First of all, it allows children to:

- employ their own views of life and people,
- use their own standards of evaluation,
- exercise their own terms when expressing and tempering these ideas.

It also subjects children to the demand to communicate clearly and specifically both in discussion of the ideas, and the dramatic expression of them. The linguistic demands alone may range from academic discussion of a factual point, to an emotional outburst such as a king in defence of his kingdom might make (public language) or a tramp at the door of a rich man, justifying his existence might be called upon to make (private language).

Drama cannot properly function unless the children agree to tolerate generously, and put to work, differing personalities, points of view, information, speed of working, and levels of attention. A sixth-former recently, while working as a member of a self-chosen after-school drama group, when asked what was affecting him most, replied 'I never really saw a D-streamer before; I never realized what it must be like not to understand what is said the first time I hear it. This bloke learns about life in a totally different way from me, and I'm not sure that my way is the best way'.

It gives instant feedback for assessment and rethinking. E. V. Taylor, in 'Experiments with a Backward Class', quotes the example of a little boy role-playing a Greek guard who said 'By gum, it's cold'. His classmates protested that 'Greeks don't talk like that'. He modified after some thought to 'By *ye* gum, it's cold', which passed their critical surveillance.

On another occasion a group of four year olds were interested in an 'old' map, and decided to travel its roads and seas. They chose to go in a 'Yellow Submarine'. The song was 'Top of the Pops' that week. The approved school boys who chose to kill a president were interested to see how much latitude the (new to them) teacher would allow them in their gang-warfare.

Finally drama is also at the service of the other areas of the curriculum simply because, when people are put, in the act of living, in their environment, the area of study regarding them may be as varied as their characters or environment. Fisherfolk living in the Outer Hebrides may be of interest because of their isolation, their fishing boats and particular skills, their religious and moral beliefs and attitudes, their homes, stories, folk-lore, understanding of the tides, means of communication, spending or voting power, hobbies or a multitude of other facets of their lives. Set them in another century and the possibilities are doubled. Which of these aspects is to be isolated and brought to special notice, depends upon the teacher's present purpose.

## Aims and assessment

Because of the many purposes to which drama may be orientated, it is often difficult for teachers to discover how to plan progressive work, and how to recognize progression – indeed it is impossible to do the latter unless aim and assessment are kept firmly together in the teacher's mind. All too often the aim is too vaguely defined, and the assessment based falsely on 'showing' rather than 'experiencing' aspects of the work. Teachers find it hard to observe what is the real experience for the children inside the overt action which has been stimulated. An example of this was seen when some seventeen-year-old boys chose a theme of 'Mods, Rockers and Drugs'. They finally decided that a gang owning motor-cycles should meet in a garage to draw lots to decide who should do the 'ton-up' on the M1 in order to carry urgently-needed blood plasma (and incidentally to collect some purple hearts *en route*). They used chairs as motor-cycles, and spent most of the drama session discussing plans and arguing on a corner of the hall (the garage). The teacher (looking for development of the drama – the shape of the play) was frustrated and felt that session to be a failure. What she failed to notice was that the boys' real experience during this session was that of owning a motor-bike. One can sit on a chair and it becomes the finest vehicle in the world – to have to wheel it out of the garage and drive off would be to turn it once again into a chair. The boys knew this for they were inside the situation, while the teacher remained outside. This kind of misreading of children's drama occurs all too often.

One of the broad aims of education is to help people to achieve the fullest and most varied and subtle changes of register in relating to others. These changes of register must be in reference to role-capabilities, language, and physical relations.

It is in this field that dramatic activity is of most direct help, whether at the 'wendy-house' play in infancy, or the socio- and psycho-drama of adulthood, together with all other types which lie between these two extremes.

## The role of the teacher

The skills required to understand how to employ drama to these ends are not so shrouded in mystery as might be supposed. They would seem to be as follows:

1  To acquire an understanding of the six drama elements, and how they combine through contrasting with and supporting each other to make statements.
2  Vivid pictorial and aural imagination.
3  Empathy to sense the general mood of a group.
4  Capacity to put the children's needs before the teacher's plans.
5  Sensitive changes of register in verbal communication with group.
6  Ability to employ changes of register in the teaching role. This is explained more fully below.
7  Ability to *look* – to perceive the real situation. Ability to *listen* – to perceive the real statement.

## Changes of register in the teaching role

The teacher's role is often seen as a consistent one – that of he or she who knows and can therefore tell or instruct. This is too limited a register, and a barren one, except in certain circumstances. In drama the teacher must be prepared to fulfil many roles:

The deliberate opposer of the common view in order to give feedback and aid clarity of thought.
The narrator who helps to set mood and register of events.
The positive withdrawer who 'lets them get on with it'.
The suggester of ideas, as a group member.
The supporter of tentative leadership.
The 'dogsbody' who discovers material and drama aids.
The reflector who is used by the children to assess their statements.
The arbiter in argument.
The deliberately obtuse one, who requires to be informed, and the one who believes that the children can do it.

## The needs of the children

If children are to see their ideas function adequately the material must be so structured that without anyone interfering they are seen to work. The non-verbal child should never be placed under a verbal pressure which is too great to cope with – it is the teacher's task to plan the expression of the idea so that the child's strengths are used, not the weaknesses. No teacher would dream of asking children to try to make pictorial statements with badly mixed paint, and exactly the same must apply in drama work. As with art, they need not be fine artists but they must be sensitive to the possibilities of the medium.

It is urgently necessary that some means should be evolved of training teachers to use drama progressively during the child's school life – drama which is not always related to theatrical standards but which considers the children's changing needs both as individuals and as members of groups. Then experimentation can take place to discover which kinds of group drama most efficiently serve which present need in the children. All too often we press the future on them and leave them with insufficient time to experience the present. An example of the kind of error we fall into was seen when a lecturer in education watched a group of nine-year-olds battling to find which statement was the important one for them in the struggle between Pharaoh and the Israelites. In discussion sitting round the teacher they knew that they wanted their freedom to return home, but in drama all they could say was 'Give us more food'. Each time they asked and the Pharoah refused, more children became involved, and 'changes of register' began to be available to them in this difficult verbal situation of kings and soothsayers, prophets and slaves, past civilizations and remote climatic condition and costumes. The education lecturer thought that 'movement might have been a better approach'.

## Conclusion

In small groups, all people whether children or adults, wise or foolish, verbal or non-verbal, employ the taking of roles (sometimes through individual day-dreaming, reliving of situations, reading of books, watching television and films) when it best serves the ends they require. To harness this to the classroom learning situation would obviously be common sense, even at some loss of the individual's ability to do what pleases when it pleases. Rules do not restrict, they aid, if they are good and pertinent rules. The old-fashioned (and false) rules of theatre such as 'face the front', must be replaced with rules which artists have always employed when creating, such as 'use your ideas and talents honestly, serving the disciplines of the medium'.

# Subject or system?

*'Drama and Education: Subject or System?' first appeared in* Drama and Theatre in Education, *edited by Nigel Dodd and Winifred Hickson, published by Heinemann, 1971.*

Much attention has been given to drama as a subject, but in comparison very little to drama as a system. I therefore shall consider the latter. Drama in education can be sub-divided *ad infinitum* depending upon how many persons happen to be discussing it at any one moment and what interests they profess to. The terms are only too familiar – the precise meanings too vague. I refer to divisions such as improvisation, role-playing, dance-drama, socio-drama and so on. These are all conventional sub-divisions of a larger field. It is more relevant to my purpose deliberately to keep the field large and whole and sectionalize my cultivator – the teacher. What do all teachers hold in common? We can assume the wish to communicate, or at least the responsibility for communication (if only of the one-way type) to be accepted. One can also assume interest in subject area, presumably a modicum of concern with measurement of that which has been communicated, together with some basic training for the job and the need to survive in the job. No one teaches a teacher how to teach. Teachers are made in the classroom during confrontations with their classes, and the product they become is a result of their need to survive and the ways they devise to do this. In my view insufficient emphasis is placed upon this during the training period or at any time later when new skills are required.

One should be prepared to define one's terms. For the present purpose I will define a teacher as 'one who creates learning situations for others'. That is, a person whose energies and skills are at the service, during the professional situation, of the pupils. A teacher's rewards come because those energies flow into other people and therefore can make the return journey through the teacher's own ability. The total person a teacher is, is employed in this task, properly filtered through the professional principles and duties. What he or she knows and requires to communicate. What the means are of achieving this.

I define educational drama as being anything which involves people in active role-taking situations in which attitudes, not characters, are the chief concern, lived at life-rate (that is discovery at this moment, not memory based) and obeying the natural laws of the medium. I regard these laws as being: a willing suspension of disbelief; agreement to

61

pretence; employing all past experiences available to the group at the present moment and any conjecture of imagination they are capable of, in an attempt to create a living, moving picture of life, which aims at surprise and discovery for the participants rather than for any onlookers. The scope of this is to be defined by story-line and theme, so that the problem with which they grapple is clearly defined. I maintain that problem-solving is the basis of learning and maturation.

Problem-solving[1] extends the work of learning. It is the capacity to act as if an act were carried out before in fact it is undertaken. It uses past experience, product of prior learning, to predict what may happen if and when certain acts are carried out in conditions given: it multiplies interlocking learnings; seeks their conscious integration; provides a ground for more sustaining action; and sharpens need for evaluations which work out to be productive in their fitting to creation, as acts, in fact, are taken. By means of conscious problem-solving, we increase the range and depth of our conscious knowing of creation's shaping.

Looking at people to note their social nature, we can see that communication is the crucial function. Communication allows people to be inclusive of one another as members of the species, to integrate their meaning for each other, to order their transactions to be increasingly supportive, and to share more fully in communion with their natures. In the classroom setting, we have as elemental the communicative system between a teacher and a student. We know its basic nature: two creative systems intercoursing, feeding one another.

The teacher is a sender and a receiver; the student is a sender and a receiver. What the teacher sends, the student needs to be able to receive. As the teacher receives a particular sending from the student, the teacher needs to be able to organize a response which is relevant to what the student can next receive and use; the student, receiving, then organizing a response to be relevant to what the teacher can next receive and use, thus continues the sequence of communication. As each receives and sends, they have to be able to project into the inner world of the other and to sense what is forming there. Then their communication can be meaningful (a means) to the sequential and emergent development of the communication. Otherwise, communication fails; education fails. Communication is the centre of the educative system.

## Two-way communication

I am concerned then with two main aspects of teaching: the first is the way a teacher confronts the class and the way the two-way flow of

[1] *Explorations in Creativity*, eds. Ross Mooney and Taher Razik, Harper & Row.

communication takes place. This is the living vibrating matter of teaching, firmly based upon mutual respect by each for the other's contribution. A factor which may have to be taken into consideration when training teachers to use drama in education is the varying ways of thinking which are presently being researched into by Liam Hudson[2] and others. I refer to the convergent/divergent types.

*Convergent Thinking*[3] This is the ability to give the appropriate response, to acquire habits of thought and action which are most acceptable within a culture or subculture – for example, working class as compared with middle-class value systems (McGuire and White, 1957). Measures of performances on tests of intelligence, abstract reasoning, space relations, and the ability to listen combine to yield this factor in persons.

*Divergent Thinking* Some, more than others, acquire a capacity to devise new forms, come up with fresh ideas, and see deeper meanings in objects, events, inter-personal relationships, and symbolic materials. Measures, such as identifying unforeseen consequences, seeing unusual uses of problems, and sensing new meanings in common situations, now are used to identify the creative person. Although some teachers and parents value creative children and adolescents, many are uncomfortable with them and prefer a degree of conformity (Getzels and Jackson, 1960).

## The teacher's security

The second point concerns the areas of security the teacher gradually acquires and depends upon in the job: teachers require to understand their own security and practice in order that they may gradually push back these security needs and accept more tenuous positions in order that eventually they may teach from positions of calculated risk. I believe very few teachers discover their true teaching thresholds because of timetables and syllabi which prevent the discovery of natural teaching pace and rate. This applies equally to the classes taught. Many may never come to terms with their learning rate until after their school life is over. These security thresholds seem to include *the noise level*, that is the quality in the sound which first causes the teacher's 'panic stations' behaviour to come into operation. I refer to discomfort regarding the noise which the teacher cannot ignore. This is sometimes rooted in guilt, for so much so-called discipline is related to

[2] Liam Hudson, *Contrary Imaginations*, Pelican Books.
[3] *Explorations in Creativity*, eds. Ross Mooney and Taher Razik, Harper & Row.

noise level, when in fact noise quality is much more relevant. *The space level*: this refers not to emptiness but to the distance the teacher requires to set between him/herself and the class. *The group-comfort level*: that is, sizes of groups most comfortably and efficiently dealt with in the teacher's subjective view. *The way decisions are achieved* in the classroom. *The 'subject' interests* of the teacher. *The resources* the teacher employs in evaluating the work undertaken. *The variety of registers* available to the teacher in approaching the class.

*The noise threshold.* If we are going to teach at all well in any circumstances (and I am not here referring only to drama) we must understand the kind and the quality of noise we can take and the point at which we cannot take it. Questions like, Are you comfortable in class when children discuss and leave you out of it? What if children argue back, or shout at each other across you, or are shifting furniture? are relevant here. Some teachers are very uncomfortable under one or other of these circumstances, and would be wiser and more efficient never to become involved in such situations. These are not fanciful ideas. It is time to do job-study in teaching, and each individual has to make a start. It is essential that we learn to teach with a modicum of security so that we are not consequently appalled by meeting our thresholds all the time. Some are uncomfortable with even an appearance of disorganization. Headmasters looking through windows may have a very powerful effect upon that particular threshold!

*The space threshold.* I make my contacts most comfortably when classes are close together and near to me. Others require to teach at a distance. This does not make either of us better or worse teachers. Value judgements are irrelevant here; the main consideration is that teachers personally understand why they teach at the distance they elect to use and the consequent effects of this choice. For many years I wondered at my stupidity in creating such crowded situations which can be uncomfortable and sometimes nauseous, until I understood this requirement and now can accept and employ it positively. I have to create situations in which classes can first throw their behaviour in my face in order that I may make an assessment of needs and therefore of starting points.

Also, for drama, I require that a class shall be made to feel like a group. Desks isolate individuals, therefore my instinct is to discard them unless I require individual differences to emerge, then I hurry to desks in order that that behaviour may emerge. Eye impact and eye feedback is important. The teacher who requires the class to look (and feel to be) a small number in a large space, functions very differently from the one who prefers a class to seem a large group in a relatively small space. In fact both these are valuable experiences at relevant times. Once this is consciously understood, changes may be made to employ both when they best serve the needs of the class, the material, and lastly of the teacher who may be more ready to risk-take because of this conscious knowing. Teachers often request empty space for drama, but all areas are space, only some are interrupted upwards by pillars, cupboards and other compendia, some symmetrically by, for example, desks, others circularly by floor patterns, or lighting arrangements. Some focus toward one end. The teacher and class will have a subjective response to all these factors which can be most profitably employed if it is consciously realized in drama work so that strengths and weaknesses of form, for the purpose in hand, may be exploited or circumvented.

*The size of group threshold*. While relationships are still tenuous I require my classes to function as one group. For some people this is the least happy or convenient grouping. I require the large group for my personal comfort as I need to make personal contact of eye, voice, and group positioning with the class and also I require an immediate feedback of response (good or bad) from them in order to test the relationship and feel the temper of the class. Even when I first began teaching I used this large grouping. The important question is, what sizes of groups give you security? Often in training or when teachers first attempt drama the situation becomes closed just at the time when it should remain open. For example advice is often given like, begin with small groups or even individuals or pairs, the assumption being that these latter are easier to deal with. In fact, to be realistic, size of group is entirely dependent upon the subjective view of the teacher. The medium is so flexible that it can begin anywhere and function under all circumstances. Every other rule is irrelevant at this point.

Once some security is gained, teaching experimentation and other consequent dramatic forms may be explored by the teacher and class when the size of groups employed can be directly related to the aim and purpose of the work done. A whole class working upon a market situation will bring, receive and face totally different experiences than when working in pairs. It should be possible to help a teacher understand the differing consequences of saying, 'Find a partner and work out this', 'Divide into groups', 'Everybody is going to be the same character', 'Go away and lay out your market stalls', 'Find your houses', 'Listen to this story then act it', 'Start with these words, "Don't go in there"'. It should also be possible to help a teacher understand the difference between progression which aims at burnishing the drama and that which undertakes to burnish the children. Both are sensible educational aims but there is no doubt in my mind which has priority, though sometimes the play may appear to be more important.

65

A further testing aspect of grouping emerges during periods of discussion. Some teachers require to communicate via them, otherwise they feel a loss of grip when the children turn aside and speak to each other with consequent loss of audibility to the teacher. Trying to ensure that every word spoken is heard by everyone else, except under specific circumstances, leads to loss of efficiency and boredom. Personally I am most secure when the class are ignoring my presence, discussing among themselves, thus enabling me to tune in to the temperature and attitudes of their work and the messages I can receive through ear and eye. Thus I am informed of their next need. I can quickly get the gist of the discussion simply by asking. I gain much of my information about groups via identification and empathy and rely less upon verbal inter-change. The main thing is that we require to know which we rely upon so that we structure to get what we require, first for our security, later in order to risk-take.

*Decision-making and leadership thresholds.* Some basic questions here seem to be, 'How do you structure for leadership? Do you appoint your trustworthy and reliable ones proven by time? On which occasions do you require to retain leadership yourself? At what stage, and why, will you challenge weaker personnel to lead? When don't you mind who emerges?' Obviously all these situations are of value for different purposes, they are not to be set against each other. The secure teacher can employ them all efficiently and skilfully and inbuild the security of a satisfying result for the class. All this is related to the types and degrees of selection a teacher can allow a class and still retain a feeling of security, and also to the way decisions are taken. I require my classes to decide upon material to be used in order that I may discover what types of themes interest them and at what level they require to work and how they become involved. I also believe that decision-taking is an important educational experience and one means of ensuring involvement.

Group decision-taking is not easy but there is nothing quite so revealing of either the needs or resources of any community as making this demand. Drama-making involves groups in a vast range of decision-taking, and progression in this field is related to more and more subtlety of feeling, perception, language, social adjustment and drama expertise. I want my classes to learn to make decisions, and to understand the problems and rewards of these decisions, so I regard it as my prime task to ensure that they clearly understand the choice between possibilities, the nature of the decision taken and the demands likely to be put upon them because of the decision taken. This is another reason why drama is such a wonderful educational tool.

*The subject interest of the teacher*. This clearly will be biased by the intellectual and emotional capacities of the personality, the quality of training received, and the particular approach. It is obvious that the teacher's own interests in the field may be entirely irrelevant to those of the class. In drama it is especially important that teachers have no rigid rules of how to begin, which material is suitable, at what level it will be employed, and which dramatic forms are most acceptable and rewarding at any age. If teachers begin by using rigid rules their consequent development is often towards closed rather than opening and advancing methods of work becoming available to teacher and class alike as they learn to use themselves, their ideas, and gain the capacity to understand and grapple with the medium.

*Evaluation and standards thresholds*. This relates to the ways teachers observe and the things they value and therefore look for as they observe. Some retire or withdraw in order to see their classes at work, others intrude. Some identify, others enquire. A class involved in drama will throw up so much behaviour and teaching opportunity that it is impossible to observe everything or to seize upon everything. So it is essential that the teacher learns to be highly sensitive in observing the relevance of what is thrown up and to perceive the classes' needs via their behaviour. This penetration of the surface facts in order to reach the relevant data is highly important because through drama work the teacher stimulates and feeds the hidden or disguised elements in classes' or individuals' behaviour.

Another important area of observation is that of clearly seeing (that is without bias, and minus the blinkers of the teacher's previously devised intent) the present group, its mood and possibilities at any given moment. A clear example of this was seen when an ESN boy rummaging through a dressing-up box to choose clothes suitable for a slave-driver in King Herod's entourage, selected a hangman's black mask and cap. If the teacher's response had been 'wrong period, must intervene', how much would have been buried which was just on the point of emerging because in choosing, the boy was crystallizing his ideas and feelings. The teacher waited, saw the boy work in the clothes in the drama and observed the enlarged attitudes bringing to the boy a sureness of approach and from the slaves a clear response to the visual threat he fed to them. At some stage the anachronism may be pointed out and a compromise made but the child's need should dictate the timing of this. This boy eventually said in response to an interest being shown in his choice of clothing, 'I'm not bringing these women much life, am I?' And thus some of the reasoning behind his choice became clearer to boy, class and teacher. He had taken a reading of the situation of which he was capable at that moment and this is at once both the very stuff and opportunity offered by drama in education: to permit present readings to be exposed and explored and through that widened into more subtle and generously-based readings.

At first attempts readings (or soundings if preferred) especially of unfamiliar situations are bound to be shallow, socially ramshackle, linguistically hesitant or unsound, artistically tenuous. Time and experience bring a tempering and a tightening of all these. We all take our first readings via our prejudice – a mother's reading of 'mother-type' will employ her direct experiences of being a mother, her own childhood memories, the experiences of others in the group, and in time this range of experiences will become available to challenge, deepen and temper her original reading. So in the action of the drama these experiences become exposed for consideration – either of audiences if that is the final purpose of the work, or of the group only, if that is the purpose. The teacher requires to be unprejudiced and receptive to a vast range of readings, helping the situation by receiving, challenging, helping to develop ideas and above all creating and preserving in the class attitudes of receptivity, non-value judgements and artistic integrity.

Surely it should be possible for us to devise situations whereby teachers may learn how to do this filtered through their own personalities. Because of my personality, much of the drama my classes work upon is sociologically based as I see a class of children trying to work together as a social group, so I give a strong lead in this area with a correspondingly weak one in others.

*Teaching registers*. All teachers develop a range of these as part of their survival kit. The difficulty is to be aware of the uses made of them and their real value to the teacher. Drama reflects registers of approach to and confrontaton with other persons at times of change or crisis. Therefore the teacher requires a sensitivity in this area and in particular must have a conscious command of the register used in confronting classes and understand the reasons for the selection at any given time. It is dangerous in any teaching situation to employ the 'I'm telling you' register too often – in drama situations it is suicidal. What of teacher as catalyst? (When I switch on the red light 'it' has begun.) As reassurer? (Don't worry, put yourself in my hands.) As devil's advocate? (That's surely not true). As good listener? (Good idea, what happens then?)

Register is related to authority and impact, and all teachers require to know which authority they dare not or cannot forego at any price. The teacher with a range of kinds of authority and ways of asserting them can employ them to serve the needs of the various classes rather than the teacher's own, and will obviously be more flexible. Our secondary and comprehensive schools demand this flexibility, and the timetabling which usually operates demands a speedy variation also. The teacher of drama can employ this for conscious effect. *The authority of role.* 'I have my river pilots' licence and I am empowered by law to escort this boat and crew to the harbour bar.' *The one who knows.* 'When you've decided what you require I'll help you to find out about it.' *The teacher leader.* 'I'm in charge here.' *The authority of being in a position to switch roles.* To run with the hare and hunt with the hounds. Children rarely consider that they could also do this!

For me the most secure authority has always been from within the drama situation rather than the teaching one – the authority of role. Not only can I be more flexible in the use of registers, but I fear the teacher authority because I mistrust my ability to cope with a situation which may arise of teacher against class. The role-authority gives me shifting power and a variety of register to be at the service of the class. I may suddenly gather authority to deny or accede to requests, or be minus power but have strong opinions or resist a class in order to strengthen its opinions and decisions. My belief in my attitudes supports their belief in theirs, but this type of teaching takes courage at first and is always a calculated risk.

A further facet of the authority spectrum is that of status and stature. Teachers who 'can be wrong' are likely to last longer and go further! This question of status is the most basic question of all, and requires concern when we train teachers not only for drama, though because drama brings the child's subjective life into the classroom the problems of status and stature are thrown up very quickly and the teacher requires support and preparation to deal with them.

## Drama as an educational medium

So much for the thresholds. How does drama function as an educational medium? Improvisation is essentially living at life-rate, in the present, with agreement to pretence. Dramatic activities are concerned with crisis, the experiences of life, small or large, which cause people to reflect and take note. It functions via these disciplines. The role-taker draws upon all previous relevant experience, all information, factual and subjective, abilities, failings, blind-spots and skills, character and personality. Thus when studying and seeking to understand the 'pretend' situation the role-taker draws all relevant information to the surface and forefront and puts it into action but interacting with others who are also in the same situation. The important difference between life and this make-believe life is that in the latter there is the opportunity for one problem to be faced at a time with consequent selectivity being possible, and of course for different permutations of response to be tried.

69

As stated before, it is prejudice which usually emerges first and often at first this is reinforced. I believe the teacher must accept this hazard, but also be prepared to do something about it in due course. However, the first drama discipline for the teacher is to accept the present condition of the group as revealed by their work. A group of boys chose to rob a security car bringing to their work all their notions about the police, property, wilful damage and right and wrong. No one was arrested even though the police saw the robbery – it was not in their present range to give the police the stronger hand even though their present real condition (living in an approved school) was living testimony to the true position. As teacher I saw no point at all in forcing the issue, other than offering a mild challenge to the authenticity of the situation, for groups must forge their own truths for themselves. The sculptor and painter work via external materials, the truth of which they presently reveal. Others to a certain extent may share this truth for the materials remain to be consulted. The role-taker's material is individual skill and can never be static or perfect. It is therefore essential in educational drama that the teacher be skilled in helping to reveal the presently emergent truth to the group creating it.

Another natural law is that the statement must be achieved in the present and it must be seen to occur, therefore the personalities must behave at life-rate, though as stated before, there will be degrees of selectivity depending upon the skill and sensitivity of the group performing those acts and saying those words which would be relevant to the situation, and period in time, and as in life show no future or advance knowledge of what will occur as a result of those actions. All too often we plan the immediacy of the moment right out of the picture so that persons can never be confronted by themselves. We plan so that everyone knows what they ought to do next, whereas in fact we should plan so that they discover what they did do next. The element of surprise is one of the most important bases of work in educational drama.

For classroom purposes the values of drama seem to me to be these:
It is sociologically based, employing individuals within groups and the interaction of their active processes.
It is also play-based, having a defined area of intention (as in games – a football team knows it will not end up playing at darts!) and employing elaboration.

We often deny our classes elaboration time, in fact it is often taken away by the teacher's own worry or impatience. Elaboration experience probably contributes more than anything else to the process of becoming a mature person. The rules of drama are definite but they are so infinitely flexible and basic that they offer a very wide range of elaboration. In football the brilliant player 'plays' the rules to their limit and good drama experience is as concerned with its rules as with the exploitation of them. So improvisation is really an elaboration procedure which employs all relevant knowledge to this data – factual and emotional information – and tests it in action. It gives immediate feedback to release energy for more elaboration because it is what Harold Rugg in *Imagination*[4] calls 'A gigantic working model'.

Theatre itself is a game of elaboration within a strict framework of intent. In a sense theatre and improvisation begin at the same point. When a group of minds come together to work on the problem there is already available within them the finished product (whatever 'finish' may mean, depending upon aim) but as yet all is obscure and cloudy because the avenues by which it may be expressed and brought into focus are not yet open. If I say to a group of children 'What is a good play?' all of their answer is there available but avenues have to be opened to get the processes of elaboration working to take away the cloud so that they may perceive their answer. We then have, as in the theatre, the brilliant sparkling detail of matter which is related to the present capacities of that class. In theatre the author defines the area of intent and certain of the procedures which must be followed, for example words to be spoken, order of events and especially the process by which the problem will be exposed and resolved. Some plays make us aware of their aims by deliberately emphasizing the difference in persons, others by style, some by the words spoken. Some achieve it via surprising and shocking the audience, others by absurdity.

In educational drama, it is the awareness of the class creating the play that we want to stimulate. In order to do this we create an opportunity for a collection of attitudes to relate together in problem-solving. All the attitudes available in the group can provide the spectrum for solving the problem, thus as a result there is opportunity for a 'widening' sphere of attitudes to be experienced, a widening appreciation of scales and numbers of problems and therefore a greater number of relationships and associations with the experiences of others to be brought into orbit and made available to the group. This is not a teaching process in the conventional sense. It comes about by a series of confrontations between persons and their ideas. The game provides the safe framework for such confrontations.

One of the reasons why teachers may experience a feeling of failure in using these procedures is that they either do not understand or fail to perceive the initial phenomenon of group inertia. A group of persons gathered together, facing another person generate a kind of inertia of expectancy, and look to the one isolated person (the teacher) to solve it. We must consciously train our teachers not only to expect it as a natural

[4] Harold Rugg, *Imagination*, Harper & Row, 1963.

phenomenon but to deal with it fruitfully and at least cost to themselves. After all, the average teacher faces it a considerable number of times each day and so must learn to 'carry it lightly'. The first element in solving this group-inertia problem is that of having a wide range of focus to offer. The group must become focused in order that it may begin its work. Out of this focus can emerge that moment of arrested attention which launches that work. So the teacher projects energy firstly to focus attention, then to direct it toward the defined area of intent. It is at this stage that teachers must know the size of groups; spaces and other risk areas they are prepared to cope with at this moment, for in defining the area with the class they can at the same time create the active situation with which they may cope. To clarify this let us take an ordinary classroom situation which often arises. We will define the teacher's thresholds as thus:

*Space* – there is only a classroom with moveable but not stackable desks. The teacher prefers a hall.

*Noise* – Another teacher on one side of the classroom prefers *not* to hear the dramatic work! The drama teacher tries to respect this and anyway worries a bit if the children begin talking or moving rather freely.

*Decisions* – The teacher prefers to plan but is learning to risk just a tiny bit, however, as yet always introduces the idea they will work on.

*Size of group* – The teacher prefers children to work in groups of about five but is aware that the classroom makes this rather a difficult feat.

*Teaching registers* – The teacher likes to be friendly but the children know the voice of authority which appears when they take too much into their own hands. For example the teacher will always prevent a 'fight' developing, see it 'a mile off' and deflect it, unless it can be planned and known in advance (a) who will win, (b) how many will take active part, and (c) what all the others will be doing. The class is a group of lively ten year olds – equally divided between boys and girls, and the teacher is male.

*Understanding of the medium* – He realizes the significance of selecting a problem, but is not yet good at or swift in helping children's own ideas to take the lead but wants this to happen and recognizes the extra quality present in work where ideas and disciplines are acquired together.

*Subject chosen* – The Easter Story because it might be pleasant to 'work it up' for the other classes to see, he knows it is exciting, especially the entry into Jerusalem, the Last Supper, the arrest in the garden of Gethsemane, the trial and Peter's denial and finally the carrying of the cross. He sees that the material is relevant to girls and boys but he doesn't wish to foist a heavily moral viewpoint upon them.

Now, remember, he has as yet no space, he doesn't wish to make much noise, he doesn't want the children to become too excited yet he *does* want to use this theme and initially with smallish groups. So he must find first a focus which is relevant to boys and girls so that attention will be arrested. Because he wishes to work with small groups he immediately, before he even opens his mouth, must have decided whether mixed-sex groups will be chosen by him, or whether he will allow the boys and girls to select their own groupings and if he does this he knows in advance that his groups will be composed of either all boys or all girls! So *that* must be settled before he decides that the time has come when girls and boys must start working in mixed small groups. He therefore must examine his theme to find a focus which requires mixed small groups. *Any* theme will yield problems to suit any type and condition of class. These immediately leap to my mind if one looks at the Easter Story: families out in the evening in the Garden witness the arrest, groups of soldiers and women at the well during the entry into Jerusalem, witnesses confronting Peter and accusing him; a disciple's family at any of these events, the room below that in which the last supper takes place with women preparing food and disciples occasionally entering to collect and return dishes and to report. It can readily be seen that because of his group size and noise thresholds, most of the conventional visions of the Easter story must be bypassed. This is not necessarily a disadvantage but he must be extremely flexible in conjuring up small group areas to be explored. He will be at a distinct advantage in using small groups to explore some of the personal agonies, fears, and bewilderments arising out of the larger panorama of events, but he cannot do these large panoramic events, because he has 'cut his crowd scenes' by sacking his actors.

All of the small group scenes mentioned however (and there will be hundreds of others within the theme – what of Joseph of Arimathea? Did his family welcome the idea of a notorious stranger occupying their beautifully constructed tomb?), may provide a nucleus of experiences which may be then fed into the larger panoramic view and this can be another advantage to him. All his desks can be easily utilized for any of these small-group ideas.

So before he meets his class he must already have examined his theme to discover the size and intensity of his small group problems. He then must present his theme via focus upon 'family' situations. For example should he choose to focus attention by using a picture, say of the entry into Jerusalem or the Last Supper, he must *not* discuss the crowd situations. Instead he must lead immediately into study of smaller 'kin' groupings (for example friends, families, shared feelings) otherwise his focus will be irrelevant to the development he can afford to permit. He has created for himself one enormous problem which, if he does not realize it, will cause all the work to be hard graft instead of a pleasurable exciting evolving of ideas gradually crystallizing into form.

This problem is, that because he has chosen small groups he is placing an emphasis upon language in the main, and to a certain extent upon the more subtle relationships and emotions. His ten year old class may be at a loss to do more than touch the fringe of these problems, and he and they may be disappointed and frustrated. One of the early tasks of the teacher is to create experiences of intensity (not necessarily of depth) because these are the ones which will commit the class to further work as they give instant success feedback. Only the teacher can ensure that no failure is experienced – the group cannot. It is at once simpler and more economical to achieve this for the whole class. Looking at our Easter story again, which are the moments when intense experiences may be easily created? Usually these are easiest and most powerful when all the group are focused upon one, for example a crowd watching a Christ carrying an obviously too heavy cross will have a reaction; whether it is obvious or not is irrelevant. A crowd watching a soldier taking a crown of thorns, pass it amongst them then place it upon the head of Christ cannot avoid a kind of involvement though it may be inactive, a crowd of happy citizens suddenly hearing the voices or marching feet of troops in the garden in the evening will have their attention arrested even momentarily. If our teacher understands this, he will naturally see that tension of this nature are within his small group situations. It can readily be seen now that his material of focus, whether spoken, seen, handled or heard must have this element in it. Strangely enough this experience element is the one most often omitted, yet this is the very experience which will release energy to get further similar experiences.

A further tool in the hands of our teacher will be his ability to employ a flexible range of linguistic registers. He does *not* require to be an actor or a vocal sensation with hundreds of dialects and accents in his repertoire but he does require to indicate attitudes, different strata in society, periods and style, by his own choice of words, tone, pitch and pause when he makes his contribution. Remember we do not ask of the children that they shall act in the stage actor sense, only that they shall take up attitudes and viewpoints and for the time believe in them. Ability in this area gives the teacher the opportunity to become one with the class because he can without apparent effort select words which are in the children's own register, put them at their ease or draw their attention if that is necessary. The odd curse, and cutting off of conson-ants, together with a slight roughening of tone have 'saved my bacon' often in the early stages when working with tough town boys. A variety of registers is also essential for helping groups to capture mood, quality and type of tension, social strata of personnel, period and style, provided it is a hint and not a performance!

Lastly it can be employed to put in a press toward further development of the group by advancing them into less well-known and understood territory and a deeper consideration of the situation.

If we again look at our Easter Story situation, the teacher will conduct his early discussions in rather different idioms if his class is from the stockbroker belt than if it is in a down-town area, and also his 'Joseph of Arimathea' family require a different verbal register feed than that given to a poor fisherman's family watching the struggle to Calvary. Please understand this is not to suggest that our teacher becomes a chameleon or a mountebank, only that he can indicate verbal changes (sometimes crudely, sometimes slightly). I recall an extremely bright class of forty-two top juniors living on an ice planet called Isagon developing an original verbal style in keeping with their culture because as their leader I slightly stressed the 'S' sounds in words. This was taken up by them and gave rise to a whole new conception of motor development. We travelled via a type of hover-system and it arose entirely from the slight sibilance of my words.

The last important linguistic area is that of knowing what not to say and when not to speak – the hardest area of all. This is only achieved when our teacher is so secure that all his attention, except that necessary area of detachment which is his teaching life-line, is focused upon the working group and not upon his own image and status.

So we focus, then we define our area, then we elaborate and out of elaboration comes the next stage: the demand, which I believe is basic in all human beings, for form to be achieved. Again it is the teacher's responsibility to perceive when a press towards form may be made, and at what level that form may be achieved. A class of six-year-olds making a tournament achieved form by ordering the events, the places in which the events would happen, the processions to and from the winner's and loser's prizes and the harmony of the head-dresses of the ladies. This was 'doing' form. A class of fourteen-year-olds, working on the voices of the Sybil in the cave, worked entirely on juxtaposing and texturing sound-effects. Form in educational work must be achieved in conjunction with the needs of the class.

What is form? Like drama we all understand it when it happens. The first component would appear to be the ordering of the miscellaneous and reducing miscellany to order. In drama this miscellany is all the variety of life experience available in the group, and their range of ideas for solutions to the current problems, all their differing ways of approach (whether convergent or divergent), and the way they actually perceive their work. Elaboration reveals the miscellany.

75

The second ingredient would appear to be a process of simplification. In *Imagination* Harold Rugg notes, 'The essence of creative activity lies in a simplifying process which automatically involves not only the selection and rearrangement of the available material but its modification in process of developing a simpler form'.[5] Louis Danz says, 'Form is that kind of organization to which nothing can be added and from which nothing can be taken'.[6]

Third, form is 'fitness of purpose' of all the material contained in it. Form making is not a process of finishing something, it is a forward moving procedure constantly simplifying, seeing more clearly. It is not a static repetition for we can never exactly repeat an experience: would it be worthwhile?

So in the creative work we have focus, definition, elaboration and form. There is a further area – that of maturation and casting off. Maturation in educational terms seems to me to be 'the total end possible at this present time'. Some creative work can be preserved and daily lived with, met freshly and re-savoured over and over again, clay pots, short stories, paintings, recorded music, fabrics, and though this can be naturally cast-off in favour of other visions, it is not a lost thing but a no longer needed one. A positive casting off is a feature of living, and in the drama field it may take many forms. Showing to others, humbly or with great style, is the most often used. Sometimes however the material achievement is such that it requires to be written up as a record (for example the third year remove class of girls working on a drama of 'How to select a husband' decided to create an advice column as the end product), crystallized into economical film, developed into a series of lectures (the first year girls' grammar school class dramatizing the development of Christianity in Northumberland decided that they had too much material for a play!)

I have dealt with what I believe to be the fundamental areas we should be considering if we are to help teachers to employ drama creatively in school: to confront their thresholds in basic drama 'rules' in the classroom, and now finally to choose material to use in relation to age and ability levels in classes. Good material serves all classes and circumstances. One selects an area of the material upon which to work which serves the needs of the children. All material will be concerned with 'people, now'. Variations will be used depending upon the strata in society, and the verbal, emotional development and imagination of the class. Harold Rugg, again in *Imagination*, says:

the principal function of imagination is to enable the human being con-

[5] Harold Rugg, *Imagination*, Harper & Row, 1963.
[6] Louis Danz, *The Psychologist Looks at Art*, New York; Longmans 1937, p. 80.

stantly to build thought models of the real world. The inventor conceives in imagination new arrangements of his machine-parts to bring about described movements. The creative dancer conceives in imagination the right movements for the objectification of his or her imagined conception. The mathematician imagines alternative hierarchies of symbols of relationship. Recall Einstein's never-ending task of imagining 'what would happen if . . . one were to run after a beam of light or ride on one . . . if you could run fast enough . . . would you reach a point where it would not move at all?' Or the imaginative work in Cezanne's perception-in-depth of the strong hidden skeleton beneath the surface of his valley landscape.

The steps involved in thinking point to the crucial role of the imagination: the capacity to delay responses; to manipulate symbols in imagination; to sense and hold the direction dictated by perception and recall; and to generalize, that is, to form and use concepts. Much of our thinking is done by imagined body movements. A little boy in Lincoln School's first grade said, 'I can't say it, but I can draw it.' A four-year-old girl said, 'Mummy, I'll dance it, you write it.' The chief distinction between men and animals is this capacity to work out solutions to problems symbolically, in imagination. To use Koestler's phrasing, 'Artists treat facts as stimuli for imagination, whereas scientists use imagination to coordinate facts'.

I find the best kind of guide to help me in considering material is a short basic list: Drive (what makes a group want to do something); Feedback (what satisfactions are achieved by doing it); Signals (the range of communication within the group); and Rituals (the experiences which seem to be required to be made again and again – individual and group) and finally Content (the level at which children can work). A list of the areas into which culture may be divided: work, war, education, health, food, family, shelter, travel, communication, clothing, worship, law and leisure (I realize there are other groupings equally relevant). All material yields some aspect of all these and all classes will find some excitement and relevance in one or other of them. The more flexibly teachers can learn to approach material the better, if only to achieve constant rejuvenation rather than deprivation of self and their ideas. If we look at this list it is easy to see that some areas are more obviously 'beginner's areas' than others, able to be achieved with less subtlety of design, making fewer verbal or emotional demands. For example 'worship' in drama can cover a range from a personal silent prayer to the most complex academic argument in the church's philosophy. It is a matter of the teacher finding the level and area which will stretch a class yet give satisfaction in those five areas of the first list.

So it would appear that in helping teachers we require to devise situations free of tension which will enable them to define their present teaching needs as far as thresholds are concerned, to understand as well as they may precisely what makes drama 'tick', to be flexible in selecting, presenting and handling their material and to observe honestly their teaching results. Obviously the operative words in the above sentence are 'free of tensions' so value judgements and relationships concerned with status are not relevant here. Until we can train so that the end-product is open to receiving positively classroom experiences, teachers will go on teaching behind the closed doors of their classrooms. This means that teachers must be able to discover and healthily recognize their real strengths and also to understand that strengths and positive qualities embody their darker sides – punctuality in a person can make them intolerant of others who are less time conscious, for example; to teach as much by intake from their classes as by output to them; to forgive themselves for their failures and start afresh; to *structure* (in terms of 'Build') their drama lessons rather than plan the children's contribution out of them and so spend precious time trying to keep to the plan; to observe clearly what is really happening as the children dramatize; and lastly to bring to school not only their information. This way the realness in the teacher can keep alive and present the realness in the children.

Included in almost all our recent statements of aspiration in education – to educate more scientists and more mathematicians, to teach more foreign languages, to produce well-disciplined, nondelinquent, responsible citizens – are diatribes directed against the school system by professors in liberal arts colleges, irate parents, high military officers, public speakers, but they seldom go to the heart of the matter, and that is the chance we give teachers to teach.

The truth of the matter is that it is not teachers we look down on, fail to value, fail to reward – it is teaching itself.


## More than lip service

Medicine is an art regarded with reverence. Why should the ability to stimulate and shape a well mind be less valued than the surgical skill to remove a tumour from a damaged one? This is itself a measure of our present lip service to creativity. We want people who are original, creative, spontaneous, innovative. But we want them to be produced by teachers whom we condemn in a hundred ways to be overworked and uninspired, unrespected and underpaid. We have seen what a related activity has done in the arts where we overvalue the product while we undervalue the living painters, allowing them to starve or to eke out a miserable living with commercial art, while we auction off the works of their comfortable dead predecessors for £100,000 a painting. So, also, we would like children – as a product – to be creative, to learn about creativity, while we make the best chance they have to learn, to respond to teaching, as uncreative as possible.

There is only one sure way to develop creativity in all the different kinds of children in our schools. We must cherish all the way through – in the school and the teachers' college, in the way the teacher's job is set up, in the freedom granted to the teacher to teach while others perform the thousand chores which are no essential part of this task and this art, in the time given the teacher to read and explore and think and plan and search for new materials – the creativity of all those who have elected to become teachers because they want to teach.

If we are to give more than lip service to creativity in children, we must actively support the creativity of the teacher. That is to say, we must come to recognize fully the creativity of good teaching.

# Drama as challenge

*Part of this paper first appeared in* The Uses of Drama *edited by John Hodgson, and published by Methuen, 1973.*

It is generally acknowledged by teachers in most of our educational establishments that the arts offer children certain experiences which other subjects cannot give. With regard to music, the plastic arts, and painting, the work of Cizek, Herbert Read and for example, the BBC's work in music and movement, have established music and painting in our schools. Teachers feel they understand these media at least sufficiently well to try them out. Because these art forms may be preserved, music on the tape-recorder, art on our walls, teachers can see their results and make evaluations of this kind of work. With regard to drama, however, because it is such a transient medium, incapable of real preservation beyond the moment of its creation, it has not yet become established as a teaching aid in our schools. Teachers do not feel, except perhaps a very small minority that they either understand this medium, its techniques, its possibilities or that they know how to apply the medium to a child's development. There has been much emphasis in past years, via books and certain pockets of dramatic activity in England, for example Birmingham, Mr Peter Slade, the Rose Bruford Training College, the odd isolated teacher working well in his or her own school, on the value of dramatics in a child's growth; but there has been very little attempt to really examine the nature of dramatic activity in relation to the nature of the child's changing needs as he or she matures.

The Oxford Dictionary defines drama as 'a stage play, dramatic play-like series of events' and dramatic as being 'forcible, theatrical and striking'. The Greeks used the word drama with a rather different meaning, 'to live through' and it is in the latter context that we should consider drama and a child's growth. Kenneth Tynan defines his personal meaning of drama in *Declaration* (MacGibbon & Kee, 1957) as 'Good drama for me is made up of the thoughts, the words and the gestures that are wrung from human beings on their way to, or in, or emerging from a state of desperation.' He further defines a play as being 'an ordered sequence of events that brings one or more of the people in it to a desperate condition which it must always explain and should, if possible, resolve.' In these two sentences lies the key to the essential nature of drama.

The teacher's[1] role in education surely is to provide learning situations At times he may instruct, but in the main he is concerned with the growth of the personality to whom he offers facts and information and skills as they are required. Therefore, his main way of teaching, if we are concerned with maturity rather than factual knowledge in education, is in the provision of situations which challenge the energies, the intelligence and the efforts of the children in his class. It is as a releaser of energy that drama is valuable to him. This, to a large extent, is not fully understood by teachers through no fault of their own, but simply because their own experiences of drama lead them to consider the finished product as paramount, and the energies of the participants and contribution to the growth of the child are pushed to the background.

This does not happen so much in music and painting because rarely are these activities carried out with an audience in mind. A child may hang a painting on the wall and so complete the creative process. He may stand his model on the window-shelf and look at it and live with it and perhaps later discard it. To a certain extent his music can be created and enjoyed without necessarily involving an audience. But somehow the creative urge in drama cannot be completed without an audience to participate in what is at once its birth and its destruction. So, it is easily seen that the emphasis will be placed upon this final situation and this is rightly so. However, if our purpose is to release energy then we cannot afford to work only to the finished product. Certainly we must make opportunity for the product to be concluded, probably with an audience, however small, but we must not overlook the fact that it is the making of the drama which is going to contribute most to the growth of the child. Therefore, we are concerned not with rehearsal for the event, but with 'living through'.

Let us consider ways in which people the world over, through all time, dramatize instinctively:

1   We all dramatize, whatever our age or intelligence, each time we read a book, for we become lost in the adventures or thoughts expressed in the story or the personalities. An ex-soldier, reading *The Naked and the Dead* in this respect will be having the same experiences as a child reading about *The Little Red Engine*. He will be entering another world voluntarily for a space of time and will believe in this world and will 'live through' the events recorded.

2   We all dramatize in order to feel secure: for example, before an interview we project ourselves into the room and try to plan in

[1] This article was written using the pronoun 'he' to denote the teacher, child, etc. For ease of reading this has been left as it is, but should always be taken to mean he or she.

advance the way the interview will progress. We may even think up
the questions. A small child knowing he has to go into hospital may
well do the same. He will, however, quite possibly take this a stage
further than an adult, whose main commerce of communication lies
in language, and he will 'act' the situation in advance, either
through the medium of another toy or by playing with dolls – (Slade).
Quite often he will do this secretly and the adult will have very little
idea of what actually is happening.

3   We all dramatize after the event, for example all of us have our
frightful hazard stories. The times when we faced serious crisis.
The near accident, the operation, the embarrassing or frightening
situation. We get rid of this situation by telling it to someone else at
the earliest opportunity. We retell it because of the pleasure gained
and the effect we have seen it make upon others many times, and in
the retelling we embroider, we fill in detail which perhaps in reality
was not there, but fits the story. And with time, we believe in the
reality of this detail and the story gradually takes upon itself an
orderliness. We tell it with anticipation, we almost act it. And the
time may well come when our story can be triggered off by the
slightest reference to anything remotely concerned with our theme
and how great our disappointment when the listener says 'you told
me that before'. The young child has exactly the same instinct after
important things have happened to him, but because his verbalization is less he will dramatize the event, for example a child returning
from hospital will gather about him either other children or dolls
and it is significant that he will not be the patient. He will not enact
the role of patient, he will rather enact the roles of the people who
have the authority, the doctor, the nurse. Why does he do this? He
does it partly to get rid of the fear, as we do in our operation story, he
does it partly to understand what the doctor and the nurse were
doing, what their actions meant. He does it partly to crystallize the
situation and come to terms with it, to make it part of himself. As his
control over language develops, so this so-called 'play' diminishes
and it is significant that in adults who have little command of
language there is a tendency to much more mimetic communication, particularly of hands, stance, etc.

4   We dramatize, whether we are adults or children, each time we
watch a play, or the television or puppets or a film. We 'live through'
each time we hear a story told to us.

So drama is a means of learning, a means of widening experiences even
if we never act in a play or stand upon a stage. It is a human instinct to
have 'a willing suspension of disbelief' (attributed to Coleridge). That
from the moment we open a book, or our ears and eyes, we are willing to

discard all prejudices, all pre-knowledge and wait for the story or the play to take control of our imaginations and for the time we believe in the action. We follow the cowboy on his horse and feel the tension as he nears the place of ambush. We seek to know in the beginning of the film who will be the hero, the heroine and the villain. We see in the glimpse of the revolver in the drawer, forthcoming violence and wait for it, believing in it, exactly in the same way as does a child. To dramatize is instinctive. It belongs not to the artificiality of the first night theatrical production, to the so-called 'practices for the night' in a school production, to the painted books on the stage flats and the wine gum jewels on the ladies' costumes; it lies in the nature of people at once to escape from their own existence for a short time, into those of others and to learn from the events they see, read and hear about, by sharing the emotions conjured up by the author. We are thereby given fresh acquaintance with humanity. We are offered a further opportunity for insight into human actions and feelings and some of this which we share is brushed off on to our own lives though we may not fully understand this.

When the New York audiences wept their tears during Arthur Miller's play *Death of a Salesman* no one knew, least of all those men and women who wept, what knowledge had entered their lives, what awareness and sensitivity had been given to them. When the Greeks on the hillsides watched the stories they knew, 'lived through' yet again, who knows what strength was given to them by this re-acquaintance with their myths, this new look at the warp and the weft of their heritage. Michael Ayrton says 'I do know that we live by myth, inventing it when necessary, returning to it with satisfaction when it seems useful.' (*The Testament of Daedalus*, Methuen, 1962).

When we have had acquaintance via the story tellers, the poet, the author and the playwright with the emotions and situations of other people, who knows what energies may be released in us for greater sensitivity, greater comprehension, new knowledge of our society and others (and even of ourselves) and of new awareness of our relationships with those near to us in the community in which we live. It is this which must concern us when we consider drama in our schools. The teacher's role is to harness drama to his own needs. To use it in the way in which it will most aid him in challenging children to learn. Its purpose will never vary, but the activity will vary as the child matures. In the young child there is need for play (which is real work) for feeding to young children the myths, the legends, the fairy stories, the real events around them and the opportunity for making these the basis of their own dramatic play. This playing out of situations challenges the child's social attitude, his verbal control and language ability, his unselfishness, his physical energies and his imagination as he 'lives through' the situations of interest to him. He learns to understand them in his own way. He relates them to his experience and makes them comprehensible in the light of his experience. Therefore, the teacher's role in this situation is that of feeder, whether of stories or of ideas. His task is to create a permissive atmosphere in which deep involved play may take place.

As the child grows and his ability to verbalize becomes stronger there may be less need for the playing out and more need for a challenge towards the verbalization and real planning of the situation. The shape of the story will become much more important than erstwhile and it can be seen that though children are still using their own words to express the emotions aroused by the story and their own gestures and actions, greater demands will be made upon their ability to organize their material. So gradually Tynan's second sentence is being incorporated. 'The play is an organized sequence of events'. We are already over the barrier from the so-called informal side to the so-called formal side. We have been challenged not only to feel, but to organize our feelings into some kind of expression. In other words, we have challenged the children first to feel and comprehend, then to make their knowledge clear to themselves. We have challenged their language, both emotional and intellectual, because in any play-making situation, language demands vary considerably. Sometimes the language required is based upon emotion, at other times the language will be social as the children discuss the pros and cons of their play and come to terms with their own different ideas upon the matter in hand. At yet other times the language challenge will be towards clarity of expression.

So we have challenged children not only to play out their ideas, but to organize them. This is surely educational. At a later date still these children need challenging further, possibly to become interpreters of someone else's writing and though at any time in their school life they may have been challenged to show their playmaking to others they have not yet been challenged to interpret another person's writing. This challenge must come when they are ready to meet it, and of course, it is understood that certain children will never be ready to meet it. For example, the educationally sub-normal child who may never reach the stage of interpretive work. As soon as children are ready to be challenged to interpret and as long as teachers realize that before interpretation can happen, 'living through' must be achieved, then the children are using theatrical art and this means that their eyes and observation should be turned towards the theatre, for they are working in the direct way of the theatre as soon as they concern themselves with an audience and a play. Therefore, we have now progressed through playing for ourselves, in order that we may better understand the world and make acquaintance with it and its heritage and legends, towards learning to create within a group and finding language to communicate to each other in that group, and now towards the interpretation of other people's ideas of the world which leads us to our own understanding of the world and to our awareness of the place of the theatre or the television or the film or the novel or the poem in our world.

In other words, our eyes have turned outwards to the place of the arts in the world of the adult. It should be possible to give the arts the same consolidated position in our classrooms as we have given at present to the skills of reading, writing and the sciences. If only we can give our teachers real insight into the nature of the arts they will be working in, and sufficient techniques to enable them to work with the children with some measure of success; if we can train teachers to be themselves sensitive and to use the arts in their own lives, and achieve a measure of continuity of experience through these teachers for the children in the classroom, then who knows what new success we may have in educating our children to become sensitive, aware, mature citizens, able not only to see the world from their own viewpoint, but through the eyes of others.

Three factors must concern us in training teachers to use the arts. These factors are not necessarily different from, or opposed to, factors required in the sciences. In fact, there is probably a very close relationship: Attitudes, Knowledge of the subject, Techniques of teaching.

## Attitudes

In drama the teacher in a way suffers a reversal of his usual role, which is that of one who knows. In mathematics he knows the answers to the problems. He can read better than the children, he has more experience of the application of mathematics and in general, he knows much more than the child. In drama, this is not so. He may have more life experience to draw upon having lived longer, but when it comes to the interpretation of ideas it is the child's viewpoint which is important, not the teacher's. The child is not measuring up to a pre-set situation, he is discovering through the situation of the play. Therefore, he is not asking the teacher for the answer, he is offering the teacher a viewpoint and in return the teacher may offer another one. Neither one will be right or wrong. Each will differ because the two people concerned are different.

For some reason this attitude is a difficult one to engender. The role of onlooker, guider, is somehow a very difficult one for the teacher, partly because his training leads him to feel he must know in advance of his pupils; that his role is that of the instructor and that there may be some loss of face in admitting to a younger person that that person's view may carry equal weight with that of the teacher. Once, however, this barrier is overcome and teachers are induced to leave their pedestals, which have generally been built from fear in the past, (fear of inspectors, fear of not measuring up intellectually to their jobs, fear of ridicule in the eyes of the children) it will be seen that this situation, whereby the child is challenged to bring as much as the teacher into the classroom, develops on the teacher's part a very special advantage. It brings with it a new relationship which can be best likened to that of the Renaissance painter with his school of students or sculptors. This relationship of the teacher offering to the children his extra live experience and the children offering to the teacher their own fresh way of looking at things can be of tremendous advantage to both. Not only does it free the child to bring himself to the situation rather than the personality he thinks the teacher expects, but it offers the teacher a freedom which he cannot possibly obtain in the role of the 'all knowing'.

This new relationship brings with it certain instinctively felt disciplines which children will not cross. One very rarely finds children in this relationship to the teacher being rude or lacking class discipline, because each recognizes the strength of the other in the situation. This attitude which we in the Newcastle Institute feel to be of the most supreme importance will colour all the teacher's school life. This attitude will encourage the children towards greater maturity, greater courage in expression and carrying out of ideas and a more realistic approach to adult life. It produces trust, self-knowledge, care for others, integrity and an ability to respond freshly to each situation. If we can engender in teachers, through dramatics, the idea that they are releasers of ideas, rather than interpreters of ideas, we have some chance of success.

## Knowledge of the subject

We must aim to give teachers as thorough a grounding as possible in the actual dynamics of drama. The heart of this lies in Kenneth Tynan's first sentence and if we can carry them through from this first basic conception of dramatics being first feeling, then the selection and expression of those feelings, to all the techniques which they will require in the understanding of the presentation of the theme to children, through to the final stage production for parents, etc., then they will be equipped to exploit the energy-giving factors of the attitudes section.

## Techniques of teaching

Following this real knowledge of the medium we can feed to teachers the necessary techniques knowing that they will not be misled into using those techniques blindly because they achieve results which are acceptable to headteachers, parents, etc., but will use them as and when required and not lose sight of their aims for the particular class with which they are concerned.

In the Newcastle Institute we have these basic aims in planning our full-time Drama Course for teachers:

1   To give them a thorough understanding of the nature of the medium.
2   To give them opportunity to develop their own skills in the medium of drama.
3   To offer them a variety of experience from which to draw when working with children.
4   To give them opportunity to study the changing needs of children by visiting schools of a kind other than the ones in which they regularly teach.
5   To develop their own techniques in using drama with children.
6   To have some knowledge of the subsidiary arts, for drama uses many other arts to achieve its main aim, for example music, crafts, art, dance, and keeps them always in a subsidiary role.
7   To consider the role of the theatre or television or the cinema or the novel in the life of an adult in order that the main purpose of dramatics in school is not lost in the producing of plays.
8   To awaken their own personalities to the fullest extent of which they are capable and in part to strengthen their ability to look upon life without making moral judgement, but to use life as the artist uses it, as food for their creative work.
9   To offer sufficient techniques and tricks to achieve success in the medium.

Now let us examine the demands made upon the actor, whether he be a child or professional in the adult theatre, when he works upon a play which has already been written. First, a written play is someone else's creation. The author 'lived through' the experience as he wrote the play. He wrote it from his own experience, the ideas released by these experiences, the people and events he has met and been attracted to or repelled by, his own intelligence, his own emotional responses to these events and to these characters. In this respect, the written play is already complete. One man's energies have been released. The actor meeting this script can only glimpse the author's intention through the medium of 'worn out words'. For words do wear out. Their meanings change with fashion. A good example is 'I couldn't care less', which now is given a very lighthearted interpretation and the real meaning has been worn away. So the actor converts the 'worn out words' and must re-breathe life into them. Michael Ayrton says in *The Testament of Daedalus*, 'to make a thing is to touch dead things and to breathe on them', and the words of a play lie dead until the actor breathes upon them.

To bring them to life he has only the same elements as the author had when he first created the play, his experience of life and his reflections upon life, his observation, which in the actor, as in all creators, is acute, his memory, his kinaesthetic ability, his sensitivity and his intellectual powers. Therefore, the actor must seek behind the written word to find the dynamic thought and emotion, using only the above factors. Having done this he must, again using only his personal experience of things seen, read and felt, create another personality based upon his interpretation of the author's intention. This personality will be made up of fragments of observation, memory and experience remembered and recalled as needed. Having done this, the actor must then speak the lines left to him by the original playwright as if they were just conceived spontaneously and at the same time he must remember that it is not what he says, but what he listens to and responds to which is most important, in other words the actor's medium may be said to be that of the pause between the words spoken where the emotional response of the audience is drawn into the play, and the actor is as much a listener, a responder, as a speaker.

Rehearsals offer the actor two opportunities. One opportunity lies in making his acquaintance with the author's intention. He never practises for tomorrow, as we often expect the child to do; he 'lives through' today's rehearsal in order that tomorrow will have fresh life and new insight. The other opportunity offered by rehearsal is that having felt a situation or an emotion, the actor must then select, using his memory, his kinaesthetic ability and his acute observation, the appropriate gestures, movements, responses from 'living through' that he has conjured up during acquaintance with the play. Having done this, the actor is now equipped to put his feeling aside, and concentrate on the expression of that feeling. Because the actor's task, once he has conjured up the feelings, emotions and character, must be to balance the play, to evolve the play's expression, so that the audience who have paid their money and their time, feel the play and 'live through' at performance. This, as can readily be seen, is a very complicated structure. If we are going to use play production as a medium of education it is absolutely essential that teachers understand the fundamental nature of this work and the demands which it makes upon children. These demands are not insurmountable and provided emphasis is laid upon the fact that play production means 'living through' rather than showing to, then it is not wrong for children to interpret plays.

A barrier has grown up and people have taken sides. The two teams are the advocates of the so-called informal dramatics, whose creed is that children shall use their own language always, versus those who consider the so-called formal production is best. One glance at Kenneth Tynan's remarks quoted earlier will show that there is no reason why these two teams should necessarily be opposed. If our purpose in education is that children shall learn by doing as much as by listening to, then both these fields of activity, the so-called formal and the so-called informal are only two views of the same thing. Whether a play is to be taken from a book or conjured from the children's own experience depends not upon a teacher's but upon the child's needs and abilities. A child of seven years old is not yet ready to be an interpreter of other people's ideas; a child of seventeen should be working as an interpreter. So it is in the light of the child's needs that our selection is made and our programme planned.

Returning once again to Kenneth Tynan's definition, the heart of successful dramatization so that children are involved and concentrating and being made to think and use their energies, physical and mental, lies in the words 'wrung from'. Much of the confusion which teachers have with regard to drama lies in the fact that it is so intransient. They can hear when a musical instrument is tuned properly; they recognize the need for this and it is easily apparent when the tuning is wrong. The same applies to paint and clay where it is easy to perceive wrong mixing of paints, wrong size of brush, and this can easily be put right. In drama, the equivalent of too liquid paint or badly tuned instruments is not easily apparent and one of the first essentials for teachers is that they learn in dramatic terms how to mix the paints.

The clue lies in Tynan's first sentence, that drama is concerned with people whose normal tenor of life has been disturbed and who are either about to be, or are already involved in emotional disturbances. The playwright in the adult theatre knows this; far too often the playwright for schools ignores this. Drama is concerned with the thoughts, words and actions which people are driven to use because they can do no other, and it is this which if carefully used in education, will release the energies of our children. This is the reason for putting the word drama on a timetable in a school curriculum.

# Drama and learning

*This paper first appeared as 'Drama as Education' in* Children and Drama, *edited by Nellie McCaslin, published by David McKay & Co. Ltd, New York, 1975.*

It seems sensible to me that, if there is a way of making the world simpler and more understandable to children, why not use it? Dramatizing makes it possible to isolate an event or to compare one event with another, to look at events that have happened to other people in other places and times perhaps, or to look at one's own experience after the event, within the safety of knowing that just at this moment it is not really happening. We can, however, feel that it is happening because drama uses the same rules we find in life. People exist in their environment, living a moment at a time and taking those decisions which seem reasonable in the light of their present knowledge about the current state of affairs. The difference is that in life we have many other things to consider at the same time and often cannot revise a decision taken, except in the long term. So drama can be a kind of playing at or practice of living, tuning up those areas of feeling-capacity and expression-capacity as well as social-capacity.

Poets do this in their poetry, painters in their painting, writers in their books, and film-makers in their films. All these art forms, however, require technical understanding and often elaborate equipment; drama requires only a body, breathing, thinking, and feeling. We begin this practice of playing at an early age because we realize that identifying with others is a human act of which we are capable. It is in the nature of drama that we start exactly where we ourselves are, with our own prejudiced views. The diagnostic potential in drama is, for teachers, therefore very valuable. I believe that classes have the same privilege as other artists in ordering and reordering their worlds, as they gain new information and experiences.

So for drama with our classes we must select an incident for review (not an easy thing, this isolating of key incidents), and this incident has then to be clothed with such elements as place, period, persons present at the relevant times, season of the year, or any other 'fixing' device. This fixing is really the work of the class and reflects their prejudiced view. Some fixing needs little assistance; others require much more elaborate preparation; but it must feel real to the players. Broadly speaking, I use a very simple guide if I am in any doubt. I have isolated three ways of structuring the situation: simulation, analogy, and role.

Much drama in school works on the simulation level, but it is
teachers to keep it believable when working with an uncommitted

If you choose to begin with analogy, emotion can usually be the
device. This is the easiest approach, as it is in the true theatre trad
which is about the spaces between people being filled with meaning
relationships. All too often children never get to that kind of experien
in their drama.

The third way of starting is with a person who is already fixed, for
example, a derelict or a police officer or a rent collector who demands
(because of the strongly fixed role) an immediate emotional response. I
often work in role at first because it fixes emotional reaction. I find
much prejudice against this way of working, though I maintain it is the
equivalent of good paint or clay and proper tools. The proper tools of
drama are emotional reaction and the state of being trapped, a state
from which one can escape only by working through the situation.

Now we have a starting point. Next we need to know what this
starting point is likely to teach our classes because of what it will
demand of them.

Some work started in classes has a short term objective, for example
when I recently introduced a class of infant children to the Goddess
Pele (the guardian of volcanoes in Hawaiian literature). I wanted to
make a double thrust into learning about volcanoes because I considered it more efficient to learn, on the one hand, that modern humans
have a scientific explanation for events, and on the other that in ancient
times we had other explanations for the eruptions. I introduced the two
kinds of truth. Both kinds seem of equal importance to me, depending
on which point of view stretches a class the most at the time. Both
certainly deserve recognition. A much longer project, which altered
radically the behaviour of a class of eleven-year-olds, was the founding
of a city-state in which only eleven-year-olds could live. The city-state
made laws, developed a system of education (school every other year!),
dealt with sickness, negotiated with adults, arranged for food, and
handled finance. In the Goddess Pele experience the class stayed as it
was and entertained her presence. She could come and go as required.
In the city-state, however, though the children were themselves, they
began to live according to other rules and to take on different burdens
of responsibility.

All drama, regardless of the material, brings to the teacher an
opportunity to draw on past relevant experience and put it into use;
language, both verbal and nonverbal, is then needed for communication. The qualities of sympathy and feeling are demanded as well as
aggression and its results. This is not always comfortable for the
teacher, for the expression of the class sometimes threatens her or him.
But if we grant that it is the artist's right to begin from where he or she is

with their view of an idea, then we must also grant that right to our classes when they create. A second opportunity, of course, is our right to insist on the other side of the coin – that of reflecting on the results of our view of the event. In such arts as pottery and painting this is easy; it requires only the hands to stop and the eye to view. It is more difficult in drama because the means of expression is the same as the means of looking, namely, the individual person. Art cannot exist outside the person and take on its own life. It becomes a memory of the event.

I am much criticized for 'stopping to consider', especially when 'it's going nicely, thank you', but it is for this very reason that I can stop. I know that the event can be rediscovered. Reflection about work is one of the best ways I know to elicit trust, for I can stop work in order to show enthusiasm, to challenge, to demand more, and to show my own involvement as well as my non-interest in value judgements. The outsiders of the work matter to me only when they begin to matter to the class; of course, some classes like to feel that they are doing a proper play from the start. I want them to feel this, too, in that case, until they find themselves more interested in the ideas than in the shape. The shape is just as interesting; but not everything can be done at once, and I prefer to leave that aspect until later. I am primarily in the teaching business, not the play-making business, even when I am involved in making plays. I am engaged first of all in helping children to think, talk, relate to one another, to communicate. I am interested primarily in helping classes widen their areas of reference and modify their ability to relate to people, though good theatre can come out of this process, too. But first I want good people to come out of it. One difficulty of drama is that often the behaviour of a class threatens us because it seems inapplicable to the circumstances we are interested in exploring. Purple trees in paintings do not threaten us as much, for they stay on the paper and are obviously the personal viewpoint of the artist; drama, on the other hand, threatens the very spaces we occupy, and the attitudes of others threaten the very air we breathe.

The procedures are as follows:

1 We make the world smaller by the isolation of an area of concern.
2 We involve groups of people who, in turn, are involved in group decision taking. Groups can work in fantasy or life situations (truth). These are the same; only the rules are different. But whichever they choose, they must realize that in drama there must always be the acceptance of the 'one big lie'. This is an agreement to pretend that we are in the situation we have chosen. The truths are the truths of how we see the situation, our own behaviour, our own language and expression, our own significant actions and the truths we find to be important to us in the situation. I have discovered that

all people understand the idea of the one big lie. It is like giving well-mixed paints or good wedged clay to classes, and it eliminates the silliness that often characterizes children's work at first. One reason for self-consciousness is, of course, that the person of the child is used as the material; another, that the rules are hard to perceive. This is unlike the rules of paint and clay, where the clay falls apart and the paint runs off the paper if the mix is not right. The mix in drama is just as fundamental to the success of the work as it is for the visual arts.

3   We establish certain ground rules:

(a)   First the situation must be defined. There must be a beginning that each person can recognize as true to the situation. In games the rules stand at all times when the game is played, and the players learn them once and for all. Drama rules may appear to change because the actual start must use the present capacity of the class to relate to each other. In drama what is important is the social health of the class, and the nature of the game – which will change with each playing. This demands very special skills to be mastered by the teacher; books alone cannot teach them, though as we learn how to isolate factors, it will become possible to teach teachers more rapidly than we do at present.

(b)   Group views must be put to use so that the drama starts where the groups are (simply because you cannot start from where you aren't). This means that the leader/instigator must find a common starting point. If the common starting point is negative, then the negative must be used – positively, of course. This is why, when I am asked what I teach, I can only give the answer, 'I teach children'. What else is there to teach at first, whatever the subject area? It seems to me that we all teach children until such time as the classes are committed to an interest in the particular discipline and a desire to learn the skills of that discipline. To commit classes, however, requires strategies. Far too little time is spent in training for strategies or for holding staff conferences regarding those usable strategies that successful teachers stumble upon. Indeed, there should be no need to stumble upon strategies. The study of these should be a constant in-service part of running a school.

(c)   There must be some instigation to review progress. Progress can easily be seen in the visual arts, but drama often disguises progress or shows it falsely; for example, if the action moves quickly, the result can be mistaken for quality. A slower approach can suggest lack of progress. I usually take on the responsibility for reviewing progress at first because it is difficult for a member of a group to get the ear of the class. Once the social health of a class has improved, however, it is easy for others to assume responsibility and they should be encouraged to take it.

The first leaders are often those who have language confidence, though not necessarily the most ability. Later the demand shifts from talk to action, from the repetition of facts to the understanding of feelings, by the demand for skills of different kinds (often not socially acceptable, such as picking locks or brazening out a stand against authority).

As I have said I am much criticized for instigating early review. I do it because one thing that must happen in learning is the development of a sense of commitment to work. I will not guarantee that classes work; what I will guarantee is that I will always keep the work interesting. Another advantage in early review is that it prevents rot from setting in, without its looking as if one had stopped for that reason. So review can be a 'failure saver' as well as a 'slower down into experience'. Reviewing, to me, is a strategy.

(d) Strategies must change according to the class and the drama. Because I often work in role at first, there is an assumption that that is the way I shall continue to work. In an organically changing situation such as teaching, one is constantly seeking to make the first strategies redundant, while seeking to serve the class in other ways. I am weary of explaining to my profession that I do not do the same things every time; I start where the class can start and from then on, as we become more understanding of each other, I try to build a working relationship, in which we can take more liberties with feelings, make more demands upon each other and move more as a team.

A class with poor social health requires a more delicate strategy than one in better health, where there can be some self-help. So strategies are of two kinds: those that stimulate the class to working and those that further the action in the drama. Progression lies in the growing ability of the class to accept the discipline of the drama form and to put the work before personal interest. Concern for each member of the group, ability to take more thoughtful decisions, the courage to risk making and rejecting suggestions – all these are progressions.

There are also the art-form progressions. These are closely related to the above, of course, but there are the extra dimensions of awareness of the overview: the avoidance of anachronisms, the checking of facts, the groping with unfamiliar skills and pursuing them past weariness, the never giving up until it feels right. In other words, it is conceding that sometimes the work matters more than the individual.

There is also the confidence of making the form work for you, revealing how those rules, which seem so limiting to the inept player, help to release the brilliant player. When a class can take liberties out of knowledge rather than out of ignorance, we can rejoice. This is rarely achieved in drama because much of the time students never really understand the rules.

(e)    The work must go slowly enough to give a class an experience. This is very difficult with classes of poor social health because they do not want to go slowly. Another reason for strategy! I never object to any ideas the class wishes to work on, but I do interfere with the pace. I cannot say that this is right, but I believe pace is an important aspect of work and I do much to ensure that it contributes to the best experience. This is an area that a class cannot manage for itself.

(f)    Tension of some kind must be present in the drama. Teachers rarely understand how to provide it. The simple factor in making tension work is that something must be left to chance but not more than one thing at a time. So long as there is that one factor and no one in the room knows precisely when that thing will occur (though everything has been set up so that it must occur), we have tension.

Subtle tensions are useless in a class that will only respond to cruder ones. An example of such a tension might be waiting in the dark for an intruder to enter a room. Or a less crude one, demanding more patience, awaiting one's turn to be interrogated, knowing that one of the group will be found guilty. The pressure must come from within the situation, not from the teacher/role insisting that it be done right.

Every conceivable situation can provide the tension to suit any type of class. I remember a group of delinquent children (fourteen-year-olds) who moved very quickly through a series of such tensions, each one making the group work harder than the preceding because each one demanded more of them while allowing them satisfaction. The first was a mugging; the second a verbal threat to a lady of wealth to blackmail her son; the third a painful forging of a document that would fool the guards; the fourth a telephone call made under the nose of the police, warning a friend of a police raid. Finally, the wait outside a temple to find out whose baby – yes, baby (and they themselves were the mothers) – would be chosen to be sacrificed in a prayer for rain. They also did the ritual mourning.

One feature of using tension in teaching is the opportunity it offers for using the same situation while it apparently changes for the class. An example of this was seen with a group of retarded children working on the theme of *Macbeth* (not, of course, the text, for they could not read):

*Tension 1*: Aiding the king safely through a forest in which dwelt a wild, often hunted, but never captured boar of great strength and size.

*Tension 2*: Finding that the lair of the boar was occupied and needing to be sufficiently silent while in that area.

*Tension 3*: Finding that the boar was loose and might attack at any moment.

*Tension 4*: Finding that the old guide, who would have been able to predict the boar's reaction, had fallen sick and could not help them.

*Tension 5*: Realizing that darkness was falling and they were lost in the forest.

This class explored fear and responsibility each time, while apparently changing their play. Each time they carried over more of the factors involved in looking after kings. They also 'grew' a vocabulary in order to discuss the subject of fear. This came about because of 'teacher interference'. Before the teacher can interfere, however, the class must understand or make a decision as to which factor it will reinforce and why, while apparently changing the tension. I chose the problem of having to keep the king safe because I believed it helped the class to avoid using their own instinctive aggressive behaviour, which would have been to kill the boar and thus rid themselves of the situation quickly. If a solution comes too easily, there is no opportunity for a class to be stretched.

(g) Feelings and thoughts that exist inside persons have to be made explicit to the group so that it can see and respond to the expression in the group. In drama this expression takes place through what can be seen to happen, what can be heard to happen, and what can be felt to happen.

The elements of darkness and light, stillness and movement, sound and silence are held in a constantly changing expression of life. In drama these must be in use from the very start and I personally try from the beginning to introduce classes to the use of them so that they begin to be selective about the way they will make their statements, thought I do not necessarily discuss them in any technical way. I might say,

'How will we first know that a monster has been here while we were away?' From the answers I receive I move the class to active decisions, which can be seen to employ these elements.

It is the use in common of these elements that make classroom drama and theatre kin. In theatre they are used for their effect on other people whereas in teaching they are used to make the impact on the very persons who create the work. Drama is about filling the spaces between people with meaningful experiences. This means that emotion is at the heart of drama experience but it is tempered with thought and planning. The first is experienced through the tension and the elements; the second, through the reviewing process. Out of these we build reflective processes, which in the end are what we are trying to develop in all our teaching. Without the development of the power of reflection we have very little. It is reflection that permits the storing of knowledge, the recalling of power of feeling, and memory of past feelings.

All too often we phase out emotion in our classroom work as if it were unimportant. (Certainly emotion is harder to deal with than thinking because children do not expect to use their emotions in school.) If we take the emotion out of drama, there is only the burden left. I recently heard of a group of 'Roman soldier juniors', who were expected to attack a British fort in a 'noisy way but without making a noise'. I do not blame the teacher, who was trying to avoid disturbing the class next door. I do not blame the children, who mouthed all the words they would have spoken, had they been permitted. They were neither fish, flesh, nor fowl as they tried to do a noisy thing quietly, while trying to be the efficient fighting machine they understood the Roman soldiers to have been. They had to do all the external things while being denied the internal experience they needed in order to find their truth. If they could have made a silent attack, out of the necessity of a silent approach, they might have managed it.

I blame only the training of the young teacher, which led him to think that what he was doing was drama.

Please note that I am not quarrelling with the fact that the children could make no noise – only that they were expected to do and believe in noisy things while keeping silence. If they had decided to try to attack in silence, then their movements could have been a real experience of battle. Likewise, if they had been allowed to assume a bargaining position, which would have demanded a careful choice of words, they might have experienced the significance of the spoken language while facing the enemy who misunderstood the words and the promises.

I believe that the child and the actor have to follow the same rules. It is not possible to simplify these rules; it is only possible to simplify the demands we make. Some potters make clay work harder for them than others do; some painters do the same with paint; some actors say more with fewer gestures; and some musicians get more out of fewer notes. The processes are the same for the great and the mediocre, but the expressive use that is made of these processes is the varying factor. Surely we owe our classes the real material that our artists have to use. Drama is possibly more liable to criticism than other art forms because the rules exist in use, by people in action, and they never exist outside that reference except in the memory.

The elements of darkness/light, stillness/movement, and silence/sound offer an incredible range of expression. They embrace all clothing worn, all places in which persons find themselves, all words said, all groups formed, all sounds made, all gestures employed; and the teacher must master the flexibility of the elements so as to make them available at will to their classes.

The method of teaching classes is usually via the theatre exercise. But exercises have a built-in, self-destroying force, particularly when used with uncommitted classes. They have a drive toward ending themselves. True drama for discovery is not about ends; it is about journeys and not knowing how the journeys may end. Once there is real commitment to this way of learning, there is a reason for studying the factors we employ in order to isolate and practise techniques.

But let me give a few examples before we start on the means by which ideas are communicated. We have crippled our children beyond the breaking point by insisting on rewardless labour before they are given the opportunity to experience any reality. Learning about being a person comes from trying out, not by practising for it. I am not saying there is no value in exercise skills. I am saying that we must have some motivation for doing a thing before we start imposing our theories. When drama is exercise-driven, the natural discoveries that come from emotional involvement cannot arise. Pace, pitch, tempo are discovered in the heat of the moment. Exercises exist to take emotion out, so that coolness and repetition can exist. I know you can devise exercises for emotion, but why should you with children who have the real thing so readily available just waiting to be tapped?

Recently I was working with a class of nine-year-olds who were just becoming interested in the Luddite rebellion, which took place when the first spinning frames were destroyed by the incensed weavers in

1812. The children set up a frame in 'heat'. That is, they knew nothing about such frames but in confrontation with an owner of a mill, who was impatient to see the frame working, they not only built it slowly from hints given in role but they also developed a sense of responsibility as skilled workers who dared to build such things in troubled times. They developed at the same time a distinct feeling of the rhythm of building together. Exercises do not work so efficiently. Their value lies in the way they help to isolate a factor and let special attention be paid to it. I say that exercises are for those who have already tasted the riches of a tough and real experience. Far too many classes never get to the reality of their art because of time spent on exercises.

Drama, then, teaches in the following way. Taking a moment in time, it uses the experiences of the participants, forcing them to confront their own actions and decisions and to go forward to a believable outcome in which they can gain satisfaction. This approach brings classes into those areas that in the main are avoided in school: emotional control, understanding of the place and importance of emotion, and language with which to express emotion. We expect good parents, partners, honest citizens, fine sensitive friends, tolerant and understanding neighbours to emerge from the classes we teach but we have done very little to prepare them for these roles.

I should not criticize our educational system so much if we did not profess to be doing more than making children literate. We talk of career classes, for example, and then we proceed to ignore the relevant areas of responsibility that are emotionally based, except for a little advice in the form of cool discussion. We talk about religious education in our schools and behave with arrogance towards our children. These and many other subject areas demand a steady reaction of emotional input for thorough exploration but we often present our material in such a way that emotional material has to be treated without emotional response.

Though drama is probably discussed more today in terms of teaching and learning than it has been in the past, it is far from being fully exploited in our schools. It continues to limp along, never quite able to show its potential because the system, as it stands, preserves jealously the 'one class, one teacher' syndrome, the 'everybody has to be the same age in the group' syndrome, the 'teacher has the secrets' syndrome, the 'we can't have more than one person making decisions' syndrome, the 'let's keep everything in short periods' syndrome, and above all, the 'let's not have too many children surprising the teacher' syndrome. I know, of course, that pockets of superhuman experiment do exist, and I do not want to denigrate these in any way. But the basic problems remain and give rise to the apathy and the social ill health in our classes.

## Procedures and practice

First, let us examine a simple table.

*Informal Approach* (often referred to as left handed):

emphasis on applying experience in the act of learning
using the emotions to aid understanding
being involved in the teaching
being able to challenge the teaching
taking decisions to modify the pattern of the plan

*Formal Approach* (often referred to as right handed):

emphasis on learning from others' information
learning through the mind
convergent learning
objective learning
strong reliance on the proven

I think that the best learning takes place when there is a balance between the two extremes, but I present them here as opposite sides of the same coin. When I am actually teaching, I am happiest in an area that lies midway between the two methods as, for example, in the Goddess Pele work mentioned earlier, where the truths of scientific explanation and myth were taught simultaneously.

It will be readily seen that these two methods need not be in conflict; some kind of happy medium can be found in order to give the teacher security. Indeed, it is not factual information and emotion that oppose one another; it is the approach to the class and the strategies employed. The left hand relies heavily upon mutual appreciation and mutual decision making between teacher and class. Drama is not an efficient means for straight factual teaching, but it provides a rich ground for making facts understood in action. When building a spinning frame, for example, if you are not certain of the details and are asked if all the cogs run smoothly, you either ask questions about its construction or some-one tells you (there is always more information in the group than emerges at first), or you do the thing that feels right. It may elicit the question, 'What about those under the shafting?'

And so it goes on until looking at a plan seems a good idea; then you may either gather around the board and draw what you think you have been building or look at a picture of a real frame. The main thing, of course, is that when you do look at a spinning frame, the illustrations must not only be of good quality but may be more complex than they might otherwise have been. The class studying the Goddess Pele worked simultaneously in the areas of correct vocabulary, technical detail, ancient beliefs, the power of Pele as seen in her person, peril to people, and the formation of new lands. In a formal approach the class would have dealt with these elements one at a time, gradually building up a factual picture. With Pele to challenge and be challenged by them, to offer her explanation in reply to theirs, the students absorbed many layers of feeling and information at once. Also, it was possible to test the understanding straight away, for many diagnostic techniques can be used during the action to test the grasp of concept and factual understanding.

The basis of all my class contacts seems to depend more and more upon a few relatively simple techniques. I plan the areas where the class will make the decisions. I also plan strategies that I shall use to get the class committed to work. This planning is always done from an inside experience approach rather than from an external tasks approach. I try to know the impact of every verbal statement I make as I make it. I select all signals with extreme care and sensitivity, even when working with my back to the wall with what I call 'dragon's teeth' classes. I spend much time examining the uses of questions and the types of questions asked. I recognize a dud question and set about recovering from it immediately. One dud may take ten or more other good questions to make a recovery. I decide when and why I shall leave role and become interrogator-leader. People assume that because I use role early, I mean to go on with it. I use role in order to teach the class that emotion is the heart of drama. Talking about emotion is no substitute for feeling it. This is the advantage of being in role but, of course, it is a complicated tool and takes some patience to learn how to use it. I have not yet met a teacher who cannot use it and who does not learn more about the use of drama in their teaching as a result of its use.

I seek rather than plant information. And I never mix plans. In other words, I decide very clearly what the lesson should achieve. It may be an unplanned session when I deliberately decide to test the class in order to find out where it is; all subsequent sessions can be based on what I learn in the beginning. Or it may be a session especially designed to introduce some aspect of learning, such as the Pele work discussed earlier. It may be very specific, such as the work done to readjust opinion or to bolster confidence in order to answer questions in examination. Or it may be to help study how the text comes alive on the stage.

Drama is so very flexible because it places decisions in the hands of the classes; the teacher acts as midwife. I select all the best artifacts, literature, and reference books I can find (adult materials for the most part, as I find them superior). I do not withhold information if I can find a way to impart it. I believe far too much information is withheld from classes, or children feel that it is being withheld, which has the same effect.

I work slowly in the beginning. I do not move forward until the class is committed to the work. This does not mean that I stand still; it means that I use many strategies to keep in the same place while apparently moving forward. The social health of the class dictates this commitment, and it is my belief that all the real difficulties of drama come from social ill health. Therefore, if we want to train teachers to make use of drama, we must begin by training in strategies that develop social health as the teaching progresses. This strategy is also geared to success and approval. I work to stretch classes. I expect students to work very hard, and I show that I work hard too. I never withdraw help nor do I ever praise falsely. I give positive comment at all times, and when I want to urge further effort, I often quote my own experiences (always true but often edited to make the strongest impact and timed so as to shock the class into new awareness).

I do not expect classes to like drama automatically. I guarantee that I will do nothing to make them feel foolish, but neither will I allow them to get off the hook. I use the rules from the beginning and especially make the point that all signals, whether positive or negative, affect the work. Finally, I stress that at the present time with the emphasis upon the children's expectations, the teacher will have to initiate, guide, ask for proof of work, time the work, and be the guide and mentor throughout. With some initiative developing in the fifth and sixth forms, we are bound to find this way of working difficult and slow. Children have not been trained to trust their own ideas or their own ways of approaching work. Therefore, for the time being, we not only have to carry the burden of working against the stream but that of creating classes who will revel in taking decisions, in using emotion productively, and in exercising their skills.

# From the particular to the universal

*In 1978, Dorothy Heathcote was one of the contributors to a two-day conference on drama and theatre held at the Riverside Studios, Hammersmith, London. The conference gave rise to the book* Exploring Theatre and Education, *edited by Ken Robinson, published by Heinemann, 1980.*

Robert Frost, when asked by a budding poet what he thought of the young man's work – the young man already considering himself to be a poet – said, 'Poet is a gift word. You cannot give it to yourself.' I think the same is true of 'teacher'. Some days I am given it and some days I do not earn the right to be in the lists at all.

For a long time I have known that I am an 'amateur' in educational circles. By this I mean that I always feel that, beside other people's thinking and talk, I stick out like a sore thumb. I read another book recently, however, and was immediately heartened by the realization that my 'amateurishness', comes from my never having learned the language of depersonalization. Perhaps that accounts for why I am so bad at explaining what I am about to do and afterwards why I did what I did. I always understand it very clearly but find it difficult to depersonalize it in explanations. So do we slowly grow into understanding and change our perspectives ever so slightly, inch by inch.

The following quotations illuminate for me three important aspects of the teacher's work. The teacher's reason for the work done is summed up for me by Josephine Miles: 'I think that an art gives shape and stability to the valued materials of life, in order that they may be stressed, attended to and preserved.' That is at the root of the way I work.

The rights of all my students – children, adults and of myself – are clarified for me in De Quincey's words: 'It is the grandeur of all truth which can occupy a very high place in human interest, that it is never absolutely novel to the meanest of minds; it exists by way of germ or latent principle in the lowest as in the highest, needing to be developed but never planted.' I believe that every child I meet understands deep, basic matters worthy of exploration but they may as yet have no language for them. One of the languages they may develop is through dramatic work. As yet we do not give this grace freely to all our students. Often we deny to others that which we value for ourselves.

The relationship of artistic endeavour to the ordinary and the awesome, in our lives is summed up for me by Stanley Kunitz: 'No poetry is *required* of any of us. Our first labour is to master our worlds.' This sounds so dull until you place 'ordinary' beside 'awesome'. Then you realize the roots of poetry and all high endeavours which grow out of the need to understand – to explain things to ourselves. What a privilege to be there when a bit of understanding happens to someone!

I am concerned, in my teaching, with the difference in reality between the real world where we seem to 'really exist' and the 'as if' world where we can exist at will. I do live but I may also say, 'If it were like this, this is how I would live.' It is the nature of my teaching to create reflective elements within the existence of reality. Brecht calls this 'visiting another room'.

The main differences between actions in these two rooms are to do with:

1 The freedom to experiment without the burden of future repercussions.
2 The absence of the 'chance element' of real life.

If we needed a *reasonable* reason for including the arts in schools, surely it is here in these two rooms. But the arts are not depersonalized and it is because the schooling system is, for the most part, that they are not valued as yet. I wonder if they ever can be? What changes in our aspirations for our future and for our culture will have to come about before they are?

The thesis of Erving Goffman's book *Frame Analysis* (Peregrine Books, 1975) is that the real world of sociology has embraced terms which the theatre has used for many generations because theatre, like sociology, seeks to examine the nature of social life. He looks at how we function socially in the roles of participant and spectator and talks about different 'framings' of experience. The key word in his analysis is 'purity' which he uses descriptively rather than judgementally. The road from existing in your life to demonstrating how life is lived can be thought of as a continuum: 'I live . . . I show how life is lived.'

Between these two poles there are many different types of social situations in which we have to find our way. In doing this we read signals in the events of which we are part and place them within a particular frame of reference. This guides us in our actions and responses. In some situations our behaviour is, to a high degree, fixed and pre-ordained by traditions, circumstance and the very nature of the event, particularly whether it is private or public.

Goffman divides the various types of situation into 'bands' (see Figure 1). The most formalized situations he calls the most 'pure'. By this he means that in them our behaviour is strictly pre-ordained and chance, or random behaviour, is reduced to a minimum. Broadly speaking, the more public the event, the more planning it will require so that 'fitting' things are done.

104

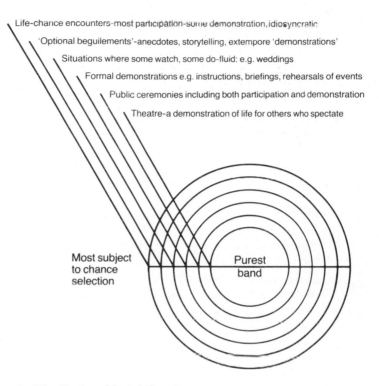

Life-chance encounters-most participation-some demonstration, idiosyncratic

'Optional beguilements'-anecdotes, storytelling, extempore 'demonstrations'

Situations where some watch, some do-fluid: e.g. weddings

Formal demonstrations e.g. instructions, briefings, rehearsals of events

Public ceremonies including both participation and demonstration

Theatre-a demonstration of life for others who spectate

Most subject to chance selection

Purest band

*Figure 1. The Purity of Social Occasions*

The point at which we move from being a participant in, to a spectator of, an event is critical: as soon as there are 'those who do' and 'those who watch' the event, it begins to move towards the right hand side of the continuum. Actors are clearly at the extreme right hand, because for the time they are removed, by the theatre convention, from showing their own lives. The lone individual in a private event is clearly at the extreme left hand and spontaneously 'selects' behaviour which is fitting to their own reading of the situation. Goffman calls such occasions 'the least pure'. Theatrical presentations are 'most pure' in that the actors prepare an event for others to experience. If the audience does not come, there is really no sensible purpose in going ahead with the play. Within such a pure situation the actors have a different range of experience from the audience although both forms of experience are equally real: the actors and those who watch are both visiting other rooms consciously and productively; both are freed for the time being from the burden of the future and the chance elements of real life.

There are many different blends of purity. Social events may be elaborately planned and be long awaited or they may arise spontaneously. They all reveal how we function as social animals trying to explain and make sense of the world.

It can be readily appreciated that one important aspect of experience which this 'other room' of Brecht allows us to see is the 'degree of selectivity' which different occasions require of us. The observer can see which kinds of behaviour have been selected. Those times when we must participate by providing a bank of stored information to be drawn upon. How 'pure' then is the occasion of a bedtime story or a raconteur telling a story at a bar? What of those times when we watch and take part – weddings, funerals, enrolments and passing-out ceremonies? What of times when one gives careful instructions to others? Is the purity of Hamlet saying, 'Speak the speech, I pray you,' akin to when a craftsman briefs an apprentice at work? And what of briefing before battle and meeting friends and asking, 'How was the interview?' One of Goffman's beautiful terms for such spontaneous occasions as the latter is 'optional beguilement': a magnificent definition.

As a teacher I seek to keep people's experiences 'real'; that is I try to bring about a change, a widening of perspective, in the life of the real person, as well as to offer systems of learning and knowing. I feel bound, therefore, to take account of Goffman's notions because they seem to me, better than any others, to give meaning to the many blends and manifestations of drama activity.

## Four faces of dramatic activity

I can find no basic conflict between those teachers who prefer to make and show plays to others and those who prefer to base their work on games. Between these two there are many subtle shades of activity. The learning which might come about is not really to do with the activities themselves. It is to do with the quality of the experience for the group and the relevance of the activities to the underlying purposes of the teacher. I have struggled to perfect techniques which allow my classes opportunities to *stumble upon authenticity* in their work and to be able both to experience and reflect upon their experience *at the same time*: simultaneously to understand their journey while being both the cause and the medium of the work. My techniques embrace all the ways which enable classes to do what seems important to me. In learning these enabling techniques, I have neglected others.

The four faces of dramatic activity which I can see are explained below.

*Making plays for audiences*. This can be a meaningful experience for children, or adults, or for anyone doing it because they are interested, and not only because they wish to live in it and earn their money by it. Making plays seems to have gone out of fashion in education possibly because people did not learn to do it well with children who were not necessarily committed. When we ask this of children, we must treat them as the artists they can become. For too long in schools we have refused to let children function as artists. We make them learn about it.

*Knowing the craft, history and place of the theatre in our lives.* The study of the history of the theatre, of different styles of acting and playwriting in our own and other cultures is surely of great value. When they are placed in a sociological setting they stand with architecture and art: to help us to understand people in their cultural context. They help to reveal what all people and all cultures have, in their time, found to be significant.

*Learning through making plays.* This uses the materials and conventions of theatre to build upon the children's reflective energies: to limit the world to certain agreed aspects freeing them of the burden of the future; taking out some of the chance elements; being more selective in their responses and recognizing their reasons in doing all of this so that they may reflect upon what is changing in their perceptions of others and of themselves.

*Using the conventions of 'as if it were' to motivate study.* A great deal of my work is concerned with this because I see it as one of the principal ways in which schools could be humanized. It is using the conventions of the depicted world to motivate study of the real world and of humanity, providing a framework of purpose for and within the school curriculum.

These are all education. They are all exploration and allow children to function as artists and they all produce changes in perception. But their processes are different and demand different skills from the teacher/ leader. Their basic materials are the same: people exploring their own attitudes, reflecting upon living and expressing their point of view as precisely as possible but realizing that it is a temporary moment of perception and may change in the act of expression.

It is impossible to contemplate all of this without running into the terrifying complexity of the word 'role': a complexity which is to do with the varying ways in which we function in different social situations under so many different kinds of authority and power. It is to do with the many levels of our existence within a vast range of social patterns and the many different meanings we make of how the world uses us and our personalities.

The word 'role' runs straight through Goffman's analysis. Our actor who is this night Hamlet is also at other times a father to his children, son to his parents, citizen of his country and so on. He is also an actor who is also a spectator. All of these aspects of role concern me as a teacher. The children are in role as students while I am placed in the role of teacher. But as a teacher when am I functioning as a director, as a playwright or as a counsellor?

Perhaps we might look for a different centre to drama as a way of learning, in order to find our way out of the drama/theatre abyss. So far we have tended to put the word 'artist' at the centre, without of course allowing children to function in that way. But should we meet in sociology? Should it be in psychology? Would the theatre see this as a true centre? If we embrace Goffman's idea of purity framings, we must make some attempt to clarify the centre to our different-seeming skills.

Brecht has really said all of this very succinctly indeed in his terms as a playwright.

... I am a playwright. I show
What I have seen. In mankind's
⠀⠀⠀⠀⠀⠀⠀⠀⠀⠀⠀⠀⠀markets
I have seen how humanity is traded.
⠀⠀⠀⠀⠀⠀⠀⠀⠀⠀⠀⠀⠀⠀That
I show, I, the playwright.

*As a teacher I have to be selective too, helping people find frames of reference, understanding tension as an aid to learning.*

How they step into each other's rooms
⠀⠀⠀⠀⠀⠀⠀⠀⠀⠀with schemes
Or rubber truncheons, or with cash
How they stand on the streets and wait
How they lay traps for one another
Full of hope

*This is the spectator in me, the sociologist who perceives the manifestations of people and their concerns. It is also the technician who perceives the means of the manifestation.*

How they make appointments
How they hang each other
How they make love
How they safeguard the loot
How they eat
I show all that

*As a teacher I cannot afford my own monitoring-out of what interests others. It is very easy to say that and very difficult to live up to affirming and valuing the ideas of others.*

The words which they call to each
                other I report.
What the mother tells her son
What the undertaking asks of those it
                takes under,
What the wife replies to her husband.

*The perennial watcher –*
*the teacher's life-style,*
*that of becoming*
*concerned.*

All the begging words, all the
                commanding,
The grovelling, the misleading,
The lying, the unknowing,
The winning, the wounding,
I report them all.

*The psychologist and the*
*sociologist, able to per-*
*ceive, acknowledge and*
*allow the reality and the*
*humanity of social life.*

I see the onset of snowstorms.
I see earthquakes rolling forward.
I see mountains in the middle of the
                road,
And rivers I see breaking through their
                banks.

*The artist in the teacher*
*accepting nature as a*
*means of inventing new*
*forms. One of my tasks is*
*to fore-shadow for chil-*
*dren the outcomes of their*
*present acts.*

But the snowstorms have hats on.
The earthquakes have money in their
                wallets,
The mountains have arrived by motor
And the headlong rivers control the
                police.

*The artist/teacher trans-*
*lates and transforms easily*
*from the seeming ordinary*
*to the new view – the*
*awesomeness of a new*
*look, a new outer form for*
*a universal inner meaning.*

To learn how to show what I see
I turn up the representations of other
                peoples and other periods.
One or two pieces I have adapted
                precisely
Testing the techniques of those times
                and absorbing
That which is of use to me.

*The struggle for form to*
*communicate the ideas.*
*The acknowledgment that*
*we can borrow from those*
*cleverer than ourselves.*

I studied the representations of the
                great feudal figures
Through the English: of rich
                individuals
Who saw the world as space for their
                freer development.

*The recognition of the*
*past as a model.*

I studied the moralizing Spaniards,
The Indians, masters of delicate
                    sensations,
And the Chinese who represent the
                     family
And the many-coloured lives in the
                     cities.

*The teacher as respecter of different ways of doing things.*

Finally, there are three ingredients to my growth as a teacher:

1   To remain accepting of the ways and present conditions of others while considering how best to interfere, and that I seek to bring about shifting perspectives and understanding. This includes me as well as those I am responsible for.
2   To be able to affirm and receive from others.
3   To remain curious.

It is the spirit of the accepter of what children bring to the situation – always the receiver, the curious one, the playwright, the creator of tensions and occasionally the director and the actor – that I have to function.

# Part Three

# The function of drama in the curriculum

# Introduction

As teachers began to assert that educational drama is a process, a mode of learning, an agent which brings about change, so the place of drama in the curriculum required fresh consideration. As a learning tool it began to cross subject boundaries, and such cross curricular functions implied that drama could offer a vital contribution to the entire curriculum.

Inevitably, the changes in the function of drama across the curriculum throw up new areas of difficulty and debate. In the primary school it has always been potentially easier for drama to act as an integrating force in the curriculum and for teachers to draw on different subject areas in order to create a wide range of learning outcomes for drama, than in the subject and examination orientated secondary school. However, in secondary schools there is increasing recognition of the value of drama strategies in English, the humanities, social studies and moral education in spite of the rigid framework of the timetable. It is this flexibility, inherent in educational drama, which poses problems in its relationship with other subjects in the school curriculum. Whatever subject is approached through drama the kinds of learning which may arise will not primarily derive from inputs of new information by the teacher; besides the material which is to be illuminated through drama strategies, the teacher will be working with what the children already know. The task for the teacher is to structure that understanding, 'the teacher "hot forges" into form, ideas brought about and into play by the class'.

Gavin Bolton in his paper 'Philosophical Perspectives on Drama in the Curriculum'[1] demonstrates that the contribution of drama to education depends on what general educational philosophy is in the air at the time, and its place in the curriculum depends on the kind of assumptions that are made about education and knowledge, the status of drama as a subject and the status of the drama teacher.

In many ways Dorothy Heathcote's work and writings about drama with the handicapped deserves a separate publication, and it was a difficult task selecting one paper which would encapsulate all that her

[1] *Drama and the Whole Curriculum*, ed. Nixon, Hutchinson, 1982.

work with these exceptional people means. The paper is placed in this section because, in one way, this special work throws into slow motion all the considerations made at lightning speed by teachers in normal schools. Dorothy has stated herself that the benefits to her and the students she has trained are many:

the chance to recognize another kind of logic;
the chance to slow down and recognize the other meanings in that logic since the slowness gives time to pause and listen to oneself as teacher and person;
the chance to reflect on how one struggles with a new idea;
the chance to value and name one's gifts, while giving names and recognition to theirs, and
the chance to renew the innocence of meeting familiar ideas, because of the demand to make them newly simple.

These benefits to the teachers she considers are passed on to the 'ordinary' children; when these teachers return to them, they will never be tempted to berate children for not instantly understanding. They will know the difference between 'telling' and 'devising the means' which help others to understand and they will select their materials for need, and devise all manner of outer forms to bring about real learning.

113

# Drama as a process for change

*This is an edited version of a paper entitled 'Drama in Education', given as one of the Jennings Lectures at Cleveland State University in March 1976, and published privately by the university.*

I should like to first examine what the essence of drama is, in order to see whether it has anything to offer us who concern ourselves with education. The second point I wish to examine is what drama would be if it were drama as education. The third area is why aren't we using drama, because it is no good pretending that at present we are using it. Fourth, is it possible to train people to use drama? And last, how could we make a start so that something happens, instead of only all of this talk about it?

Let us first of all look at the arts in general to see what they offer us, and then look particularly at what drama might offer us. The arts employ humanity and the ideas about humanity and the places in which we live, and because it is people who use the arts and create the arts, they look to humanity for their material. They needn't always draw people or play music about people dancing, or dramatize using the human as the catalyst in the struggle. But they use the conditions of humanity.

The second thing is that the arts isolate a factor of human experience. They particularize something to bring it to your attention.

They use life and understanding of life, but they make you examine it through a particular moment of life; whether it is the frozen time that a painter captures for you or the ongoing struggle that a playwright captures for you. Therefore, art creates selection. It demands selection.

It seems to me that effective teaching is about selection. It has to particularize. It has to isolate. And because it does this, it distorts. You cannot have art that does not in some way distort. It distorts productively. Therefore, you do not see the whole, you only see a part through this distorted view, this particularization. As soon as you get distortion, you have the struggle for form so that the ideas are encapsulated in a style, a fashion. You begin to understand what lies behind this particularization.

So, in art, you have: isolation of the human condition, particularization, distortion, and forming so that you may contemplate it. It is given shape to synthesize the importance of the distortion.

I am thinking as a teacher. I am not trying to think as an artist, but I seek to marry the truth of the art and the truth of the teacher who is trying to create learning situations for people.

114

Let us look at what is special about drama itself. The most important manifestation about this thing called drama is that it must show change. It does not freeze a moment in time, it freezes a problem in time, and you examine the problem as the people go though a process of change. If you want to use drama as education, you have to train people to understand how to negotiate so that the people go through a process of change.

Is education a process of change to you? It certainly is to me. To me, it is bringing about a process of change, hopefully for the better. In drama activity, change must be seen to happen. Second, in drama, there must be interaction of people and forces. Third, these people, or these forces, must be given a framework within which they negotiate their change, their interaction. It might be a lifestyle or it might be a place. The playwright is not bound to one thing or another. A place need not be created by actual objects. It does not have to be two pictures of your Auntie Fannie or a candlestick for it to be located in a place, in a framework. It may be in limbo, but we have to be able to perceive where they are, and 'where they are' is going to contribute to the process of change. So, if we desire to train teachers to use drama as education, we have to be able to help them to structure so that the place where the people find themselves to be contributes to the process of change, contributes to the process of new awareness. And finally, teachers have to be able to trap the people into an agreement that for now they will believe in 'the big lie' in order that they will fight through to the process of change and not say, 'I don't like this, Miss', and go away. There is an awful lot of 'I don't like this, Miss', unless you train people to lure their classes into traps.

Now, because in drama we involve people in a situation, a circumstance, which pressurizes them and causes them to work through the problem, we have to at the same time understand what the final process is going to be. You cannot go on struggling forever; otherwise people say, 'I'll have to get out of here. I just can't cope with this any longer'. So, as you struggle through, you have to reach a stage in drama where there is some easement of the struggle. Some temporary feeling that, 'Oh, it feels a bit better now'. This is, for instance, when children reach a point in their struggle where they can say, 'I could leave it for a bit now. I understand it a bit, enough to know a bit about it'. Or, it occurs in a theatrical play in a conclusion where you know that they 'got married', or, 'he dropped dead'. The feeling of conclusion. That is not the same as easement. Sometimes the situation only brings easement and not conclusion. As teachers, we need to consider very carefully when a class needs conclusion because they are not ready to tolerate the more difficult easement of the problem.

As well as conclusion or easement, there is a third area – to get a new view out of it, for us to learn that it did not solve anything, but at least we are looking at it differently. 'I'll never again think that about people like that' might be the new view we get out of the theatrical event. That is not necessarily the same as easement, and of course this new view may be very disturbing to us. Sometimes, in education, a new view is the most disturbing element that a teacher might set up: so risks must be calculated carefully.

A fourth response might be that we can perceive that 'there's a new start to be made'. It is not only the idea that the problem is concluded, but that there is a whole new beginning.

The fifth development from the struggle may be just a new awareness, not an understanding, but a slight feeling that 'There's something I haven't conceded before'. This is what the theatre can do for us. As a teacher, I ask myself if I want to use dramatics to help this happen to my students in my classrooms and if I want to do it constantly for myself.

In the past, there have been a minority of people (we call them actors!) who have been prepared through some alchemy in their make-up to spend their lives upon this struggle of humanity, within the framework out of which people can receive reflective energy. Actors are called by psychologists 'productive schizophrenics'. They productively live a double truth for other people, not for themselves only; they try to produce a change of view, attitude, awareness, and understanding in other people.

Common people, such as you and I, have only entered this kind of territory at times of festival, at times of mourning, and at times when public statements of feeling are symbolized through action, public action. All of us at some time have taken part in such things: and, for that brief moment of time, we have met with what the actor does. We haven't done it as the actor does it, but we have been privileged to enter this world of sharing in an experience and publicly finding the images whereby the meaning of the experience is spread about the community.

At times of enormous public presentation of a nation's idea, we enter this world of the actor, where not only do we feel something, but the statement is publicly made. Whether it is in the church, or in the marketplace, it seems to me everybody has this privilege. Every teacher must decide for themself whether there is any value in this.

If you do decide that you want to use this as part of your students' education, there are three very important things you may not abdicate from, I warn you, because if you try to abdicate from these, you not only cripple yourself, but you won't make any education out of drama.

One of these is that you must accept you are going to use human material, not fancy ideas, not cool abstractions of facts. You are using the human condition of your students, their attitudes, their philosophy, their ideas, and you have got to use them as they really are. You cannot pretend that they are different. So, you are going to be involved in human material and there are some teachers not born to be involved in human material. Am I still worthy of being involved with human material? is a question I have to keep asking myself. So, it is your human material and their human material that is going to somehow come together.

Secondly, you have to accept that you will be involved with distortion. You cannot examine all aspects of everything simultaneously. You are involved with distortion the minute you start to breathe. You are certainly involved with distortion as soon as you build a school, but it looks more respectable when called selection. What of the historian's distorted view of The Declaration of Independence? We are always concerned with distortion, but drama brings it to notice. Isn't it worrying when the distortion you are dealing with inside your classroom doesn't please the people who are walking past your classroom who would prefer another aspect of distortion? They would rather it wasn't so blatant, or they would rather it was pushed under the counter or made to sound more academic. You cannot make drama sound academic. The academic aspect is there, with all the bias, the distortion that people bring to it. Their readiness for change, of course, is part of this too.

The third area you are going to be involved with is fighting for form to give shape to these ideas, so that as the shape is fought for and crystallized there is more reflective energy available in your groups of students.

Now, of course, the 'freedom lovers' in art do not want you to fight for form. They want all people to do what they like. They do not want them all to do what they like in history, but they do want them to do what they like in art. Anything goes, you know. Don't interfere with little kiddies when they are thinking, and certainly don't do anything to check them when they are wrecking the joint or the drama.

So, these are the three elements you have got to train for and you have got to be prepared to accept. I use the human condition. I use distortion in order to examine, and I seek for form, so that in the examining I may create reflective force to consider what I am learning. I repeat, these three things you may not abdicate from.

Now, for my next point. There is, in any teaching situation, the inner structure of the teaching you create and there is the outer apparent look of the teaching you create. I have always planned, though I did not realize this until recently, for the internal structure of my lesson building. This week I had to teach a high school class. I wanted them to come to some understanding of loyalty within a feudal situation. I had been given a 'history brief', you see: loyalty within a feudal situation – this is an 'English' class. I did not, therefore start thinking about how the

117

place was going to look. I did not start thinking, 'Right, we need a Tudor mansion'. Instead I said to myself, 'How do I introduce the whole idea of loyalty? What strategy will I use whereby there shall be a slow realization that the choices between loyalty and disloyalty become available to the class? And, how do I do this within a Tudor framework? And what shall be the dilemma? What will make it possible for them to make that choice?' They were fifteen years old.

I call this 'classic form', the careful looking at the internal structure of how you bridge between one part of the learning and the next development. I find that teachers are not trained in this. It is not the pretty outer romantic form that teachers must examine. You have got to look at the internal form: What is the value of doing this? What is the purpose in doing this?

Drama particularly, and much of our teaching, has suffered desperately about this inner and outer structure, because somehow or other we have looked at the outsides of how other people look when they are teaching. We have never looked at the inside of what they are aiming at at any particular moment. A lesson changes from second to second. Often, others have torn my work apart and the work of each other by saying, 'Well, of course, I would never dream of teaching the way Dorothy Heathcote teaches'.

And so we get this manifestation in our profession, whereby people say, 'Well, I've looked at what she's doing and I don't like it'. They have not looked at what the teacher is doing at all. They have only looked at the outer manifestation, and they have decided, as people often judge my work, 'Oh, I wouldn't work in role like she does. She makes it too easy for them'; or 'Why does she have to make it so difficult?' These are all the external romantic forms.

The internal meanings are so important, for example, when I say in the *Tudor Mansion* work, 'Good morrow. Have you walked from your homes today?' I am trying to establish, 'You had a life before you came into this room, and that is the attitude you will bring to my Tudor house'. I am changing my language slightly to limit the view and distort the world.

A child says, 'Yes, I walked all the way', and I reply, 'Is your hovel far from here?' If the onlookers look at the outside, they might say, 'There she is insulting him again, calling his home a hovel'. If they look at the inside, they see how I am upgrading whilst I am using the word hovel because in the act of saying hovel, I am actually starting to draw the house on the board to begin imagery with the class. The boy says, 'Yes, and it isn't a hovel, it's my home.' 'Forgive me. I had assumed you had all lived in rather poor circumstances.' I am slowly establishing in my class the ability to fight my own role attitude. The internal form is going to grow a strength in that class that will tell me where I am overstepping my rights because I am trying to build a group of people who are proud of their origins, and this demands training. And this demands much more careful training, a much more delicate training of this selective ear and tongue.

It demands the selective use of words, the selective use of gesture in the teacher. We have mistaken casualness for the ability to get on with people. Casualness gets you nowhere in teaching. A semblance of casualness might often be a useful strategy, but unselective casualness is death to the teacher. One of the most important elements in teacher training is high selectivity of the way we will signal our relationship to our classes. Every teacher in this world is functioning within a variety of roles. You know this. You know sometimes you fetch and carry for them, sometimes bully, and sometimes you don't let people 'off the hook', and sometimes you listen, and sometimes you give, and sometimes you share, and sometimes you dictate. All these roles we use, and many others beside, in our daily teaching. Drama demands we use them even more specifically and with a greater range of flexibility and consciousness for effect.

So I now reach my main question. Do you think this 'trapping of people within a life situation', however small or lengthy (because drama can be two seconds or it can be two months) has anything to offer you in the teaching concerns you have? Can it help you to draw attention to something? You have to answer it for yourself. And, try if you can, to put aside fear. Drama is such a normal thing. It has been made into an abnormal thing by all the fussy leotards, hairdos and stagecraft that is associated with it. All it demands is that children shall think from within a dilemma instead of talking about the dilemma. That's all it is; you bring them to a point where they think from within the framework of choices instead of talking coolly about the framework of choices. You can train people to do this in two minutes, once they are prepared to accept it.

Do you think this thing called drama offers you anything? Can it help you to extend the understanding about something by thinking from within a framework? Do you believe it might help you to help your classes bring about any behavioural change? It might be the behavioural change of 'stop chucking the books about', or it might be the behavioural change of 'notice the archaeology or the architecture of it more'. These are all different aspects of behavioural change, for they are the beginning of perceptive changes. Do you think it is valuable to help you extend with your classes the range of attitudes they are capable of examining, and do you think it would help them to develop ordinary gumption?

The children in the Tudor mansion met their final moment when they had to make the choice of being loyal or not. They were raided by

119

three men sent from her majesty, Elizabeth I, to look for hidden Catholic priests. They could betray me as Lady Norris, or they could keep me safe. I had done nothing to win their loyalty. We had only grown into a feeling for this building, this house, this responsibility for the Norris family. There had been no proselytizing. There had been no religious teaching. There had only been the furnishing of a mansion, ready for Lady Norris and her family to occupy. And, in the course of the furnishing, they discovered that there were certain spaces in the house that seemed unnecessary. As soon as the three soldiers arrived, with their pikes, seeking for evidence of popery, every child jumped to the conclusion that they were searching for the great Bible which I carried, and would not be separated from. Slowly, they had realized I valued the Bible. Children had kept coming up and saying, 'M'Lady, uh, do you want me to do anything with your book?' And I would say, 'Not yet. I think I would rather keep it with me until I have seen all of the house that you have created.' I do not think they ever realized it was a Bible I was carrying, but as soon as those troopers came, every one of those children realized that Lady Norris's book would give the whole game away if they were to find it. And from then on they hid it. It disappeared. I never saw where it went. They did not know they were going to have to choose whether to be loyal or disloyal. They just were caught in 'a moment of authenticity', of real choice and real concern. Drama gives us the opportunity as teachers to allow our classes to stumble upon authenticity.

What mattered then to me was that suddenly they were in a very real situation with their capacity to understand it being employed in the process of change. It is not for me as a teacher to dictate how they should go about choosing. I have set it up. It has a form. But how they choose is for them to decide. We can then all reflect together upon the choices they made. So a choice becomes consciously understood and pondered on. They were in a difficult position, because the three soldiers who were teachers in role were very, very clever. They knew about priest holes and they searched every inch. I did not give those soldiers any orders about whether they should find or they should not find anything.

One of the things I must do as a teacher is know why I want to bring that class to that moment of choice. And this is the fourth element in using the arts. You must know why. You must not do them 'because they are fashionable'. You must do them because you have decided that they will efficiently teach the precise thing that at the moment you want. In my Tudor work, I wanted to introduce two things. One was something true, as far as there is any truth about history: the reality of the Norris family and Speke Hall which they built and they lived in and in which they hid thirty-four priests. They were fined constantly, 500 guineas, by the king for hiding priests and would eventually have gone to their deaths if their people had not been loyal. I also wanted to bring the children to the realization that a teacher and a class are in each other's hands. They were in my hands at that moment when the soldiers came, and I was in theirs.

And so, I have two reasons. The choice of the Tudor mansion was the curriculum choice – they were learning history. The choice of how to use the Tudor mansion was a teacher choice to do with my teaching ethics. You have the double choice. In the choice of the curriculum, you have bound yourself to try to further learning as meaningfully and as educationally as possible and in your personal teaching understanding of the procedures, you want to set up for real learning to take place. What I want is the reflective energy that comes out of the experience – an examination of that condition we are now in, as people, because of how we handled the Tudor situation.

What I am always saying in the drama situation is, 'From where you are, how does this problem seem to you? And when it's been dealt with, let's look at where you now are.' Because what I am really saying is, 'It's where you are that makes you deal with your life. It's how you under-stand that makes you deal with your way of life so that all the time the growth you bring about is the reality of the class you've got.'

Let us consider two trees, the tree of knowledge as it is now.

The trunk of this tree holds: the child, the family that provides us with the kids, the teacher, and the school building. What we have done is to build a sort of tree-top based upon a lot of different kinds of growth. There is a little bit of French blossom up there, and there is a little bit of mathematics, and drama. Drama is in a very little corner for very special people.

It is nice if you can speak three languages. Obviously, you want to be able to fly a Boeing 747 if that's what you're going to be, a pilot. Obviously, you do need the blossom element in education. But what we have done is to say, 'All right, here is the trunk. We will put all the energy into fighting for a little bit of time to grow our own blossoms.' So every time I want extra drama, somebody in geography gets a bit less of time for their teaching.

In the school we try to bring three things together: the matter of the mind of the people, the matter of the being of the people, and the matter of the doing for the people. And those three things have to come together in a quality relationship. This seems to me where, in our education, we have missed opportunity. Art is high quality endeavour. The difference between high quality endeavour and 'just doing it because there's nothing else to do right now' is the difference between setting the task for the student and seeing he or she does it, and creating the fusion between the mind, the manner of the being, and the matter of

121

*Figure 2.*

the doing. And this is what my Tudor mansion was trying to do, to bring about the quality-task relationship.

We have to set up a situation in our schools where all the time, every time, we introduce a new element to children, it has the effect of cracking all their previous understanding into new awareness, new understanding. This is what growing older is about. This is what being more mature is about. This is what being educated is about. The moment whereby all the understanding you had before is sharpened into a new juxtaposition. Drama is about shattering the human experience into new understanding. It uses the facts, but, in addition, it fuses the new understanding all the time.

I think that the second tree of knowledge is more realistic (see page 124). We have as our roots now the attitudes the child brings to school.

122

Often we try to push those attitudes under in order to try to get some kind of conforming from our classes so that the curriculum can be taught, but the real roots of the inner attitudes are going to be there all the time. One of the big problems of teaching today is that as more and more cultural ideas become diffuse and people become their own experts, it is much harder for a teacher to handle the variety of different roots that the children bring into the school.

What are the roots of our tree of knowledge now? The first root is that children have already tried and failed a bit before they come to us. That is one of the roots they bring. And we have to keep that root of trying, failing, and picking yourself up and growing strong. That is a root to cultivate. The second root is they have already often faced the choice of whether they will, or will not, care about anything. And that also is a root that we have to keep growing. The third root is they have to decide for all their lives whether they will, or will not, get committed to doing things with quality. They have already at the age of five had a lot of experiences that have grown this root system. They already are beginning the process of reading, writing, and numbering skills. These are roots, not blossoms. These are keys to all our education forever. It is the means by which the trunk can get the sun, the person to mature.

Another root is the skill to look with perception. They have already learned to perceive. They have already learned to read people before they come to school at five: that is a root they bring. They already have begun a process of reflection about their experience. Every child we get in our classes has begun this to a greater or a lesser degree. So, a common root all teachers have to grow is reflective power. Another root is the business of accepting others and being accepted by others.

What is the trunk of our tree? What are the parts of that trunk?

1   It is a personal monitoring system that makes you (no matter what you are doing, learning French, geography, history, or baby care) examine how you are tackling the job. Children are perfectly capable of giving an honest assessment about themselves as workers.
2   It is the ability to see there are many faces to truth. The truth of the proven, the truth of the myth, the truth of the other point of view. The many forms of truth is a trunk system that needs nurturing from the roots. We all know what happens to people who can only see one point of view.
3   It is the understanding of the difference between the outer forms of things and the inner forms of things so that we are not fooled into buying cars because they are red and shiny. But neither are we fooled into saying, 'Mmm, that's a good strong engine. That will be all right'. Instead, we have the ability to look past the outer symbols to the inner understandings of things. This is for all teachers to teach.

123

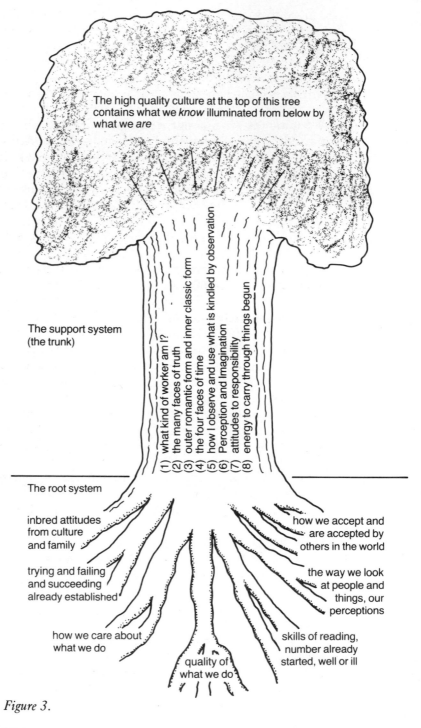

The high quality culture at the top of this tree contains what we *know* illuminated from below by what we *are*

The support system (the trunk)

(1) what kind of worker am I?
(2) the many faces of truth
(3) outer romantic form and inner classic form
(4) the four faces of time
(5) how I observe and use what is kindled by observation
(6) Perception and Imagination
(7) attitudes to responsibility
(8) energy to carry through things begun

The root system

inbred attitudes from culture and family

trying and failing and succeeding already established

how we care about what we do

quality of what we do

how we accept and are accepted by others in the world

the way we look at people and things, our perceptions

skills of reading, number already started, well or ill

*Figure 3.*

4   It is the understanding of the four faces of time: (a) The clock time which rules us all in a social community, the acceptance of this, to handle for ourselves. (b) The great time that is our feeling of time. I feel younger as I grow older. I feel more active as I presumably will become less physically active. I feel I have more energy. I feel time is shorter for me, but a great deal of my feeling is I had a very long youth. The great time that school hardly mentions, but the children sit in the classroom with that at their centre. (c) The third area of time, the time of how the world is speeding up the world time, the pressure of time, this news is coming in, those advertisements are coming at me. (d) The body time, the pulse rate, the how I feel today time. These four areas of time every person must learn to handle. Lucky people handle it. Unlucky people break up. And most people stumble along.

5   It is observation skill. Skill not only to look, but to know what you see.

6   It is perceptual skill. Skill to be able to tell yourself how you're looking at something, how you are learning something. This is for all teachers to work at.

7   It is the business of how responsible are you prepared to be, whatever you are learning or doing.

8   It is the energy to carry through, to understand your own energy, to know when you need rest and when you will stop and why you will go on.

These seem to be the trunk. Not the teachers and the building and the kids. They are in the roots.

And what is the blossom of this tree? The blossom is high quality culture. That is the only blossom worth having at the top of our tree. I cannot make much effect in my small lifetime, but I am not settling for less.

# Material for significance

*The work described in this paper is analysed in detail in a booklet entitled 'The Treatment of Dr Lister: a language functions approach to drama in education', John Carroll, Mitchell College of Advanced Education, Bathurst, Australia, 1980, which accompanies a videotape of the work.*

When children dramatize what do they have to be able to do? Once teachers understand this they should be able to make the work more successful in school. Children should not be required to perform the tasks of actors, which is to convince other people who are called watchers or onlookers, that what they see is authentic as to action and spontaneity. The supreme skill of the actor is to appear spontaneous while being very deliberate in everything he does. Is this skill ever appropriate to the schooling of children? And if so, when? It is a waste of public money to spend time learning to be deliberate while appearing to be spontaneous, especially if you are quite a young child.

On the other hand, is there any point in letting children play at social affairs? And for what ends? And at what ages? Both actors and children in dramatic play are playing at life. One group is choosing a companion and creating a depiction of experience, and the other is submitting an experience of life to making a rigorous demonstration of events so that onlookers of the event feel that they are experiencing spontaneity. Both kinds of drama depict life. Both kinds of people know they are not actually living through the events they have activated. That is, they both share in art. They know it is a depiction. What actors learn is how successfully they managed to appear spontaneous, and how authentic an experience they gave to the others – the bystanders, the audience. What children learn is less easy to define. They use what they have noticed. That is for certain, for we can see that occurring. They copy what they have seen others do. They also select from all their experience that which seems applicable to the present time. They use their observation, power to select and power to imitate. So do actors. And yet the outcome for the two groups will be different. At one pole of this activity is the actors' art, and at the other end, the children's playing. Both choose to do the activity in the first place. Actors are called 'productive schizophrenics' when they do it, and are considered mature members of culture. When children do it, it is called playing at life. In the present cultural climate both are regarded as non-producers! This problem also confronts teachers who wish to use the skills of playing and portraying as part of a learning process. No wonder they often despair, especially considering the present teacher training.

I have already mentioned depiction, and quite a large number of teachers will say that depicted worlds are 'not what we want to be doing in schools'. But all the curriculum of schools is based upon depictions. All teachers talk. Language depicts real experiences; geographers use maps-depictions for places; pictures are used by most teachers in one form or another; writing is a depiction, so are engineering drawings; depictions are in. They have always been respectable because when you can't be in direct contact with the actual event, or place, or person, you must use depictions. The whole school's curriculum is founded on the idea that depictions are respectable. Drama is also a depiction; of living in social situations. Why is it that the other depictions mentioned above are seen as work and drama depictions are seen as 'only' play? I suppose we can't get away from the fact that a good map looks 'like it will be serious'. After all, you can really get lost without a good map. And the same might be said about pictures of Henry VIII. After all, 'the fellow really did live, didn't he?' So it is with engineering drawings, chemical formulas, or symbols in physics. They are all serious business. Some of us believe that drama can assist that serious business.

It is in the nature of schools that depictions are used, because they are a good way of representing the world about which the children are expected to learn. The serious depictions are deemed to be those which actually take on a solid existence of their own. Books, with their written depictions and taped languages, make you feel that they're a substance to be reckoned with. 'In the bank' as you might say. And you can see that their contents are 'for real' too. However, it is my contention that most of the very real and existing depictions are employed in schools as part of a huge 'con'. These real-looking things are employed for 'dummy runs' (I owe this beautiful terminology to a student of mine). The reason schools are dedicated to the 'dummy-runs' is not that they do not mean to be serious, but that almost everything they ask of children makes it impossible for the children to believe they are serious in asking it. What is serious about a situation which prevents the children having any influences on outcomes?

What I'm trying to do here is to shake the reader out of the conventional view of the curriculum, by using the principle of 'ostranenie' defined by Viktor Shklovsky as being 'that of making strange'. We very readily cease to 'see' the world we live in and become anaesthetized to its distinctive features. The arts permit us 'to reverse that process and to creatively deform the usual, the normal, and so to inculcate a new, childlike, non-jaded vision in us'.

Dramatic work is undervalued because in the present age the conventionally acceptable view of situations seems more stable and less disturbing. Art experiences insist upon a restructuring of ordinary perceptions of reality so that we end by seeing the world instead of numbly recognizing it. We cannot say that drama is just 'acting stories' in the light of those poles of playing and acting.

Obviously there is a range of experiences available in between, and it is those we need to name. Think of it like a cake, or a loaf of bread, which has two crusts one at either end. The crusts are the poles of playing and of making art. We now need to slice all the cake in between, and lift the pieces out to specify the different balance of play and art in each slice, and remember the same applies to every subject in the curriculum. Playing with water is playing at alchemy. Being a chemist demands the same interaction of a person with a serious intent and responsible outcome. The chemist is seen as having power over objects, which always appears a serious endeavour. Perhaps it is the lack of the object in drama which our culture can't take seriously? Perhaps this is the reason why drama at both poles is seen as non-productive. Poets don't seem to have much in the way of objects to shift around. Actors appear to have even less sense in moving their own bodies around. Poets at least get their words written down but actors are transients and their work ephemeral. Most of the activities we ask children to participate in inside school buildings lack the urgent need to do them. All the activities tend to be introduced through teacher-power, with little to aid children to experience the urge to perform the tasks.

This 'provision of urgency' is omitted, because it seems impossible (or maybe unimportant) to provide such a thing in the protected world of school. Some situations in school rooms have urgency, because the actual materials cause it to be present. Domestic-science rooms on cookery days, and engineering labs where tools are used, to name but two, provide immediate context, where materials get in direct contact with the worker, rather than the teacher and class discussing the problem. Don't think I'm urging an oversimplified practical school. I'm arguing for something far more radical. I'm arguing for a school in which teachers don't intrude between materials and children, but work as 'enablers' to put children in direct touch with the tasks set for them, in a context of meaning.

## The no-penalty area

Drama depicts life, and teachers can choose just how much of the material of any drama class will provide context for curriculum, either as work or play, which is undertaken in the no-penalty area of art. That is, participants will be able to test out their ideas, try them over again, and generally examine them, without necessarily having to fulfil, in actual life situations, the promises they have tried out in the depicted one. The material of drama then consists of, first, our ability to make

128

'another room' for ourselves, in order to examine something. You can call this plays, or playing, or the theatre, or make-believe, its name doesn't matter, so long as it takes the burden of future responsibility temporarily out of the picture. It becomes a no-penalty area in which the two parts of people can have equal status. The spectator part, which allows us to stand back and see what it is that we are experiencing at any moment, and the participant part, which has to deal with the event in a practical manner. So the immediate environment with its classroom contents can be transformed into the environment a teacher might need for present teaching purposes and it can be done with a minimum of fuss.

There is no need to fuss because of the next ingredient of drama; namely our ability to identify 'as if we were' in the place of another, in a specific situation. This is of paramount and far-reaching importance, because it involves a shift in time which is often not made so specific in the ordinary context of school. Placing yourself in the shoes of another suddenly brings you into time-pressure which is a feature of dramatic activity: the need to do something about it now. It becomes imperative to take decisions because the event you portray or explore demands immediate process. It involves you in trying to ease the situation, and in eternal time-present. People in drama are now, here, and under pressure to act in situations. That is the tension of dramas. T. S. Eliot says in his *Four Quartets*:

> Time past and time future
> Allow but a little consciousness.
> To be conscious is not to be in time
> But only in time can the moment in the rose-garden,
> The moment in the arbour where the rain beat,
> The moment in the draughty church at smokefall
> Be remembered; involved with past and future.
> Only through time time is conquered.

And in an interesting parallel from the Sioux Indians Levi Strauss says:

> Everything as it moves, now and then, here and there makes stops. The bird as it flies stops in one place to make its nest, and in another to rest its flight. A man when he goes forth stops when he wills.

Usually the media, whether as news or art, show rather extreme situations, so we tend to think they are far-fetched and unrealistic, dealing with the more extravagant aspects of one social existence. Here is another feature of drama. It is a social art, and demands consensus from participants, and this makes it extremely difficult for teachers to 'make it work'. This is partly because consensus is not easily achieved with modern children, for they are no longer in awe of people called teachers. Teachers also lack training in the necessary negotiation skills required to make consensus in largish groups. So drama is a no-penalty area, using people in groups, in immediate contextual time, which forces the pressure to act in an event. This is the contribution which drama could make to the school curriculum.

The materials now bear scrutiny. There is a tendency for people to think that the materials of drama will be stories, because they seem like events in which people will have to act. Stories suggest diachronic time, and seem to follow on in a logical way, so teachers are lured into a false situation by stories. Let you be warned! Learning through drama demands synchronic time; the web of interaction within the frame of a selected environment and event. The act of dramatizing is the act of constructing meaning, which may also involve the interpretations of meaning. Play makes constructs of reality which are then available for examination by the spectator which exists in each participant; that part of us which observes what we are doing. We take up a position from where we can look at it, from outside of it. It exists for itself, not as a process. Art does the same, but it is done for others. Being the closest to actual living, drama more than any other art has had to create a special frame. This frame is called theatre. Theatre is life depicted in a no-penalty zone. It looks like, seems like, but is not actuality. Irving Goffman says it 'is that arrangement which transforms an individual into a performer; the latter, in turn, being an object that can be looked at in the round and at length without offence, and looked to for engaging behaviour, by persons in an audience role'.

Drama is a social art where people are and do, and other people may see them doing and being.

## Tension

Drama involves groups, small or large, sharing in some immediate occasion. The material of such occasions is always people, under conditions of tension. Tension is not conflict, such as occurs between people. Tension introduces 'another' element, usually above and beyond people-power. The existence of tension in actual life is often disturbing and non-productive. In the depicted world, because of the no-penalty zone, it can be used productively because participants can be free of worry about the outcome, and so become concerned in the process of resolving the situation. It is this process which requires drama and employs it as a vehicle for becoming concerned. Because in drama, social situations are explored, participants employ the actual laws of social living. One aspect of these laws is that persons have to manage to pay attention to others who are present in the circumstances, at the time. In a social situation every person is an initiator and a responder, and the person fluctuates between participating and being spectator of others. This law of actuality must also apply in the depiction of the drama.

Society has developed rituals and symbols to be used as messages of meaning – the syntax of signal and response – and these change in intensity according to the type of communication required, in order that all present can construct meaning out of the event.

The teacher, in using the no-penalty area of dramatization still must employ the messages of meaning used in real living. The theatre frame relieves us of 'the burden of the future arising from our actions' but employs the communications structures of real life. The actor transforms these signals into poetic style; the teacher must use the same signals, but at the transactional levels of meaning, because the teacher is not training actors but developing the communication and constructional skills of the student.

## Significance

Drama depicts matters of significance. School exists to make matters significant to the child. In the actual world outside both theatre and school, social events are endowed with different degrees of significance. These degrees of significance are those 'slices of cake' previously mentioned. Each social event demands variable and selective kinds of ritualized and symbolic behaviour. These different levels, as we acquire understanding of them, become the language of social competence, by which individuals construct meaning when amongst others.

Goffman's hierarchy of ritualization processes are of immediate help to the teacher who is seeking for the materials of drama. The wise teacher uses materials according to the kind of interaction the class will become involved with, while they are constructing the meaning of the event. Any 'story' will be constructed by a different form than that of narrative because theatre is a synchronic art form not a diachronic one, and events are constructed semiotically not in literary mode. Thus stories must be broken into episodes and each episode made to yield the learning experience the teacher requires. (See further picture.)

Let us now examine a situation in which drama was used to construct meaning and what the material consisted of. A woman teacher of junior age children wanted them to learn about Lister the surgeon, and in particular to realize that his life (together with that of Pasteur), caused a watershed in medical history, which is still affecting our total world.

The story of Lister is gripping, so in selecting a drama approach, it is necessary to be quite clear why the actual interesting story of his life was set aside. The story would have placed the facts in clear order, and dates and events could have been precisely laid in. There is no doubt that the story would have helped the class to be interested, for a while, in the man Lister, and some of them would have wanted to learn more about what he did. But it doesn't provide the opportunity for the class to have synchronic experience of Lister. That synchronic element is an important one for the teacher because she wants the class to experience simultaneously two periods – the time of Lister and its relations eternally to ours.

In order that this can occur, the teacher has to find a system which allows young children (they are nine years old) to be in their own time, looking with Lister, not at Lister. The story looks at Lister, and keeps him out of our time, as it should. That is what stories can do well. To make stories in the 'now' times, we have to use conventions. The teacher could have done this as she told the story. She needn't have used the classic 'Once upon a Time', but she would have had to say something like 'Now I'm going to take you into another place and another time – the time of a doctor called Lister'. This often works for a while, but the ending of a story leaves the receiver outside the immediate event, once the words have ceased. The participants have been subsumed in the spectator. Sometimes that is exactly what is needed to arrest the attention of classes. Every teacher knows that the hold and grip of a story will give them a respite from the constant battle to gain the undivided attention of a class. The problem however remains. That of getting the children deeply involved with the outcome and meaning of the material, not the action. To be involved in constructing meaning, during the act of getting acquainted with Lister in one form or another, was what she wanted, in order that it might lead to concern.

Furthermore, the teacher wanted them to take over her power. Not the power to control the quality of the experience (no teacher can abdicate from that), but the power to influence their own construct of the meaning in the event. Telling stories places the power of the form, and the unfolding pattern of the event, firmly in the hands of the teacher, who selects the style of telling and the relationships of facts and opinion. Acting-out stories does the same. The outer skin of stories in the events and how they follow on, one from another. The inner part of stories focuses upon the attitudes of persons which then cause response from others, and out of these events are brought about. It is by this kind of ordering that drama produces the opportunity to make constructs. This is where it starts to look respectable. Piaget in *Structualism* (quoted by Peter Caws in his essay in *Partisan Review*, Vol. 35, No. 1, Winter 1968) argues that 'structures can be observed as an arrangement of entities which embody the following fundamental ideas; (a) the idea of wholeness, (b) the idea of transformation, (c) the idea of self-regulation'. By wholeness is meant the sense of internal coherence which can be seen in drama work as in all arts. Structure is not static. The laws which govern it act so as to make it not only structured but structuring. In other words the structure is self-regulating in that it makes no appeals beyond itself in order to validate its transformational procedures.

## Construct for learning

Do you see now why drama makes a unique and important contribution to school? We must learn to set up the work so that children construct reality, so that a careful teacher can monitor the quality of the experience, by insisting that the form of the experience is suitable for the construct required for the learning. It must have internal coherence, be a process, and exist in its own right, using the power to self-regulate. This latter is usually absent in school. Teachers regulate the behaviour of their classes. The teacher in the Lister experiment has set herself these tasks, which in turn will force her to select the kinds of interaction the class must experience in order to enable them to make the constructs necessary for the children to learn what she wants them to understand.

1 Lister must be seen to have really existed, and to
2 Have affected his own time radically, but he must also be seen to
3 Be still affecting the present time, because of his own life-time.
4 He must be recognized as belonging in the twin medical fields of micro-biology and surgery, and these must be seen as
5 Interdependent upon each other.
6 He must be seen in the context and environment of his own time, but
7 Cause the present time to be closely examined, in order that
8 Comparison can be made between the two.

So no fewer than eight constructs will have to be made by this class, if they are to fulfil the teacher's intention, which can be briefly stated as; 'I want Lister to be seen as having influenced modern medicine, and we should honour him!' Choose the 'story way', and it takes you about half an hour; choose this system of construction meaning and you're going to be involved for much longer than that. Your choice is not whether you are prepared to spend such time; it lies instead, with what kinds of meaning do you want children to make of Lister and his history. It also requires some very precise thinking about how to set the whole thing up. This teacher chose to create an examination of doctors in the subject of 'The History of Medicine'. In the context of an important examination, the class worked an hour each day on two aspects of Lister. In their drama time they solved problems of medicine and later wrote up the process and their results under examination conditions.

The drama provided the context for bothering to do it, that is, the no-penalty area – the 'as if it were' part. After it was set that way, all the rest of the time other depictions, such as pictures, were used (modern and old-fashioned) to inform the class about hospitals, medication procedures and so on. Also used were real surgeon's tools of the time, desks and chairs were placed correctly for examination procedures, and children searched into books for information. The classic experiments of Pasteur and Lister, which doctors and teachers of doctors have performed ever since, including the classic AGAR experiment and growing of moulds, were carried out by all the class. They used the science curriculum in fact. So what then, can be said to be different about the construction of meaning through drama?

Well, the first matter has been to make time important. They came into the time of an imminent examination. They lived in the actual time of the rituals of written examinations. They were addressed as potential doctors and endowed immediately with the responsibilities of would-be doctors. The first meaning to be constructed was the dialogue between the examiner and the examined; the seriousness of the responsibility. Teachers must ask themselves, 'Is all this trouble worth it for the future understanding of this innovator Lister'?

Next they saw Lister as if in a portrait. A teacher was seated, dressed to give an authentic impression of the man, alongside an authentic microscope and surgeon's tools. He was not precisely authentic as to dress. Teachers don't often have those resources, and anyway, good pictures can correct errors of that kind. The placing of the microscope beside surgical instruments is a classic example of the power of drama to synchronize information. As would-be doctors, accepting the yoke of responsibility, they examined the possible contribution this man 'has made to our chosen careers'. 'That is significant. Read it again. 'Our careers' (that is, the present), 'this man' (that is, of the past – they can all see that, from his old-fashioned air and his old instruments).

They were then invited to place the evidence of their eyes together with their historical sense, and write an examination paper on 'what they thought was the contribution of this man's work to his own and our present, medical scene'. They knew his name, because it was on his medical degree which lay alongside his tools. This was correct as to the headings of Glasgow and Edinburgh Universities though the name of the candidate was changed to that of Lister.

During the other drama periods, each lasting an hour, they con-

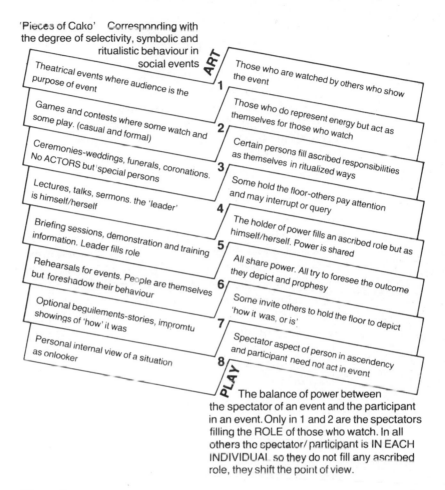

'Pieces of Cako' Corresponding with the degree of selectivity, symbolic and ritualistic behaviour in social events

ART

Theatrical events where audience is the purpose of event — Those who are watched by others who show the event — 1

Games and contests where some watch and some play. (casual and formal) — Those who do represent energy but act as themselves for those who watch — 2

Ceremonies-weddings, funerals, coronations. No ACTORS but special persons — Certain persons fill ascribed responsibilities as themselves in ritualized ways — 3

Lectures, talks, sermons. the 'leader' is himself/herself — Some hold the floor-others pay attention and may interrupt or query — 4

Briefing sessions, demonstration and training information. Leader fills role — The holder of power fills an ascribed role but as himself/herself. Power is shared — 5

Rehearsals for events. People are themselves but foreshadow their behaviour — All share power. All try to foresee the outcome they depict and prophesy — 6

Optional beguilements-stories, impromtu showings of 'how' it was — Some invite others to hold the floor to depict 'how it was, or is' — 7

Personal internal view of a situation as onlooker — Spectator aspect of person in ascendency and participant need not act in event — 8

PLAY

The balance of power between the spectator of an event and the participant in an event. Only in 1 and 2 are the spectators filling the ROLE of those who watch. In all others the spectator/participant is IN EACH INDIVIDUAL so they do not fill any ascribed role, they shift the point of view.

*Figure 4.*

structed more understanding, always in the context of modern doctors, facing examination of:

1 What made Lister struggle with these problems when it was so difficult to convince his colleagues about the urgency of antiseptics?
2 What were the hazards of the working and home conditions of his day, in regard to medication processes?
3 What developments have since occurred because of Lister's work?

The children taught Lister about these in practical demonstrations, wherein they explained kidney machines, blood banks, band-aids, plasma, aspirin, and a host of other matters they thought must interest and amaze him. A modern stethoscope and white coat was used to introduce Lister to modern medical practice. Finally they explained to him that 'There us no need to feel downhearted when you only manage to change a bit in your lifetime. The old listening-tube is only a step on the way to the present stethoscope which is always being transformed by practice and new discoveries'. Lister explained to them how he felt when he received his permission to start on a medical career, and they received their first certificates in the historical study of medicine. Please note they were not certified as doctors! That is the pretend world, and this drama has no part in the pretend world. It must preserve its inner consistent truth.

From here on, the class will conduct experiments related with Lister's time, and with modern medicine. For this they do not need a very dramatic environment because that has already done its work. They now work in the context of medical personnel thinking from within the circumstances they require to explore. They will construct meaning about the health service, or do more microscope work, or, maybe, paint pictures of the conditions under which Lister worked, and compare them to modern photographs. They will meet a real practising doctor or a medical-school lecturer who will form part of another construct where they can look at how doctors today study their subject. Whatever they do, it will have no 'dummy run' aspect. It feels real, though everyone knows it isn't actually going to teach them to be doctors. It will, however, change them into serious students.

If the chart of 'slices of cake' is now used to see the different kinds of social structures from within which the class had to construct their meaning in the Lister work, it will appear like this:

**They all entered 1, each time.** That is they agreed it was 'a depicted' event (the 'theatre' part).
A   **Meeting Lister 'as portrait'**: No. 8 (Spectating to deduce).
B   **Listening to Lister worrying** about his new system of setting bones. No. 5 (sharing his concern as fellow doctors).
C   **Questioning Lister** about his problems with other surgeons, and his life's work. No. 5 (sharing his concern).
D   **Showing Lister the health hazards** of working people in Glasgow, in Lister's own time, by making wax work scenes. No. 5 (but they take the lead. Lister is spectator). No. 1 used also (very strongly 'as if we are'). Depicting precisely.
E   **Working with Lister** in his operating theatre – preparing for an experiment with antiseptic spray machine. No. 6 (foreshadowing suitable behaviour).
F   **Teaching Lister** about modern medicine and innovations developed since his day. No. 4 (they explain, demonstrate and show).

**G** **Receiving certificates** from Lister. No. 3 (allowing the event to regulate and modify their behaviour).

Now it is possible to see in every situation, where the balance of power to affect and share outcomes lies.

In B, C, and E – class and teacher equally built the construct.
In A – it looks like teacher power, but teacher cannot move so it is equally shared. One to provide focus, the others to respond.
In D – work as demonstrators using strongly symbolic behaviour. Children have power to show another, who affirms their power.
In F – they actively take power over their teacher and teach him.
In G – the event holds the power. Teacher and children accede to its demands.

This is the contribution drama makes to the curriculum of schools, and it is capable of being varied to suit the processes of making meaning. The need may be to understand the objective world, or to understand the meaning of myth-making. To use real objects, or to construct meaning from beliefs of the past. Drama is a 'universal joint', for all the other depictions which schools respectably employ. So let us do two things. Let us refine our training processes so that we produce efficient agents of the tool, so that it can be used for learning; and let us employ it in our classrooms in such ways which allow it to be seen to implement and share in the work of our colleagues. For this we need to improve training, and unfortunately in the present western climate, where the worship of facts and the explosion of knowledge dominate, we may require technicolour, or at least flashing lights before people will listen. Maybe one day the other 'respectable' depiction-users will wake up to the potential of context making, so that classes can get rid of the 'dummy-run'.

# Drama as context for talking and writing

*This is part of an account describing work done at the Broadwood Junior School, Newcastle upon Tyne. It was written with the aid of teachers from the school and Ric Hovda from the State University of Ohio.*

There is one tool without which we now cannot work. It is the word *implication*. We find it to be one of those keystone enabling devices we all collect in the course of our careers. It makes so many things possible that we are always amazed when we first meet classes (of all ages), and find they haven't been inducted into its use. It makes every 'foreground' experience immediately have 'background'. It makes every child – and we do mean *every* child, except the severely brain damaged – able to look behind facts to meanings.

This paper is about how children can read implications, transform them into meanings for themselves, and then teach someone else. It began with a conversation between teachers of two classes and the head teacher in a primary school: 'They're nice children, not too well off but they like to learn, most of them, and their parents are interested. Last term we looked at *The Morality of Conquest* with the children in the two classes. One class examined the overthrow of the American Indian, while the other studied the British and their colonial system. Both classes are "mixed ability", top juniors in an urban school. Would drama be useful now in helping them to examine *The Morality of Conquest* at a deeper level than we have so far managed?' There is the challenge to drama. How can it meet such a need?

So much is falsely claimed in the name of drama that it will be wise to take a close look at what it can do, and how it does what it can do. We interpret the word aright when we understand it to mean living through, struggling through, and doing. But it does not mean that stories and events are the things we live through. The arts, by their nature of being like life but not life itself, free us temporarily from the burden of the future. They hold this feature in common with play, one of the seminal factors in art. They can also take liberties with time, places and perspective (the point of view we have in life often cannot be changed, but in play and art we can adapt different ways of involving ourselves in the occasion).

The arts are metaphoric and analogous, and we can be spectators of ourselves in ways often denied in a life situation, because we can distort time to give opportunity for reflection to be encountered. We can also use conventions so as to highlight situations differently, as in games. In drama work, it *seems* as if the participants are engaged in exploring and showing how people behave in events, so we anticipate there will be a logical development of the central idea and a story to follow. This is in fact to get the whole thing backwards in a very illogical way. Attitudes shape happenings, and events are their result. Each event, which is a result of attitudes, creates another shift in attitude (either by change or by refusal to change) and so creates another event. So the story is what we find we have made, as a result of the see-sawing between attitude producing action, and action changing attitude.

One of the goals of education is that children shall become able to handle complex social and personal relationships, which means developing the ability to assess the situation in which they find themselves from a diversity of angles, and find appropriate responses within their framing of the situation. Another goal is that they can grasp, as many as lie within their capacity, various types of depictions which allow people to find expression for the complex and different ideas of which they are capable. The mathematical depictions; the artist's depictions in space and colour; the languages of talk and writing, are all different ways of depicting reality. All represent something else and stand for it, for one important function of art is to retain the essence of experiences which cannot be gone through exactly ever again. So art defines, holds the image, depicts the reality it holds kinship to. Some types of depictions allow us to look back, others predict. Paintings are of the present – they are like 'frozen' time. Television, radio, film and theatre all use 'mobile' time, though they are also of the present. Writings of various kinds are in 'mobile' time also, for they depict change and development through, from attitude to event, in the same continuum as drama.

A further aspect of depictions is that they can bring the absent (for whatever reason it is now absent) very close. They cause us to think from within the frame of the depiction and actually establish things outside of the frame. This has the effect of highlighting that which is inside the framing. Depictions deal in significance. Anything not in the framing must be significant by its absence, and vice versa. Furthermore we always know the difference between art and life by the rules which can apply in the former and which cannot apply in the latter. These are: freedom of the burden of the future, productive distortion, and conventions established to communicate the statement. These three together push a switch in our minds which, once it is developed (and it seems to develop in very young children) always works if we have had experiences which allow us to learn to read the frame.

It is therefore in the context of the above that we can see whether using drama for the examination of the morality of conquest would be viable. Will a mobile depiction be the most efficient way of enabling these junior classes to examine the nature of conquest from within the frame of conquest rather than thinking it over from outside? Conquest presumably is deeply rooted in attitude. It is also a developing situation, ever-changing as events arise out of attitudes. Drama also can start at any point, and travel backwards, forwards and even take a sideways glance if necessary. It would therefore seem a good choice of strategy.

From this it is possible now to plan the approach most suitable. What stages does conquest advance through? There seem to be nine which could clearly emerge:

1   There must be established a place and inhabitants of that place. To them would arrive others from another place.
2   There must be a meeting of the two nations, some interchange and sense of differences and likenesses; possibly a time of mutual interest and need.
3   A time of assistance and sharing in endeavour.
4   Some delegation of power, of lands, of authority.
5   A formal alliance of mutual benefit to both.
6   A time of struggle of the two traditions with blending of their cultures.
7   A time of changing the status of the new and the old established peoples.
8   A time of increased power being taken by the newcomers, 'for the good of both'.
9   A time when the established community of the earliest time is subjugated.

We suggested the nine stages.

We wanted not to moralize on conquest. That is often the bias a teacher is tempted to bring to the situation when using drama. The children could be offered evidence of nine stages of change by the implication of written stone tablets, but we did not need to work with a bias either for or against the strangers. Our opinion was successfully removed in that never did the children ask what we thought about conquest. They formed their own opinions.

Nine stages of relationship to be depicted, and four days for the children to build and establish the peoples, perceive the slow changes of power and to realize at conscious level, the aspects of morality inherent in the events, and finally to debate them. The first and often the most difficult teacher task is over: to define precisely that which is to be done, for without that, it is impossible to make clear plans. In this case it is necessary to find a convention whereby nine stages of a developing situation can be seen both minutely and with an overview, for it is the spectator who sees the approach of the avalanche not the climber busy with the details of the climb. Blessings on an art form which allows us to begin thinking from the back, with hindsight!

It will be possible to start there if the children work as archaeologists seeking to understand the past. Archaeology, which gropes its way to knowledge through the taking of infinite pains, enables us to start at the end of the situation and gives opportunity for overview – for it is possible to know the outcome.

Being archaeologists will allow the minute examination of each factor in the situation. There are other roles which would give us the opportunity to work with hindsight, and perhaps a glance at these will help us to check before we make the final choice. Lawyers in a court room work backwards; historians reconstruct; biographers and novelists can do this also; the elderly recollect in tranquility with hindsight. There are indeed many roles from which to choose. But archaeology allows for the finding of actual objects, if they are needed for the concepts to develop. And the children can work at the site if necessary, so the whole experience can be more concrete.

It is perhaps important at this stage to note that the usual interpretation of drama, and therefore the typical image in the minds of readers, is that of people interacting with each other in the present situation which will have an outcome. This is too simplistic a view for educators, who must be concerned with framing situations in ways which enable their classes to be taken into very precise situations demanding kinds of thought, depiction, interaction and use of power.[1] Throughout the Ozymandias work, the shifts in language were created not by direct acting with the effigies, or the waxwork museum, but by differently depicting and identifying in the metaphoric situation. Behaving and thinking like and as archeologists was the new frame which completely altered the behaviour of the children. That was the drama. Within that responsibility and power the children employed other kinds of depictions too – painted depictions, written depictions and spoken depictions – the professional lecture, the 'I was there' accounts, the waxworks depictions and finally the lectures in the wax museum.

Percy Bysshe Shelley surely wrote Ozymandias for such a project? And certainly he would not be so mean as to begrudge our use of it with the classes of children about to exercise the skills of archaeologists? For here is the conquest to outshine any other conquest, and it belongs neither to period nor place. Archaeologists are detectives, as are historians. They detect the past on very little evidence and have to understand implication thinking, and from a little read a lot.

[1] Goffman, *Frame Analysis*, Chap. 5, p. 123.

I met a traveller from an antique land
Who said 'Two vast and trunkless legs of stone
Stand in the desert . . . near them on the sand
Half sunk, a shattered visage lies, whose frown
And wrinkled lip, and sneer of cold command,
Tell that its sculptor well those passions read
Which yet survive, stamped on these lifeless things,
The hand that mocked them and the heart that fed;
And on the pedestal these words appear:
"My name is Ozymandias, king of kings:
Look on my works ye mighty and despair!"
Nothing beside remains. Round the decay
Of that colossal wreck, boundless and bare
The lone and level sands stretch far away.

This poem was our starting point. As archaeologists we listened to it and read it as 'evidence' of a dig, not yet excavated. Our task was to see whether it seemed worth the opening up, and if we felt able to undertake it. That is the difference drama frame brings to work. To have to think from inside the responsibility of a situation rather than to think it over and about it. It places the charge of decisions firmly in the children's hands. And they never refuse a big job. They concluded that we should open the site, that there had been some terrible event; that it was 'probably around Egypt way', that the 'shattered visage might well be a great castle with the lips and sneer of cold command as the entrance to the inner rooms'; that the 'two vast legs of stone could be tall pillars which were really high buildings' and 'that there would possibly be much more hidden in the sands'. And it was worth the effort to open the dig.

As this debate was going on among the children, nine Ozymandiases quietly manifested themselves around them. No one moved, but the teachers who sat around had placed upon their chins rope beards formally arranged and highly stylized. Each beard had woven into it a number of black beads, perfectly round, ranging through one to nine, and before the feet of each one there was a piece of writing (later to be known as the tablets of stone). We selected effigies in order that

The children could find a language style to question the effigies;
They learned to listen to implication when dealing with spoken language;
The teachers could learn to talk with implication on the spur of the moment because they too were listening to the children;
So that teachers too, could find language shifts and body signals to fill out an encounter with meanings revealed not only in words but in 'presence'.

142

The children in groups had the awe of occasion, and yet the confidence to deal as archaeologists. This made their protection.

The tablets of stone were in fact simply paper glued upon thick card. Their borders corresponded with the number of beads upon the beards of the effigies, but instead of beads in the drawings they were knots, to symbolize slavery. The effigies sat in classic stillness around the discussion and so we were at the site immediately.

The nine statements at their feet were as follows. It is necessary to see all nine in the context of the stages of conquest.

1   . . . although the winter had been quite mild. During the spring of the fifteenth year of the reign of Ozymandias, three strange vessels coming from distant lands appeared for the first time. The visitors were received into the royal precinct, and rumour has it that gifts of splendour were presented to the Great One and joint thanks were offered in the temple. Later goods were traded, and it was noted what skilled tradesmen the strangers were. Many were eager to buy. . . .

2   . . . and after the hurricane, when many of our boats were lost and many of our men perished, the strangers from across the seas whose ships were more seaworthy than ours, helped us willingly to redesign our ships and even aided us in our rebuilding. . . .

3   . . . On this occasion, our leader bade us rejoice in the building of the dam to hold The Great Lake which would keep us safe and give us water in the dry season. He bade us offer 'the hand of friendship' to the Newcomers who have helped us in our enterprise. This dam further cements our mutual 'Bond of Friendship'. Truly what a blessing their coming has been. . . .

4   . . . At sunrise Ryrakali – daughter of Tkaka – arrived beneath the mighty red rocks. The Newcomers who had safely guarded her on the long journey could come no further. She alone climbed the long path to our Golden Temple. . . . Overhead a black crow screeched. . . .

5   . . . Today is a happy one in our land. Our princess, the daughter of our ruling house, embarks on the long journey which will culminate in her marriage to the son of the house of those who live across the big sea. It is in this union that our hopes of peace and prosperity lie. Many men of our land offered themselves for the honourable task of supervising her journey and presentation, but it was unanimously decided that volunteers from among our foreign friends should be trusted as emissaries. Their ships are better built, their seamen more skilled. The safety of our princess is thus ensured. Our profound gratitude and blessings go with our friends as they depart. . . .

143

6  . . . at the burial of our soothsayer, the populace noted that certain new elements foreign to our traditional ceremonies, were present, namely the coffin lid was firmly in position before sunset, and possessions were placed in a separate chamber, making it difficult for them to be viewed. It was explained that the expert craftsmen from abroad had been allowed to work according to their own traditional ways, because of their belief that evil would befall them otherwise. It was deemed polite to permit these small changes, though. . . .

7  . . . it had already been decided by the newcomers who chose to settle near the sea that new timber would be required to refurbish their old ships. They planned that timber from the Sacred Grove should be felled. Four trees were taken and stripped before anyone realized. In spite of protest from diverse persons, including those in authority, more timber was taken, amidst some argument. . . .

8  . . . All our young people had to attend, everyday. I could no longer go fishing with my father. When I protested he warned me, 'Son, keep your own counsel in the matter of these thoughts, for times are changing'. The changing times not only refer to the rest days but it would appear that the most private matters come under the . . .

9  . . . Alas we have no choice. Even our Holiest Places are threatened now. . . . Who knows in what small ways mighty events begin? And who can see the manner of their endings . . .

So the archaeologists set themselves to decipher and unravel the meanings of the cryptic and deliberately ambiguously worded statements carved in stone. They worked in self-chosen groups and the choosing was in itself a large endeavour! The first context for talk was in the reading and group discussion of the implications of the tablets. The next context was to give a public lecture upon each of the stone tablets. The archaeologists were expected to avoid talking as if it were all proven evidence. So a language not very often valued in school had to be employed, and words like opinion, suppose, consider, began to be heard. During these lectures the blackboard was used to make public recognition of the archaeological skills they were showing as they spoke. These appeared in the first session on the first day! Explanation, supposition, making connections between disparate elements, separating fact from opinion, interpretation, identification with events, careful unprejudicial examination of artifacts, seeing implications in them, precise description, differentiation between one 'time' and another 'time', recognition of tradition in cultures, understanding that chance and design have their parts to play in events, recognition of the technical skills in the information on the tablets, appreciation of hierarchy in the culture they were investigating and recognition of the resources of the country. Writing these on the board as they became apparent in the speeches, made it possible to demand that they be consciously used in future work.

The next context for language was the need to build a group picture of the event they were investigating. To do this and to arrive at a consensus, they had to talk and agree upon their images and paint them on a large paper. This was a difficult exercise because they could only use either their own readings of the tablet to create their images, or the exact descriptions as far as there were any in the texts. So they were thrown back on re-reading the tablets within a new context. Following this they then had to talk to each other, while looking at their depiction in paint and crayon, as if they were there at the time. And after this to give their second lecture on the event but this time, speaking as if they had been present at the time of the occurrence.

These different aspects of the archaeologist's work took until break time of the second morning and during all this time the effigies had sat in classic silence listening carefully to how the context was shifting the style and framing of language. The effigies were teachers on an advanced diploma course so it suited them to take these roles as part of the observation of children's thinking and behaviour.

After the lecture on 'I was there', the children next tackled the difficult art of asking questions 'so that you get the information you need'. Before they spoke with the effigies, therefore, they questioned a teacher about her ninth birthday. This subject was chosen for two reasons; it was the recent past, and really to listen to the answers and the implications underlying the answers meant laying aside expectations. There must be no blockage in their listening. The children quickly learned that they asked questions with an expectation of a kind of answer. During this time the effigies were listening even more carefully to the kinds of questions they might have to answer and to consider the best ways of forging their replies so as to challenge the archaeologists profitably.

The purpose now of questioning the effigies was to create yet another frame – that of approaching a very classic* role, one that would not answer lightly, nor in contemporary style, nor yet in words of the kind they were used to in their everyday talk. It is quite an awesome experience to approach someone you have been treating as an 'it' for two days. The answers they received were to be used to scrutinize their own interpretation of the tablets and to re-assess their other information and make intelligent guesses about the time of their reign. They

---

* 'Classic' here means highly selective as to position, language, tone and pace of communications.

were then helped by a scribe to write in classic language their version of the events carved on their tablet. They were also to pay very special attention in this document as to whether it were proof, supposition, or conjecture, and to name their sources of information. Afterwards all these nine new writings in formal language were placed with the relevant tablets in correct order as to beads and knots, and they formed the basis of a reference library in which they spent an hour under strict time controls, checking whether, by consulting all the other tablets and historical records, other than their own, they could add anything further to *their* sense of the total picture. The talk here was private in the groups. When this was completed they were thanked by the 'librarian' for their researches, and they then began the very responsible task of 'publishing their findings'.

They were asked next to create 'wax' figures (using themselves as the waxworks) which, when placed in order, would explain carefully the events as they were believed to have occurred. Before starting on the waxworks, the whole group met to decide on nine titles to be the basis of their explanation to others. The conversation again changed, because the frame was different. The emphasis now was on convention, clarity and economy without loss of meaning. Nine titles were selected as follows: The time of the Arrival; The time of the Rebuilding; The time of Friendship; The time of Trusting the Strangers; The time of saying Farewell; The time of the New Foreign Ways; The time of the Robbing of the Sacred Grove; The time of the New Laws; The Fall of Ozymandias. So nine moments of time were created in wax figures to show the slow fall of the dynasty of Ozymandias to the strangers who finally conquered. This took the whole of the last morning and the talk now was different than any hitherto demanded, that of spectators of their own work, depicting for visitors who would know nothing of what had transpired before they came into the wax museum. They devised statements to show their interior thinking, and guides were chosen who could explain anything the visitors might ask about. The wax figures could also answer for themselves when it seemed relevant.

The first visitors were a class of younger children who came to the museum to draw a life class, using for this occasion only charcoal and white card. It was an awesome sight which met them as they entered the Broadwood Wax Museum and ventured in amongst the figures in their still, classic postures. During the time of the making of the figures the archaeologists had had access to paintings chosen for the way they used space very powerfully. Wax museums, like all depictions of the kind, use space dynamically. Had there been more time, more attention could have been given to the significance of space as a language of communication. During the life class a child asked the teacher 'if it will be open on Saturday then I can come again'.

146

The above gives some indication how the drama style of depiction gives many complex framings which in turn call forth a variety of language styles and purposes. Research into language and education has demonstrated the important of experiences for children which provide meaningful contexts in which to use language for a variety of purposes, and drama facilitates this need in an ideal way.

# Drama and the mentally handicapped

*This was first published in the magazine* I D Teaching Drama, *Autumn 1978.*

Come, share in a situation with me; a visiting teacher working in a hospital for handicapped people. Nurse watching. On floor, a large man dressed in a furry costume. Children gathered round trying to 'mend a paw' with a large bandage.

Nurse. 'But if he's supposed to be a proper dog, why does he have to have one big red velvet ear? And why not two then they could match?'

This is the kind of question that I keep trying to answer.

My biggest problem in teaching is that I'm an amateur. No college of education or university department ever found me inside their august portals until I entered them as a lecturer appointed to teach others to teach. So, as an amateur I tend to use common sense. Not that I am against academic study or theories, but those addicted to this form of knowing do tend to discount common sense as being 'hunch' and written-down words as 'proper knowledge'.

The real problem of learning and teaching is really the difference between knowing something yourself, and trying to use it in such a way that other people are inducted into knowing. My areas of knowing and teaching are applied in 'people' situations and all of us know how problematic people are. They won't fit into nicely pre-packaged ideas. The skills of teaching are the skills of interaction, perception and of paying close attention to signals; to learn this one has to remain curious, take risks and watch outcomes with a keen eye and note appraisal. And, above all, remain enthusiastic in the face of much doubt. Because in our culture, examination from a point of doubt is often the respectable and safe way of testing ideas.

Now, I am an exploratory teacher, not a teller. Add explorer to amateur and you can easily be in trouble with the establishment! Anyway, some years ago, I was asked to work with the mentally handicapped, which I was delighted to do as I feel as if the urge to reach the mystery of their minds and thought processes has always been with me. So, I was asked to share work with them, and there I was, an amateur among professionals.

Now this word drama is a blanket word which has many manifestations. Usually people have a mental image in their minds of 'a re-enactment of a situation, done in public, by people, while others watch'. But when you think of that it is also true of church services, and performing magicians. In its widest interpretation it simply means that we can, by a shift in the head, experience an 'as if it were' reality, and for the time perceive it as the real world. So, at one end of the scale of interpretations we have theatrical performances of great complexity, while at the other end, we have this very private exploration. The common element is, that whichever manifestation we witness or participate in, we think and imagine from the centre of the events through identification with not thinking about the situation. This gives us a sense of urgency, and a tension about the situation that can only be matched by events, which actually happen to us, which will affect us in reality. The value in the 'as if it were' experience is, that we can be relieved of the burden of the future, except when we are pre-living a situation which inexorably will come. But even in that situation, we can tentatively experiment with a variety of approaches and outcomes. So dramatic activity, of whatever kind, can be said to provide us with metaphors to our real lives, which in turn allow us to reflect about life's experiences.

All the arts have two aspects which are present in drama simultaneously – the inner structure of the process making them happen, and the outer structure of how they look when they are seen. In many of the arts there is a gap between the making and the result. The participant makes, and the spectator then appreciates. This is true in the theatre, but in drama used for teaching we are dealing with the two parts at one and the same time. So we are trying to make something 'as if it were' life and at the same time create the means of reflecting on existence. Which is why we can employ the medium in formal learning situations, that is those which are brought about deliberately. It can readily be seen that this could be an enormous force in curriculum studies and with all kinds of students.

The problems start when others think that the 'as if' world is a pretend world, leading us to unreality. In fact it is just the opposite of this. When we reflect on our world, even if we indulge in fantasy, and stage farces, we are inexorably led eventually to real events, because drama always must deal with the affairs of people – even when they are clothed in animal manifestations, or wizards and witches. Which brings me to the brown dog with a red velvet ear. The outer form looks silly and 'pretend', but in fact the velvet ear is to provide a cuddly feeling, a focus for those who do not see well, and a less frightening aspect for the timid. Because our dog is a 'serve agent' for experiences – big enough to ride on, tough enough to fight with if you want to get rough, and timid when required, if you are ready to learn about caring and tenderness. He is also capable of being very tough with you, if you are ready to learn about handling anger in yourself.

149

The mystery for me lies in the slow exploration of how we can structure 'as if' situations, in order to give a programmed series of experiences which stretch the mentally handicapped in positive and useful ways, for their practical lives and for their inner imaginative lives. How far is it possible for such a person to share in an experience and reflect upon it, because that event has (unlike the experiences of life, which are largely chance) been introduced into their experience in a timely way? All too often when drama is used with slow learners, it is used as a 'task level' thing where events are simulated, but not really explored; where stories are hurried through but not experienced, and yet I have evidence of some rather earth-shattering explorations which seem almost to be Jungian in their manifestation. As if myth were tapped and universals perceived during the action.

Derek and Jim, two forty-year-old 'lads' in a villa were looking after me, 'as if' I were their mother. They were obviously taking great pleasure from deciding where my chair should be placed in relation to the sunshine which was pouring into the room. They then decided to take me for a run in the car (two chairs, but a very real car) to the seaside. Once by the sea they pondered with me about where the sea comes from. I stimulated this by asking the question (though it sounds like a statement) 'I've never understood why God made sand'. Derek immediately answered 'For the sea to be on top of', but as we continued, we found ourselves discussing 'this side' and 'the other side' which I began to realize was an exploration of before being born and dying.

The whole discussion however was also an exploration of children in relation to their parents. They were assuring me that they would look after me till my death, while worrying in a way that they might not be able to manage without me. They also wondered 'how old you are when you're born'; Jim being of the opinion that you have to be five before you are born, while Derek thought 'a bit younger'. All of this is in a musing fashion as we 'paddle' and they look after me. Finally they took me home and decided to build me a green house for my last days – and as we worked on it their concepts about such particular work became very active and could clearly be seen, and one of their conclusions was that 'this will keep us going for when you are over the other side!'

Here we see some of the diagnostic power of dramatic methods. It can readily be used to test what information people already possess, when assessing the next stages of instruction, and can be an excellent guide for diagnosis of the conceptual maturity, as well as to reveal social sensitivity. And of course it is not only a tool for the mentally handicapped. Working with final year doctors doing gynaecology we introduced a year group to a problem person who functioned as a role in the room while they worked out ways of dealing with her.

At first sight she was like the dog and the children – an outrageous exaggeration of a patient; truculent in manner, apparently dirty, wearing clothes more likely to be worn by a farmer during the First World War, including a trilby hat; reading comics; with a handbag filled with old photographs, spectacles, pension and telegram forms picked up in bunches from the post office counter, old tablets and medical certificates, and three Victorian books on trees and flowers. She also had her home surroundings in the form of a table with newspapers, tins of opened cat food, old tea bags and a milk bottle. There was only one lie present in the room. That she owned a large brownstone house which the university wanted to buy from her for use as a medical centre. Incidentally there only ever is *one* lie in drama work – the frame of reference in which you want the problem to be seen. The young doctors in the course of a whole day trying to gain access to her home, make contact with her as a person with whom they could relate in order to present their case, revealed great patience but hardly any powers of delicacy, signal reading, or negotiation skills. They never 'gave up' on it, because they became very interested in their own lack of skills. In addition the lady could feed back to them within the conventions drama methods offer us, her view of their negotiations.

For example, every one present mis-read two of the symbolic manifestations. Reading comics made them assume she was illiterate. The outer appearance of her clothing suggested dirt and neglect, so they 'read it' into her situation. In actual fact her Victorian books could have alerted them, but they discounted them as 'probably picked up in a library'! In fact she was spotless as to skin and hair, though her finger nails were soiled with tobacco stains. During the course of the confrontation it was easy to say 'Annie, tell the young person what he/she has done just now', and for the role to answer, using Bale's interactional analysis sheet at whatever stage the negotiations had reached. Naturally, as the day wore on, our doctors were very interested in why this type of work was introduced so late in their studies, and how to gain more from this experience in the security of the drama.

So now we see some of the potential of drama as an activity for trying out roles, and skills; for testing power in situations, and delicacy of provocation skills. I do not have enough space here to give more examples of this use of drama methods for 'coping' aspects of living being tested in the security of the life-classroom. Business people have included a watered-down version of this for years, for they have recognized the value of the spontaneous response in human situations, but all too often they have worked at the charade level, where deeper commitment and study of implication has not developed.

There is, in addition, another area which for me is fundamental in working with the mentally handicapped – to try to reach below the task levels of a confrontation or problem, to the sense of the mythological or universal aspects of living with people. I find this hard to express without example. Imagine a group of people (mostly very much institutionalized) entering a hall to find a man lying in gold cloth and with a modern staff beside him, and an unlit golden candle beside his head. We have previously become a 'family' who are seeking lights for our candles – the room is actually made dark by closing the curtains. Like our dog he is very noticeable. You would find it hard to just wander off. We try to wake him but it takes a long time because it takes a long *experience* for each one there to *perceive* him and begin to take in differences and likenesses to us. During the course of working two weeks with this man/god on the basis of an hour each afternoon, relationships were built at many levels. First he was different – not the same as us, but hard to say why. He had the same legs and so on as us. He was a 'grand lad' much sought after for company, song and dance. The dance at first was of the kind they knew. But gradually he danced more symbolically – offering his staff to them, sharing his light with them, inviting them to share his space, making new rhythms for them to dance to, obeying their rhythms, made for him. It was symbolic of universal dance, and they responded with new body shapes, different sounds with their mouths, experiments with the drumming and mouth instruments, and finally, a great variety of shapes in the dance.

Later he was threatened by a great black bird (a lady) and they helped in the ensuing battle. The 'weapons' were long pieces of silk, so much space could separate the protagonists. The battle at first was supported by cries of 'Up the lads', but gradually their support took the form of helping the enemies to apportion territories which were free for themselves to roam inside, and conventions which could be used for requests to pass, offerings of sharing pathways, fruit from neighbouring trees, visiting in each other's worlds.

Thus did what I call the more universal aspects of human friendship, powers, relationships of needs and places to feel safe, develop into the situation. The man was endowed by his symbolic appearance from the very beginning with the potential universal aspects. It need not ever matter that he is known as Prometheus, but the ideas which can gather around the meanings of that god allow a natural progression to be made, not through a story told in words, but through development in relationships always available in *concretely graspable form*. This is the massively untapped aspect of drama methods. By its nature it slows time down, forces attention, and is concretely made manifest at every stage. It is essential in all learning, that we first must be able to deal at the concrete level of ideas before we can develop abstraction skills.

I have heard two school psychologists argue about the learning potential of a ten-year-old boy. One of the opinion that he was severely subnormal, the other that in time he should be placed in an ordinary school. They called me in to set up a situation which might test his ability to abstract from a situation. As he was extremely non-verbal anyway, they had not much evidence of his abilities in this direction. I introduced four huge footprints made out of the inner tubes of lorry tyres and a hideous aspect, glued to the hall floor at regular intervals. Nearby was an empty baby's pram and a torn blanket. He said 'Monster' before two seconds had passed, and 'Baby gone' and a finger pointed out of the window where the footprints ended. Together, with me being unable to take any decisions and demonstrating fear the whole time, so that he took all responsibility, we tried to find the baby. He was heard to say at one point 'Monsters don't do that kind of thing'. This was in reply to my query as to whether the monster might be 'Wanting my baby in order to have a son of his own'.

So this is where we came in! I'm an amateur among professionals. I can set things up – I cannot know the mentally handicapped in the same dimensions as the medical and caring staffs. To me those children and adults are 'thous' as Martin Buber would express it in 'I and Thou', and must be treated as such or I lose honour for myself and them. I cannot use them as 'Its' or there can be no honour won in our acquaintance. To treat a person as a 'thou' demands first that they be recognized fully as an individual with rights in the situation of our meeting. And rights means giving to people the power to affect a situation, to respond in a growing complexity of ways to that situation. One therefore has to be able to structure that situation in ways which enable this complexity to develop. I do not know how complex these powers of negotiation can become, because usually the situation is not fully geared for this kind of progress to be undertaken. This is partly a result of too many people to be looked after at once, partly because the physical caring is stressed, and it needs to be often, though at the cost of the mental stretching. It possibly needs a whole new breed of staffing to be developed in our mental hospitals, the teacher-nurse.

I sympathize with those who find this kind of work too intrusive, too upsetting to the developed power patterns in hospital relationships which have come about because of the need these people have to be kept safe, looked after physically and controlled in the warmest sense for the good of all the residents. We have choices. We can decide to protect into ineffectiveness and keep people safe, and the place on an even keel, or we can systematically break this pattern at some cost to everyone. I am never sure whether 'happy cabbages' are preferable to 'emergent exploratory people'. Nor have I the power to decide. I am an amateur among professionals. I can only say to myself when I ask that question of myself, 'please life, let me participate in my living existence'.

153

# Considerations when working with mentally handicapped people

*These are unpublished notes drawn up to aid those attempting to bring the drama experience to mentally handicapped people.*

1   What happens must be experienced in reality by them – I *never* ask them consciously to 'pretend'.

2   To keep this reality I try to make something occur to which they only have to *respond*.

3   *These occurrences must really happen*, for example:
(a)   A person may be there to meet them.
(b)   A thing needing to be done might be there plainly *demonstrating* what needs doing.
(c)   A combination of a/b may be there.

4   The occurrence or person must be *very clearly defined*. One of the ways I use often is to create a bizarre/noticeable procreation so that no one can miss it – it can 'intrude' on their vision/their space. *A gentle invasion*, capable of constant development.

5   To achieve this I tend to look to *epic material* rather than domestic, everyday, material for my provocations. Epic material bypasses little jobs *and reaches first for relationship* – out of which working together can begin. The basis of epic material lies in these areas: striking, feeling, great fearing, joy, labour, painful touch, carrying heavy responsibility, celebrating.

6   The occurrence or meeting must demonstrate the *need to take decisions* – each decision must be the choice/s of the group – using *their* information, *their* expertise, *their* choice/s. *Each decision must be tested in outcome* – by the demonstration of their outcome leading to further decisions being taken.

7   *Progression for me* lies in:
(a)   people anticipate the presence of the role or event more and more;
(b)   they recall/recount it and their part in it afterwards and between meetings;
(c)   people take power over or with the role/events;
(d)   people show opinion and *stick to it*;

(e)    there is language from and expression demonstrated which break into new language patterns – or a change in physical demeanour;

(f)    concentration begins to show, with intensity but with openness to others.

Obviously progress is often hidden because of language and often physical damage is great. A new eyelid flutter, a new sound is a miracle of achievement.

8   *I use theatre forms to declare problems*, I reveal choices. I am always highly selective in how I present the material, for example special presentation, stance, heights, etc.

9   I use no 'canned' effects – for music I will use any instrument where the musician can be seen to be playing it and I try to bring these instruments to the group also, so that they may try them, guitars, violins, flutes, oboes, etc. I prefer portable instruments to the piano.

10   All ideas must develop slowly – keeping *high energy* but slow pace – leaving time for experience, expression of response, adjustment of attitude, development of a sense of 'where we're at'.

11   Participators must put aside pre-knowing so as to avoid taking decisions away from the group. All 'other' logic, that is not according to cerebral, conforming, informational logic *must* be encountered and kept; this means a high toleration of ambiguity.

# Part Four

# The authentic teacher

# Introduction

The two papers which comprise Part 4 of this collection of Dorothy Heathcote's writings look to the future, and so, unlike the work of the other three sections, do not require to be related to what has happened, but instead, to what is happening. It is the *now* and the present state of society and education which has provoked these papers – which are without doubt more personal and urgent in style. In essence the content of what Dorothy Heathcote is talking about remains the same, but the emphasis is different.

Throughout her career, Dorothy Heathcote has challenged existing ideas and practice, not just for the sake of it, but as part of her insistence for better schools and better teaching. It is evident that now, her desire for change is as strong, and that she has chosen to appeal to and support the teacher in the classroom to effect the change, rather than stand with the administrator or the academic.

'Signs and portents' is perhaps Dorothy's chance to answer subconsciously many of her critics who feel that her use of drama as a learning tool has decreased the importance of theatrical or dramatic form and that, attractive as her teaching style may be, many of those who wish to work in her way fail to succeed. The thirty-three conventions listed on pages 166–7 could not be more explicit in their purpose of taking teachers to the water and urging them to drink in the message that the heart of all communication is *sign* – that teachers must strive to find the *sign*ificance in all they do – that, since theatre is the art form which is totally based on sign, she has not turned her back on theatre – on the contrary. In B. J. Wagner's *Dorothy Heathcote: Drama as a learning medium*, she is quoted as saying: 'Classroom drama uses the elements of the art of theatre ... The difference between the theatre and the classroom is that in theatre everything is contrived so that the audience gets the kicks. In the classroom the participants get the kicks. However, the tools are the same: the elements of theatre craft.'

In the last paper 'The authentic teacher and the future' Dorothy Heathcote describes the context of the paper herself in the Preface or Apologia, aware that a teacher working for authenticity is inevitably in conflict with the system as it stands, a system educating children yet ignoring their future, which cannot guarantee employment or peace.

158

Dorothy Heathcote urges teachers to face change and keep their minds and hearts open to the opportunities and difficulties which lie ahead.

Such advice is not given passively; by the time this is printed it will be out of date for Dorothy Heathcote, who will have moved on, refining her practice and widening her perceptions, persuading by example. Blake's 'minute particulars' (page 179) will be relegated to the jargon file along with 'brotherhoods' and 'cool strips' and new phrases will have been coined to pinpoint exactly the stage of development she has reached. We hope the following papers will prove to her critics that it is not possible to present a unified statement of Dorothy Heathcote's thinking – to do that would be to confine or trap her spirit, which continues to outpace most of her contemporaries in her pursuit of excellence.

# Signs and portents

*Specially written for and first published in the Journal of the Standing Conference of Young Peoples' Theatre, spring, 1980.*

Actual living and theatre, which is a depiction of living conditions, both use the same network of signs as their medium of communication; namely the human being signalling across space, in immediate time, to and with others, each reading and signalling simultaneously within the action of each passing moment. We cannot help signing so long as there is another human being who needs to read the signs. Actions become sign whenever there is more than one person present to read the action.

Balanced between actual living and theatre are drama used in education (in the classroom mainly) and Theatre in Education (TIE) teams. I should like to explore the relationship of these four kinds of events in this paper.

When I first began teaching, I had no training in the 'proper' ways to make contact with my classes. Coming from a theatre training I therefore used the thing I knew most about. That was, how to make it interesting and exciting to be present at an occasion marked by *conscious* signing of intent. As I had not been 'taught manners' as you might say, I didn't know about the complexities of classroom communication where the person in charge uses the mouth as the main means of communication, with sometimes the blackboard as an additional aid to coherence. However, coming from the theatre, I got to thinking it would be important to suit the word and the gesture; and the relationship with the furniture and the book; and indeed anything which at the moment assisted in the total picture becoming available to be 'read' by the class. I also knew that you don't ask questions to which you already know the answer. That is not how theatre works. You signal across space meaningfully, to get a response which will have been born from your own signal, as the person/s alongside you read the sign. So of course you listen with all your body for the messages.

Coming from the theatre also, you don't consider sign to be bad manners. I still meet colleagues who somehow manage by *their* signing, to indicate to me that there is something rather ungenteel about behaving like that in classrooms. However, I must say that I am glad that more teachers are braving these critics and trying to employ sign more coherently in their teaching. Classes deserve the best systems of communication we can give them. I wonder if we would have fewer 'slow learners' if we used a more meticulously selective and complete signing system as our means of communication to such classes. Individuals read signs very differently, and therefore decipher the code more easily if it is rich, full and highly selective, for its present purpose.

This is the interesting variation on life and theatre signing which the classroom and the TIE team can exploit. In the theatre all actors sign for the benefit of the audience. In life we sign for the other person out of need for response. In teaching we make our signs specially interpretable, so that the children are able to read all signals with the least possible confusion. We deliberately sign for the responder to come into active participation in the event. If, therefore as teachers we send out some signs to be part of the event, but demand of children that other signs, which are also present, are to be ignored, then we baffle them by the confusion of what to discount. The most developed skill which children bring to school is that of making sense for their own ends of sign in their immediate environment. So we do not need to apologize for 'showing off', which is how working in role in the classroom is often seen. One can understand why people criticize it; because the medium of expression is the human person.

Fortunately, working through role is catching on a bit in classrooms, so it is timely to start looking at the subtlety of this style of approach, which is one of many. But all these ways must use sign in order to make communication.

## Some common denominators in working through role

We probably all agree that when we say we work in role we mean that we become part of the action of the 'play' and have a voice in the dramatic encounter. There must, by now, be some emergent theory born of practice, which could be brought together so that we can see what the rules are in order to apply them better. What follows are only the basic common denominators which I have isolated; they are not complete, because I don't myself understand it all yet.

*Now and imminent time.* The factor which distinguishes a dramatic exploration of ideas seems to be the way in which time becomes different from the usual classroom time. During discussion of ideas (though we ourselves exist in life-time) the circumstances we are planning to try to exist in are still in another time-state. We talk about, 'They would be this or that', because though we are breeding future action of the event we are still only planning. I am constantly amazed by the miracle of how thinking about a dramatic idea can in an instant become that of carrying it into action. There is a world of difference between someone in a class saying, 'Well, they would take all their

161

belongings with them', and saying, 'Let's pack up and leave'. That is the switch I work for, to enable a dramatic exploration of ideas to take place. It stands to reason then, if I want to assist in this switch to imminent time, the most efficient way is to start very carefully to use my contribution to the discussion in this now time-state. That is role at its simplest. I talk like I'm there. There is a lot more to it than that of course. One does not just become a person in the play, because one is teaching as well as signing. Ask yourself this question. The last time you worked in role were you really only adding to the number in the cast? If so, you've made a start in using the power of role, but there's a very exciting journey ahead if you care to investigate.

*Role as contract maker.* I have already indicated that social encounters need sign. The sign of the person, in action, using all objects, significant space, pause, silences, and vocal power to make the meaning available to others in the encounter. This total acceptance of signing allows children to bring their profound experience to bear in interpreting the scene. A class on the defensive, which has developed resistant techniques to classroom practice, is particularly good at reading signs for its own ends. When the teacher begins to accept the total signing system, as being open for the class to interpret, there can also begin an erosion of the position of negative spectator which we all develop under stress or criticism. In role I give myself two kinds of encounter. One is the power to get out of the expected teacher system of relating with the class. The other is the opportunity to make contracts as myself and encounter the class signing system through the role I artificially and totally consciously take up. So role can work as an anti-corrosive agent.

*'The other'.* (This is a somewhat fanciful name to give to what might be perceived as just something to deflect the attention of the class. I spend a lot of time preventing classes feeling stared at. Everything else in the world except oneself is 'an other'. The actor in the theatre, the TIE team and the teacher have all made a contract to allow people to stare at them, but the children have not made that contract. And teachers of drama who take it for granted that children have given them this permission, spend useless time in eroding the embarrassment which happens during drama lessons where children feel stared at.

The obvious way of avoiding this is to give them something so attractive in the room that they feel they are staring at it. Role is one of the most efficient 'others'. Do not mistake what I am saying; I do not mean something which is merely interesting, or entertaining; it may have that outer appearance just as the teacher in role might fool the onlooker that all the role is doing is acting. Roles must never act in the

sense that an actor may, for they have a
discussing here is that 'the other' be th
exploration which will follow as the cl
When the role is used it can set fram
fact that someone has entered into a
automatically places the rest of the
selves, for they must be addressed as if they are
the same shift or the potential for such shift to be brought
other means, simply because other objects used in this way cannot
this special time. There is prejudice against using role because it is so
efficient and looks so showy. It is part of that 'improper' behaviour
which teachers are not supposed to indulge in.

*Sharing and giving of information.* Teachers are noted for their propensity to share their understanding by a process of telling in one form or another. This often tends to look like one-way transmission. A teacher in role can undermine this approach because the theatre gets its message over more indirectly through the range of signs which come into play. Many kinds of information are available simultaneously when role is inducted, especially that of frame and attitude.

Recently I was in role as a manager of a gold mine with a London class. 'The new issue of picks, shovels, screens and pans is due today. See that they are signed for, and you'd better check that they are the correct size this time. Those big meshes are useless for this soil. We've wasted too much time at the panning tanks re-screening, I just hope we haven't lost any nuggets through these wide meshes. Where's the storekeeper?' Put baldly like this, with no pitch, pause, gesture, position in relation to all the others, and a general demeanour of authority to speak while others listen, it seems like a one way flow. What is not conveyed in print is the opportunity for the teacher to observe the class response to the variety of topics introduced. Neither can it explain the reasons why the role made that particular statement.

In the case in point the class was demonstrating in a fairly patient way that they were expecting to get into action and dig. A teacher can ask all kinds of questions about such matters as, 'Where would the tools be kept?' 'Where is the actual shaft?' 'Who are we?' 'What are our jobs?' Asked questions like this children take interesting decisions but not *as if they were* miners. That time-state cannot be induced through that type of question. In the pit manager's role there are also disadvantages. You

---

⁎ Frame: in any social encounter, there are two aspects present. One is the action necessary for the event to progress forward towards conclusions. The other is the perspective from which people are coming to enter the event. This is frame, and frame is the main agent in providing tension and meaning for the participants.

163

cannot ask experienced miners, (who in this drama they will be) where they keep their tools. Everyone would know. Neither can you ask how they do their jobs. Nor can you ask who the storekeeper is. You would know. But you can induct all the miners into different kinds of information by the statement of new tools which will be arriving; the need to check these tools against wrong and useless ones, problems at the tanks, introduction of one technical term which is *only* used in the mining of gold and giving some indication of another authority figure which can supersede your power as soon as possible.

They have a chance with all this to become in action, or at least response, seasoned miners because everything can be assumed, yet explained, quite explicitly. A request for the storekeeper (even if he or she isn't present because no one in the group wants the responsibility) can yield the whereabouts of either keys to stores, or a place where stores are currently kept; this in turn will yield a shaft where miners collect their tools. Rules of behaviour can emerge as they join their mates at the shaft head. Laws about matches, pocket contents, searches of miners after shift; all these will become natural developments from 'Where is the storekeeper?' This is the excitement and subtlety of role work. Thinking like a cat while apparently signing crudely.

*Negotiation.* Artists work from two positions of power. The doing position, where they are involved in the action of their art, and the seeing position from which they perceive what is happening and what might need to be done. By sometimes working in the action of the play, and sometimes from the spectator position I can give this power to the class. Role helps them *do*, and the teacher helps them *see*. In the early stages, contracts and decisions are often best taken from the spectator position so that everyone can see there is no con-game going on. This is one of the secrets of sincere work. In a paradoxical way, then, I build trust in the drama by working as a teacher, negotiating within the actual state, while in role I build trust in the virtual state. This is a very comfortable way to work for both teacher and class, for it enables all the rules to be seen as they come into action, and especially it gets rid of the teacher power to *tell* directly.

*Shifting the position of the class.* By taking up a role one offers not only a point of view to the others, but places them in a position from where it is assumed that they will also find a point of view (see the miners' material quoted earlier). Note that I have said assumed. One cannot endow people with commitment to a point of view, but often by placing them in the response position, they begin to hold a point of view, because they can see it has power. The crudest power to give others is that of disagreeing with the role, spotting the weakness in the role's position,

164

or even opposing the role. If a class really wants to oppose a teacher it is often somewhat bitter in tone, open to the accusation of rudeness (at the least), but opposition to a role places a class in a very safe position from which to disagree, and it establishes their *right* to oppose the teacher's power. No one loses face. But the best thing of all, the role, not the teacher, can respond to the communication, thus holding it in the 'no penalty' zone. In this way good relations can be built, on a very sure basis.

## Theatre in Education teams

So far I have been mainly looking at role from the point of view of the teacher in the classroom. What of TIE teams? The first advantage they have is that, under theatre conventions, they are accepted as total signers. They have given permission to others to stare so they can employ *sign*ificance from the start. It is accepted as normal for the actor/teachers to employ such aspects of sign as clothing, properties and setting for action. This is not so easy for the teacher because of different expectations of behaviour. One of the most fundamental decisions which TIE teams have made is that of working with classes from within and from without the action of the play. However, they have the problem, and often their weakest area is here, of changing their signing systems to indicate and accommodate to these two positions. This is because of the very strength of their sign position when in the action of the play. A teacher by her or his inability to sign strongly on clothing, setting and accuracy of properties, can sign mainly in the language and body position areas, and these are more easily shed than the clothing and prop signs of the TIE actor. Thus it is I think, that the TIE teams often find difficulty in their negotiations from outside or when seeking to bring their audience into their action. Children can't help being reminded that they are not quite in the action like the actors are.

## Conventions

So we come to the fascinating area of conventions which can be used to enable children to become involved in drama experiences of many types. The ability of children to achieve truthful behaviour under both TIE and classroom drama, and to become committed to the decisions they are enabled to take during the action of the play, is phenomenal. The conventions I shall outline seem to me to be a most useful additive to both types of work. Avant Garde theatre has always used them, and film can wonderfully exploit them. I use them more and more in my

165

classroom work and they are comparatively easy to manage with a little care and practice. They exploit the use of signing and significance in a very special way because most of them shift the way in which contact with role and 'immediate time' works. Most drama that moves forward at seeming-life-rate is too swift for classes to become absorbed in and committed to. The conventions offered here *all slow down time* and enable classes to get a grip on decisions and their own thinking about matters. They all function as 'other', but in relation to people:

1   The role actually present, naturalistic, yet significantly behaving, giving and accepting responses.
2   The same, except framed as a film. That is, people have permission to stare but not intrude. 'Film' can be stopped and restarted, or re-run.
3   The role present as in 'effigy'. It can be talked about, walked around, and even sculptured afresh if so framed.
4   The same, but with the convention that the effigy can be brought into life-like response and then returned to effigy.
5   The role as portrait of person. Not three dimensional, but in all other ways the same as effigy.
6   The role as portrait or effigy activated *to hear* what the class is saying. This causes selective language.
7   The role as above, but activated to speak only, and not capable of movement.
8   The role depicted in picture: removed from actual life, as in a slide of role, a painting, a photograph or drawing. This includes those made by a class, as well as prepared depictions.
9   A drawing seen in the making, of someone important to the action, as on a blackboard.
10  A stylized depiction of someone. For example an identikit picture made by the class in frame as detectives.
11  The same, except made beforehand, so is a *fait accompli*.
12  A life size (cardboard) model with clothing (real) of role. For example, 'framed' as if in a museum or sale rooms. 'This is the dress worn by Florence Nightingale when she met Queen Victoria after Scutari.'
13  The same, except the class is dressing the model so as to see 'how it was' on that day when these events happened.
14  The clothing of a person cast off in disarray. For example, remains of a tramp's presence, or a murder, and escape as in a highwayman situation.
15  Objects to represent person's interests. This works as above, but more intimate things can indicate concerns rather than appearance. For example, a ring of a Borgia.

16  An account of a person by another person in naturalistic fashion. For example, 'Well when I saw him last he seemed all right. I never dreamed anything was wrong.'
17  An account of a person writing as if from that person, but read by someone else. For example, a diary.
18  An account written by the person who now reads it to others, for example a policeman giving evidence or a confession. The role is present in this case but in contact through their writing as an author might well be.
19  An account written by someone, of someone else and read by yet another.
20  A story told about another, in order to bring that person close to the action. For example, 'I saw him open a safe once. It was an incredible performance. I'm not sure if he would assist us though.'
21  A report of an event but formalized by authority or ritual. For example, an account of bravery in battle on an occasion of the presenting of postumous medals.
22  A letter read in the voice of the writer. This is an emanation of a specific presence, not just any voice, communicating the words.
23  The same, but the letter is read by another with no attempt to portray the person who wrote it, but still expressing feeling.
24  A letter read without feeling. For example, as evidence, or accusation in a formal situation.
25  The voice of a person overheard talking to another in informal language, that is using naturalistic tone.
26  The same, but in formal language.
27  A conversation overheard, the people are not seen. Deliberate eavesdropping as in spying.
28  A report of a conversation, written and spoken by another.
29  A reported conversation with two people reading the respective 'parts'.
30  A private reading of a conversation, reported as overheard.
31  The finding of a cryptic code message. For example, tramps or spies.
32  The signature of a person found. For example, a half-burned paper.
33  The sign of a particular person discovered. For example, the special mark of the Scarlet Pimpernel.

All the above can be used to make classes feel involved with the immediate time of the action, and in touch with the human person, but these will not be achieved if the negotiations do not endow the class with the power to influence, not only watch. This means that the participation needs to be framed.

167

## Frames

There are many ways of providing frames but the most important factor is that the participants have to be framed into *a position of influence*. In TIE then it would seem an advantage to consider the many frames from which audiences may enter the action. If they are asked to use their judgement, as themselves, or share in an endeavour with the actors, as in a spinning-mill situation, the number 1 on the conventions list would seem to be the one which would feel right. But if they were asked to *comment on* the action as if it were in frozen time (as in a museum) then the frame can be different. For example, the actors may become portraits in a gallery and the participants may then be asked to reactivate them and make them 'play it again' in another way. Or, when teaching a Shakespearean play for A-level, a TIE team might play a scene of some seminal importance to the study, but then in effigy or portrait convention, each protagonist in the situation might be 'hung' in a gallery and the children in groups invited to take one such painting and activate it to walk the scene again, asking it at each stage to explain itself.

I take it as a general rule that people have most power to become involved at a caring and urgently involved level if they are placed in a quite specific relationship with the action, because this brings with it inevitably the responsibility, and, more particularly, the viewpoint which gets them into an effective involvement. By doing this, the social encounters, either during or after the main action of the play, become more complex and various. It *is* often done, of course, when, for example, the audience are invited to be a jury or soldiers at a firing squad, or indeed any situation where they may join in the moral or action decisions. However, often the participation functions in action time, the seeming life-rate of the theatre. The list of conventions above has only one such convention – the first one. All the other encounters listed with people, their behaviour and motives, are in another kind of time. The roles exist to be rebuilt in one way or another, and in one form or another. The class can be invited to reconstruct, or reinterpret, and this has the remarkable effect of getting them hooked into the power to think about influence and hold a viewpoint, because the action is a process of *rebuilding* not sharing someone else's materials. Unlike television with its fast moving action/image, these other conventions function more like stills or slides, causing infinitesimal decisions to be made by the children.

Theatre 'proper' finds it difficult to cause audiences to re-frame themselves, for it is not the mood in which most people come to the theatre. They anticipate the security of the spectator of action. Likewise, the teacher who prefers to teach *about* things often uses the consciously cognitive approach. This type of teaching can avoid the immediate decision time of drama. TIE and classroom role work, however, are ideally suited to exploit the types of work and it pays well to explore them further.

I said at the beginning of this paper, however, that if you only join the cast of the play as it were, it adds very little to the meaningful action which takes classes through the layers from mere attraction, to interest, to attention and finally to concern. The whole negotiation of role involves delicate linguistics in vocal sign, plus the equally selective body and space sign. Both areas of signalling require the power to be passed over to others. Let us take an example to try to make this clear.

Suppose the class are working as members of the team of the Scarlet Pimpernel, rescuing an aristocrat from the revolution, and the action has involved a teacher in role as one of the revolutionaries in order to place the class in danger as the 'brave rescuers'. The first episode may be dealt in life-like style; but see the difference in thought and the social demands made, if the second episode has to deal with the aristocrat being brought into an inn where on the wall is the portrait of that aristocrat and the loyalties of the innkeeper are not known. The convention of *portrait* makes it possible here for a new look at danger, and the complexity of signing (which the class will of course handle without difficulty) creates an entirely new social and linguistic encounter. Obviously, whichever convention is selected will always be designed to serve the particular ends of the work.

Finally, having spent a long time wondering why I have for years been irritated by the cry of 'let's have more drama in our schools,' I now realize why I always wanted to say, don't lobby for dramatics, lobby for better learning! It is, of course, because the heart of communication in social situations is the sign. *All* teachers need to study how to exploit it as the first basis of their work. The theatre is the art form which is *totally* based in sign and the drama additive to learning gives the urgency possible through using now/imminent time. This is why we lobby for better schools when we ask that teachers wake up to the possibilities of the power of resonances in classrooms instead of verbal statements.

# The authentic teacher and the future

## Preface and apologia

I suffer from an unfortunate ability to take notice of lots of things all at once when they happen around me, and the capacity to forget easily those details of authorship, occasion and reference points which would authenticate and 'fix' them later. However, as a working housewife, I often have wet, floury or dirty gardener's hands while listening to the radio, pondering on thoughts arising from reading newspapers, books and articles, or taking part in the conversations of my family or guests hanging about in the kitchen, and I'm usually too busy to stop and write, especially as I might miss some other gem as it emerges around me.

So, in what follows the reader will notice that I recall or use some seed of an event or statement, without in the least being able to give those detailed references so beloved of academics. I suspect that the ability and preparedness to annotate one's sources in detail are not always altruistic. For very often that very meticulousness draws attention to the user rather than the source – we do so respect the writer who is prepared to borrow wisely, and especially one who has borrowed/ burrowed from a lot of other sources and who didn't forget to take proper notes at the time. I do also recognize that such details permit any reader to follow up the same material for themselves, which my slap-happy approach prevents. I suspect that I'm too untutored and elderly now to find myself motivated to change but there is another point to be made. I frequently find that I've been 'borrowed' without benefit of reference and it doesn't seem to bother me. There's something very positive about individuals who can process the work of others into their own fabric of writing.

In what follows I can sometimes give you chapter and verse but not consistently. If the source is radio, then I know it must be Radio 4 because I have a prejudice about moving the dials around, but publishers and dates are a problem because names continue to elude me – as all my students know from experience.

## Society needs to review its uses for its schooling system

You can't be involved in education without noticing that teachers, like most other people, must engage with the problems of societal flux and shift, and therefore with a stringent re-examination of what schools are supposed to be for. Every day when I associate with teachers and children the same idea niggles me. What am I doing at this present moment within my society which is of any use? How will what happens in this time contribute to this individual, this group of people, my community, my nation, the world of people and objects? I've been lucky enough, heaven knows, to have evolved for myself a personal philosophy of my intentions and practice, but it just isn't enough to be personally at home with one's ideas – and in formal teaching, that is school-teaching, it never has been – but suddenly it's shockingly and increasingly evident that society needs to review, crystallize and frame its demands on, and its uses for, its schooling systems. As an individual using part of the fabric of my life as a teacher, I don't believe I'm alone in my frustration as to where or to whom to turn to for a lead in this, or how to set it in motion in any coherent way.

I sometimes think a conference would help! They say that a certain language conference in the USA changed the understanding, direction and thrust of language teaching some years ago. I haven't a lot of faith in conference outcomes myself, because it seems to me they often avoid what I call 'energized commitment' to *change in practice*. Who would have to attend such a conference? I look at the word confer-ence you see, the very word suggests talk, not action, and my heart sinks. So, who would have to attend in order to get energy for action? Practitioners I suppose, those who practise ideas in action. Inner-city and rural developers? Manufacturing people and working members of unions? Builders of communication systems? People who induct, teach and train others in skills? Those who conserve, grow things, worship, make laws or co-operate with and support the needy? We'd have to choose people of passion-plus-reflection, those who have inner meaning in their acts who are articulate to the point of excellence. They'd have to be able to listen without judging in favour of their own biased interest and above all not rush to polarize. They'd have to be those who understand the dangers inherent in what Doris Lessing has called in *Shikasta*[1] 'AOWF – the absence of we feeling', and so combat that tendency.

And to be reasonable it couldn't be one big conference because people aren't made that way. It would need to be hundreds of little ones arising in every small community, where 'authentic' people can be recognized and their energy tapped. 'Cells of change' is maybe what

[1] *Shikasta* is the first novel in the series *Canopus in Argos: Archives* published in paperback by Granada.

171

we'd have to call them. How can an individual teacher start such a move towards authentic schools for now? That is what I want, and I believe my wish is shared by many of the 433,000 teachers who teach in British schools. And that's a lot of potential power!

## Straws in the wind

There are a lot of straws blowing in the wind, however, which give me a bit of comfort. In the ten days around Easter week 1983 I collected these while getting on with my ordinary life of kitchen, correspondence, phone calls, family and student arrangements:

1   Lawrence Tinkler on Radio 4 talking about the 'dammit principle', the value of questioning the status quo.
2   Vivienne Apple, 'failed teacher', in a letter to *The Guardian*, mentioning 'that something extra that good teachers have – a kind of aura' (see p. 200).
3   Andrew W. Halpen's article on 'Change: the Mythology'[2] wherein he warns us against confusing rhetoric with reality.
4   Bob Aitkin's statement on Radio 4 referring to possible educational spin-offs from the present unemployment situation and Coventry's plans in education.
5   Shirley Williams in *Any Questions*, Radio 4, who mentioned that '. . . the arts stand for the humanization of life – a force for good?' and reminded me of –
6   Marghanita Laski's statement on an earlier such programme that 'Arts destroy the present order and pave the way to new things'.
7   Han Suyin on *The Book Programme* on Radio 4 who, in an interview, said 'We need to understand each other and to know each other better' when referring to love as a world force for good.
8   Then there was the Management Page of the *Financial Times* when Robin Reeves reported on 'an unusual educational experiment' in a Welsh university where they were working towards innovative thinking in the classrooms of the engineering department. Daley's accompanying drawing neatly encapsulated society, education, commerce and industry being connected by 'innovation' which was being forced like toothpaste from two labelled cogged rollers.[3]

[2] Macmillan, 1966 in a volume of *School Administration*.
[3] Two interesting things came together that day within a few minutes of each other. I had just been shocked by the thought that something as essential as innovative thinking is considered so unusual in universities that it formed the basis of an article in the *Financial Times*, when I heard from a student of mine that one of my colleagues had told her that my innovative ideas about diagrams and drawings as an aid in answering

9    On another day I heard the tail end of an argument about peace studies between Rhodes Boyson and an unknown teacher. Rhodes Boyson seemed to be criticizing some peace study games because they were unlikely to assist the real peace in the world, and the Unknown was defending trial and error in finding ways to start such studies.

10   In my mail was Derek Stevens's statement about peace studies related to drama practice in a comprehensive school in Ripon, Yorkshire. 'I want to encourage my students to think about the world in which they live, I want them to have a better understanding of life, to help them cope with the problems it confronts them with.'

11   The final gift that week was from *A World in Common* the BBC Radio series, programme 7, called 'Let This be a Lesson' – 'Educational programmes with a practical orientation exist in most developing countries, but they are often not within the formal school system – literacy courses for adults, for example, radio programmes for farmers, craft training and the like. Attempts at integrating schooling and productive work are rarely successful, though exceptions exist – both nationwide (China) and in special projects in countries such as Botswana. Yet the pupil's demand for certificates and diplomas may ultimately scuttle even the most promising project. There are echoes of this in the educational systems of the industrial countries, where the outcome of exams also largely determines what will happen in a person's working life.'[4]

## Authenticity the link

By this time I can appreciate that the reader is wondering what all these apparently unconnected gleanings are adding up to. Well, it's because having been invited by the editors of this book to re-read the first chapter, which I spoke/wrote some three years ago in New Zealand, I suddenly connected what I was then saying, to a notion I only recently perceived, but now realize that I've been dealing with for a long time – possibly all my teaching life – without being able to grasp hold of it

---

examination questions were best ignored in favour of a good academic style! What's good for the *Financial Times* which has to sell its ideas in the real world of readers who pay to be helped to understand, is not going to sully the portals of the Academy. It shows how far at least one university teacher has to travel into the twentieth century.

[4] From 'Creative Art as an Instrument of Building up Understanding and Peace' included in *Teachers of the World International and Pedagogical Trade Union Review*, Eva Brück, January 1983.

sufficiently well finally to clearly express it. In that previous article, when I was referring to excellence, I now think I meant authenticity, for a central notion of excellence as outlined in that paper is the capacity to behave in an authentic way. As a teacher of drama, which is often perceived by society as the most artificial and therefore the most unauthentic art form there is, it seems a bit paradoxical to strive for authenticity, except that good art is its own authenticity. The concept of authenticity is the tenuous thread which links all the previous gleanings quoted above.

There are various types of links in those comments and statements. For example, the authenticity of the fabrications of artists links the Laski and the Han Suin statements. The notion that simulations and drama may provoke or prevent an encounter with authenticity, links the dismissive Boyson remark, Stevens's statement, and Shirley Williams's 'arts and humanization' quotation. Further, using real problems and then manufacturing processes to test ideas in the classroom before people need test them expensively in practice, as described in the *Financial Times*, is another kind of authenticity, and so is the attempt by some people in the world of education to forge a bridge between schools and the actual needs of communities. Artists have always related the actual to the virtual in their art, because their material is derived from the affairs of people.

We often consider the creations of scientists as being more authentic than those of artists because artists' products are related (and relegated?) to the enterprise we call play whilst those of scientists are deemed to be of more serious intent. However, that refreshingly clear writer Lewis, author of the elegantly contrived and expressed articles in *The New Yorker*, now brought together in *The Medusa and the Snail* and *Lives of a Cell*, has done a lot to make such silly divisions seem unnecessary. Yet it seems harder for society to accept the 'energy' of humans to have power in the world because they make personal links between cultures, as expressed in the novels of Han Suin, than energies which scientists discover. The latter is connected to physical need I suppose and the former to emotional need, and our world understands the physical more and certainly separates it from the emotional.

## Authentic teacher power

So latterly I've realized that a possible way forward at this time of world development might be found in authentic teacher power. Supposing those 433,000 British teachers could start an authenticity drive? What might it consist of? In my talk on excellence I named certain aspects which I would now label as being authentic. I'm delighted to find similar notions in Halpen's The Concept of Authenticity.[5] I make no apology for the length of the quotation for I hesitate to interfere with his form and clarity. He is examining the differences between 'open' and 'closed' organizational climates:

> As we looked at the schools in our sample, and as we reflected about other schools in which we had worked, we were struck by the vivid impression that what was going on in some schools was *for real*, while in other schools, the characters on stage seemed to have learned their parts by rote, without really understanding the meaning of their roles. In the first situation the behaviour of the teachers and the principal seemed to be genuine, or authentic, and the characters were three-dimensional. In the second situation the behaviour of the group members seemed to be thin, two-dimensional, and stereotyped; we were reminded of papier-mâché characters acting out their roles in a puppet show. Something in the first situation made it possible for the characters to behave authentically – that is, 'for real', or genuinely. The professional roles of individuals remained secondary to what the individuals, themselves, were as human beings. Within this climate there was enough latitude in the specification of roles to allow the role-incumbents to experiment with their roles – to work out ways of bringing their own individual style to their job and to their relations with confrères. In the language of the French existentialists, the incumbents were given the chance to *invent* themselves. Within the opposite climate the roles seemed to be overspecified. The individual appeared to use his professional role as a protective cloak, almost as if the cloak might serve to hide his inner emptiness and his lack of personal identity. (One gets the impression that these people are living their lives inside cellophane wrappers.) The role itself and the individual's status as a teacher or a principal appeared to constitute his essential sense of identity. Furthermore, in these instances the individual used his role ritualistically, so that it became a device which kept others at a distance and thus precluded the establishment of authentic relationships.
>
> These observations fitted neatly with the climate data, for the Open Climate appeared to reflect authentic behaviour, whereas the Closed Climate reflected inauthentic behaviour.

Perhaps the remarks here bear some relationship to Vivienne Apple's comment, 'that something extra that good teachers have'? In my paper on excellence I listed these factors which I now relate to authentic climates:

1   Seeing students as they really are demonstrating themselves to be.
2   Being interested in students as they represent themselves to be.
3   Having a personal 'something', a philosophy, a belief a creed, whatever you call it, to stand for, from within yourself or derived from the establishment you relate with.

[5] Andrew W. Halpen, *Theory and Research in Administration*, Macmillan, 1966.

4   Defining tasks in a realistic manner and setting about their accom-
    plishment from within the realities of the situation: working condi-
    tions, pupil attitudes, time, numbers, standards and forms of
    achievement demanded by the task.
5   Open-ness to others' ideas, ways of working, possibilities for
    improvement, change, re-orientation and preparedness therefore
    to take *considered* risks.
6   Sharing of informational strategies and knowledge, trusting
    people's capacity to grow in response.[6]
7   Realization and recognition[7] that because one *feels* to be acting with
    authenticity, it does not mean that others perceive it as such
    whether they are participating or observing. Any teacher who has
    taught in front of others knows this one!

In his paper, Halpen lists the following as some of the hallmarks of
authentic behaviour. The authentic leader in his view:

1   Accurately diagnoses the realities of any situation in which the
    leader is involved.
2   Uses this to find appropriate leadership patterns.
3   Recognizes that everyone sees reality through their own set of glasses.
4   Possesses self-awareness plus recognition of the awareness of
    others.
5   Values the worth of the organization and its goals but is not blind
    to its faults.
6   Is not involved with personal status, but is more intent on task
    accomplishment, and is
7   Ready to risk change.

He also quotes Argyris on reality centred leadership:

> Effective leadership depends upon a multitude of conditions. There is no
> one predetermined, correct way to behave as a leader. The choice of
> leadership pattern should be based upon an accurate diagnosis of the reality
> of the situation in which the leader is imbedded. If one must have a title for

[6] Interesting how much Doris Lessing is able to say indirectly upon this capacity in her
*Canopus in Argos: Archives* series, where she is able to *induct* our understanding of it
because of the novel form, so that we are able to perceive (through art again you see
because of the liberties which she can take with time to reveal future results of events)
the products of such trusting. Even if we may regret that a novel's results may not be
achieved in the actual world we at least can see a model and take time to stretch our
minds upon the idea. In that way the artist may presage the future!
[7] These 're' words fascinate me. If we hyphenate the 're' bit they seem so much more
important and open to deeper consideration. Re-constitute, re-cognize, re-call, remember, re-search.

effective leadership, it might be called *reality-centered leadership*. Reality-centered leadership is not a predetermined set of 'best ways to influence people'. The only predisposition that is prescribed is that the leader ought to first diagnose what is reality and then to use the appropriate leadership pattern. In making his diagnosis, he must keep in mind that all individuals see reality through their own set of coloured glasses. The reality he sees may not be the reality seen by others in their own private world. Reality diagnosis, therefore, requires self-awareness and the awareness of others. This leads us back again to the properties of personality. A reality-oriented leader must also keep in mind the worth of the organization. *No one can make a realistic appraisal if for some reason he weighs one factor in the situation as always being of minimal importance.*

## Drama's impact for society

All my teaching life I've been bothered by two things which I think relate to this matter of authenticity. First, while being labelled as a 'teacher of drama' and functioning as such overtly, it has irritated me that people have perceived the work as related only with play, fiction and pretence. Not that it isn't related with these: but that it has so much more potential for society. Second, that so many people have seen it as either a separate subject in schooling situations or as a rather 'special' affair. This has led me latterly *apparently* to neglect the art forms of such activity, and to discuss it in relation to other forms of *productive depiction and distortion* such as diagram maps, sketches, photographs and so on. I stress apparently, because I've always been careful to stress the laws of the form as being seminal to its meaningful use in class. There can be no useful impact on society if those laws are ignored or not understood. That they are not understood by a large number of teachers is beyond question and it is time we tackled this problem. This becomes more urgent every day. But we are bedevilled by polarization of opinion instead of humility in examining an art far bigger and more ancient than any of us.

The power available to society through authentic experiences in school has been touched upon in my paper 'Signs and portents' (see pp. 160–9) so I won't reiterate that here, suffice it to say again only that theatre law and society are akin except for one aspect which radically differentiates them. This is the depictive aspect: in art we reflect upon nature, people's affairs, ideas and behaviour. What a force for a nation, apparently to stand aside, but in reality take an inward look at events!

It's interesting to think that the 'antiseptic' and often sterile, behaviour demonstrated in school (tasks, languages and interactions) can be authenticated by another apparently unreal mode of communication in order to make school and society come into some form of power for good influence.

## Schooling as prevention

It can't be said to be so at present, for, putting it at its worst, most schooling keeps children from under the feet of most adults for six or seven hours every day, and it prevents them (those who conform at any rate) from having much opportunity to ask awkward questions about society, morality, values, purposes and laws. It makes certain that the tasks accomplished in the main inside the establishment, can't seriously affect what goes on outside, in society. So long as the study is under-taken as 'exercise for' and not 'practice of', with the debilitating emphasis upon the assumption that 'one day you'll be good enough to really do it', there's not really much danger of the young's interference. We stress pupil incapacity, hesitation and error rather than personality, exploration, process of recovery from error, and input to society. And yet, the amazing and irrefutable factor of all this is the numbers of would-be authentic teachers there are still around – teachers who immediately understand what Derek Stevens is trying to do, and who struggle daily to create conditions in which pupils can be honoured and respected as people and personalities rather than be patronized. These teachers often work all day with their groups of thirty or more in barren rooms, designed by architects who frequently work in lovely airy offices or renovated Georgian Houses. I know cost and education allowances come into this but it doesn't say much for a society which provides for the induction of its young some of the appalling buildings many pupils have to learn in. Many teachers care passionately about their subjects – literature, languages, music, science, needlework, geography, art; but unless they have 'stumbled upon authenticity' sufficient for their needs, they are unable to take their pupils into their subjects through the doorways of attraction – attention, interest, involvement, concern – to investment and, hopefully, productive obsession which thoroughly engages them for a period of time, sometimes for life. Such teachers carry a terrible burden of ineptitude, fear and heavy spirit, and that's no help with youngsters. We need mentally strong and wholesome people to work alongside our future adults.

I've always been uncomfortable pushing art rather than, say, science, as if one were more or less imaginative or in need of brain power, than the other. I'm obsessed with all the marvellous knowledge collected through our time on earth, whether it be in art, objects, ideas or skills and I also believe that the 'big' people use the same qualities of imaging and crystallizing into suitable forms, whether they be called artist or scientist, doctor or writer. Likewise, I believe all persons as social human beings require the same skills, though they may use them with different powers and for different reasons, and in different circum-stances. We seem to have progressed better in study skills related to

178

object knowledge than to experience knowledge, which often is the basis of our developing world view.

## What can a teacher do?

It's all very well you may say to write all these things. These points have been acknowledged for years. But what can a teacher *do* about it actually to get things changed? Well, let's begin with a private individual who is also a teacher, with a teacher's individual tasks to accomplish, and work on from there.

The first question obviously has to be, 'Do I want to be an authentic teacher?' If the answer to that is 'Yes', it's possible to see what then is required. It will mean devising more systems of approaching work and tasks than transmission and direct approaches. Learning to present problems differently to students; discovering more subtle forms of induction and communication; encouraging student interaction and decision making processes; giving more lee-way to students to discover other ways of tackling situations; imagining and carrying into action a greater variety of tasks; engineering a greater variety of feed-back techniques; taking more risks with materials; tolerating more ambiguity in classroom set-ups because people may choose a variety of speeds and systems to work at the same tasks. It means apportioning time differently, not necessarily slicing minutes in an orderly chronological sequence. It means, when it's all put together, and I haven't mentioned the half of it, constant attention to detail. William Blake said a marvellously apt thing for teachers in relation to a disappointing visit he had made to an acquaintance who had pressed him to stay for a few days. He said 'If you would do good to anyone you must do it in minute particulars'. And that goes for authentic teaching behaviours too. It means facing the basic fact that in devising fruitful encounters between self, pupils, ideas, knowledge and skills we have to become process-orientated. Process-orientation means devising programmes and tasks which induct through first intriguing, then engaging and interesting our pupils.

A lot of such strategies exist, and are in use in school and university classrooms, but they don't get communicated around enough. We still believe that mythology which Vivienne Apple referred to in her letter to *The Guardian*, of 'that something extra that good teachers have', and in that way we perpetuate the notion that teaching skills are related to personality. I don't believe this. I believe that style and personality need to find a fit, but beneath style can be a sharply honed range of skills which can be separated from the individual way of carrying out ideas, without being lost internally in the teaching situation. For example, any teacher knows that different experiences will happen to a class when

179

consensus is being sought among the group, and when differences in approach are being explored. The personal style a teacher uses will not interfere with the basic premise and internal structure. In fact, the more we could honour in our training programmes the *need* for personality, plus the need for internal structure, the more quickly we might get authentic relationships in learning situations. Those teachers with 'that something extra' could teach or be helped to analyse what they are doing when they're in action. The inspectors, the tutors could start putting the news around in practical ways. We could teach each other Blake's 'minute particulars'.

## Meeting the pupil's needs

A basic aspect for consideration, and one in which drama approaches can assist, is that of the ways in which teachers learn to create focus and significance, so that the *needs* of pupils are harnessed (not over-indulged or repressed) in order that the interest in externals – object-interest – (surely by this stage in human development, object-interest has become instinctive also?) can be fostered. The school curriculum is devised on the assumption that children (especially in the upper age-range) are ready for, and equipped to deal with, object-interest. Yet pupil behaviour in school often, and most uncomfortably, demonstrates that their need-interests are not being satisfactorily met, so that object-interest can begin. The great range of interactive tasks which a drama approach – or indeed any real laboratory atmosphere – can provoke, can make a match between the need-interests and the way object-interest can be developed. The 'good' pupil in our classrooms is either one who can subdue his or her need-interest in the presence of the object-interest put forward by the teacher, or one who has already enough need-interest satisfaction. The 'difficult' pupil is the one who insists upon, or who cannot help, demonstrating need-interests in class. And the same may be said to adults. There are many need-interest orientated teachers around in schools and higher education, and some days I belong to those ranks! The more helpless we feel, the more our need-interests surface.

I am not suggesting here that only the arts marry need-interest with developing object-interest. It is not the subject area, it is the laboratory atmosphere, the reality structure of the tasks, and the degree of value to be placed by the person in carrying out the tasks involved in the subject/object-interest area which brings need- and object-interest into balance. That, and the opportunity for a sense of worth and responsibility in the participant's work. The productive tension which real laboratory-style teaching engenders can be seen in *some* classrooms in most schools. The art rooms sometimes, the science labs, the engineering and cookery workshops. The very real objects generate concern for outcomes. But for those rooms in which ideas are the tools, we need better teachers who can create meaningful tasks around less powerful or outwardly appealing subject-matter, often subject-matter which needs certain developed skills to penetrate. This is where drama may make a large contribution, because under the cover of the 'simulated' situation, object-interest can grow out of need-interest being to some extent satisfied by the outer activity levels of the work. But the present barren halls and empty spaces which are often employed for drama study – here teachers are their own worst enemies often – are not suitable. To make a laboratory atmosphere out of barren open-ness or worse, a junk room full of dirty cast-off objects, needs teachers of brilliance and enormous energy.

My heart bled recently when teachers in my own course were teaching by invitation in a high school, and on one afternoon three such spaces were provided. I myself am often confronted with such ridiculous resources, deprived of all image-making materials such as blackboards, paper, reference books and pictures. It goes back a long way of course, to the notion that children will be as committed as actors to 'being stared at', and this has been thoughtlessly taught in colleges by tutors who have become out of touch with either the real art laws or the changing generations of children in a fast changing social scene. I am not without blame in this in that I cannot say that I have ever carried the 'drama teacher's load' of short lesson periods, often removed from the body of the school for long periods of time. This is why people like me must keep on engaging with need-interest-dominated classes in order to be of authentic use in training.

## Pupils' awareness of authenticity

One factor brings me a lot of comfort and faith that what I am saying about laboratory teaching could happen, and that is the recognition children have of authentic teachers, and their generosity in forgiving unauthentic teaching times. When I work with a class using authentic approaches in a climate of unauthenticity, I am often confronted by two responses which are embedded in each other. These two aspects of pupil response have to be dealt with immediately, and cannot be shelved or ignored, because either evasion technique condones and reinforces the children's behaviour.

The first response is that the class tries to make me behave unauthentically by provoking the authority stance of using teacher-power and coerce my tasks into action. The second is that beady-eyed, rat-like spectatorship which classes can demonstrate so well. I refer to the deliberately revealed double signal which presents a bland face of

181

innocent conformity to the teacher whilst making certain that the privately shared sign intended for peers is also seen by me. I have then to choose to ignore it, in which case I have been manipulated to behave unauthentically, or to respond with teacher-power to coerce or threaten. If I do either of these things I will have proven that 'I'm like all the others'. The wonderful thing is though, that when young people get through this relationship problem, and I'm not suggesting that it's easy, for I have to be at my most subtle and face it with more courage than I need at other times, they are so generous in the ways in which they will respond. It's sometimes like a miracle and I'm sure it is to do with their own understanding, which at that stage is probably instinctive, that I am using need-orientation to breed object-interest in the work.


## Helping yourself to authenticity

So, let's suppose you decide you want to be an authentic teacher. What can you do to start helping yourself? Let's take four things for a start.

*What do you stand for?* You can easily clarify this by taking note of what you find yourself teaching, no matter what the lesson looks to be about because the inner structure of the work is related with your need-interests, which in teachers has to be controlled and made usable (not suppressed, that way madness lies), so that the interests and needs of the class and the subject can be activated. Now my inner need-interests go something like this. I'm only naming a few because we only need examples here. Your own list is more important than mine. I find I need to stress form in everything. I'm obsessed with it – pattern, shapes, colour, line and design. So I'm always finding a reason to satisfy that interest and draw children's attention to it. Not overtly, I'm too clever for that. But inductively in the way I use tasks to create interest in form. I also stress the relationship of past, present and future in any given moment. I stress symbols, implications and language, that is not only word but gesture and space. The dark side in teaching, of all these is my need, the light side my object-interest. The object-interest in teaching is first the pupil. Understanding and naming need-interest then, can assist you to use it as relevant to the children's needs, and the needs of the subject you want them to get interested in. If we look at what I've just said above, it would appear that the teachers most able to be 'creative' and interesting teachers would be those in the high schools able to teach the subjects they love. And conversely, the hardest teaching would be that of primary school teachers who have to have object-interest in many areas of the curriculum. Paradoxically, we often find the enthusiastic teachers working with the younger age range, but there are other factors at work, there which are not the subject of this paper. Knowing what you stand for then, is the first step towards personal authenticity.

*When you look at your class what do you actually take note of first?* Energy? Features of clothing or physique? Mannerisms? Spatial behaviour or interactions? And when you take note do you place them against some judgemental line bred of your expectations? How do you accommodate when you are uncomfortable with what you see? Unauthentic behaviours make us want it our way now. Authentic behaviour presupposes in the teacher two skills, first to withhold judging, and second, still to get a task started which employs what is perceived by the teacher about the class. I think those skills can be taught.

*What does your working environment have to contain, or lack, for you to find it productive to work in, alongside your class?* And can you compensate from within yourself through methods of accommodating, for example, realizing that the class may not share your views and it may be right for their needs? How much variety can you find in the reorganization potential of the environment?

*How many kinds of power must you hold on to, and which can you give away?* This is not being self-centred, it is more centring in self so that you can be wholesome to be with, understanding the needs of yourself and the needs of the work and the class. This enables you to structure assurance and stability for pupils so that you are free to be as authentically responsible for mutually 'stretching' outcomes as possible. It permits realistic risk-taking.

## Teachers in groups and authentic behaviour decisions

So far, we've been considering the individual in his or her own teaching space with reference to personal drives, perception of pupils, space and working conditions and control of communication and interaction, so let's move on to teachers in groups and authentic behaviour decisions. One of the disturbing things about a look at oneself is the way it makes one perceptive about others' behaviour and it sometimes works destructively, as we all know. We may notice many aspects of unauthentic practice before we can label the examples of authentic action. We might more readily notice the way the art in the corridors is teacher dominated, or the empty conversations we overheard. Phrases like: 'That's nice dear', or 'What a clever girl/boy you are', or just 'OK put it on my desk'. We will notice the stereotyped dismissal phrases where pupil and teacher both acknowledge that it is the teacher's right to terminate any encounter, 'Right then, you run along'. It's so easy and dangerous to spot all the failures and so hard to take up the successes in personal encounters because it looks as if we are commenting on people's private affairs. But these encounters *are* the breeders of the climate of unauthentic and authentic behaviours. It is hard somehow to accost a teaching colleague with statements like: 'I did admire the way you up-graded that child's contribution in assembly to-day', or 'You are so clear to understand when you explain things to your class', and even 'You seem very tactful when you mention the coffee-fund is getting low, and people seem to respond by paying up quickly'.

We can help each other in groups by overcoming this natural reluctance to name and specify productive task-orientated and organizational based behaviour. Society functions on this. Perhaps, if the natural reluctance of head-teachers to start stressing productive establishment behaviour prevents it, individual teachers will have to start moving? Or maybe courses for heads and teachers could help it start. In one school in Cumbria they have made a beginning with staff seminars led by their counsellor colleague.

## Working with parents

Many teachers are also parents, so if they can be authentic parents they might be authentic teachers. Can authentic parents get together with authentic teachers? Recently, I had the privilege in a Newcastle Junior school of using materials which children of eight years old had worked on in the role of sociologists examining child-rearing practices in an invented tribe of sea-faring people 'somewhere in the world'. The parents came in the evening to carry on with the work their children had started earlier in the week, so they of course faced the same problems as their young children. One parent said she was realizing because of it, that she never really talked *with* her son. She tended to interrogate and tell. When others joined us I was really impressed by the ability of those present to be self-examining, and to use one process and task-orientated situation to refer to another one, their real child-rearing practice.

Likewise, once in the USA a pediatric doctor told me how much his and his wife's family and medical work situations were changed by helping me with a class of very obstructive and socially damaged nineteen-year-old boys in a special school.

We do not have to be afraid of associating with parents in the mutually responsible task of teaching children and 'growing' adults. Once perhaps they did seem to be mutually exclusive – when those who could read took over the teaching of the young, for example. In some parts of the world, England included, that is still true, but society cannot afford to neglect the mutuality of interests. We can make a start by using what parents have to offer to the school. An authentic society finds ways to do this when it wants to.

Take, for example, school dinners since the cuts in expenditure to authorities. A neighbour of mine made terrible sacrifices throughout the high school period of her three children. She could not afford school lunches. But could she send her children with an economical sandwich? Of course she could not. Surprising how that situation is suddenly changed – too late for one parent, however. I know the reader will recall that 'they could have had free dinners'. Of course they could if we ignore the authentic pride in this case, which was appalled every term as she claimed for free dinners. The 'terrible sacrifice' of the lady in question has nothing to do with the financial costs, it is to do with the inner conviction of her upbringing that you feed your own children from your resources. That need was ignored by object-need forces and she was not consulted by the school in the area of authenticity. So I'm saying we need to look for authentic mutual help. We're all familiar with the 'daddy coming in to help with the electrics' example, and I value those, of course. But some of the best kinds of help I've received has been when parents can come along to work alongside me in the process of teaching.

Drama is particularly useful here because of the way it can employ adults in role. The role-work often permits parents to feel part of the situation but at the same time to perceive the realities of teaching second by second, and the areas of arousal of interest and concern the teacher is engaged in at that time. One recent example of this was when a high school class doing computer studies became interested – because of their teacher's need-interest – with the problems of privacy of the individual and the record keeping systems employed, for example by business, the police and banks. The two parents concerned were in role – that is, they behaved as the ordinary citizens they are – but within a specific social circumstance. They were parents searching for a missing relative, so all the student tasks with regard to the computer potential to assist, and their skill potential which was being used in action *now*, related to their need of actual bodies to find their son.

Any parent can identify with that. They don't have to engage with the emotional behaviours – they don't have to portray anguish, pain, or loss. But they can make it necessary to be assisted. And they can sit there awaiting results of the student's work. And their responses can be those of any one who came to a source for immediate search. So the skills in the use of computers, feeding, reading and collating which had been approached in theory and some practical use of computers, was, in the now-imminent mode, provided for by drama, enabling dead knowledge to be activated in practice. But more than that I think what became

185

possible was that the world of information, skills, knowledge (the object-interest) was melded for a time with the need-interest of humanity. The parents saw something of the problems of creating authentic tasks and responsibilities which teachers face, but they also shared with another generation a common need-problem, in circumstances of truthfulness, to the benefit of both generations, and that of the school in its tasks. I don't think parents can make this move easily for it smacks of interference but teachers do have the power to invite help.

## Bringing schools and society together

It needs overtly stating however (and can we find some 'establishment' lead here?), that now our society is recognizing that schools and cultures need to get together more. And that it is *urgent*. How much longer have young people, even the academic ones, to go on 'getting fed up with school'? Three of the most eminent and authentic teachers I know in higher education were expelled for their own authentic behaviour in school. They got back in their day because the doors to learning were more flexible then. I myself am an example of this. But the doors of academia are becoming more and more tightly shut. Rigidity is dangerous, especially so at this time. One of the tools against rigidity is authenticity.

It is not only the academic aspects of culture which are getting more tightly shut but the other skill groups are becoming more difficult to join because they often insist on the wrong qualifying processes which are, when you get right down to it, irrelevant to the skills which will really be needed. I am not discussing here the skills of reading, numeracy and writing – the lubricant of society – but the skills which the practical life requires so that complex new structures, tools and functional objects can be maintained. The second-class citizen of the future – though God help us if we continue these feudal ideas much longer – is likely to be the theorist who cannot practise and the thinker of high contemplative skill, both will be unemployable. This is not just likely to happen. It is already happening for we even now have doctors who are unemployed. That was unthinkable in my young days.

It is on record that a letter exists from a father to his son in the time of Ptolemy (I don't know which one), which cautions him to 'not become a maker of objects. Become a go-between'. I should say of course that at present the doctors are becoming unemployed not because they are not needed but because we have begun to price necessary skills out of the market. The reason for this is that we are basically an unauthentic society. We do not charge the price things cost to make – we invent a price relative to what we can cynically educate people to pay for things. The world is full of things which need doing – all kinds of interesting activities for the good of all. And we make it impossible for all to have their rightful opportunity to work. One of the forces in this is unauthentic schooling.

I mentioned earlier the parents who came into school to put human focus into computer studies, and I'm thinking of all the unemployed parents at present in the north-east of England who might help in schools, either by tutoring individuals in some skills, helping get the need-interests of children satisfied enough to get their object-interests flowing, being taught by the children, making things alongside their children and studying beside them and sharing in problem solving. I can't see that it's dangerous, but of course it needs to be subtle and authentic. If we just invent little jobs for parents as well as for the children, we'll be in an even worse position. Local teachers could create local associations with parents on matters of local concern. I know it means dealing with matters of insurance, timetables and general open-ness for it to happen. Some teachers won't want it to happen because it means too much change, and we may after all be a peculiar psychological breed who are best working as the only adult in the room. Well, if that is the case, and it's something I examine in myself regularly, we may have to start pockets of quite different teacher-functionaries. There's plenty of room for manoeuvre.

In addition to harnessing parent power, there's also all the student power which could be utilized. Pupils writing works which are useful for others. As I write this article in Cyprus seventy primary teachers are going to create a history archive for slow learning children to work on Cypriot seventeenth-century life. I'm doing this sort of work with teachers because we are examining mixed-ability teaching of difficult historical concepts, but there is no reason why a high school class studying these concepts could not make the preparation of such archives and help other children to employ them, either as reading skill material (reading *into* things), as historical material, or as problem solving material – ('What would you have done to help the 100 young prisoners if you had been there with some power to operate?') This way we can occasionally make an attempt to get rid of the 'dummy runs' of school learning. You can see why the first question we must ask ourselves is whether we want to be an authentic teacher. It means an awful lot of change, but it can be started in localized ways, not small – nothing like this is small – but cautiously based upon *will*, not doubt. We can't begin with huge legislation nor large signs upon head-teachers' doors exhorting us to '*be authentic*'. Andre Gide has observed that no man can be sincere at the same time that he is explaining to us how sincere he is being, and likewise the same is true of authenticity. Authenticity is practice informing theory.

## Building an authentic climate

If the idea of individual teachers agreeing with colleagues what they need for an authentic climate in which authentic behaviours can occur, then leads to more shared teaching, more links and associations in class with colleagues, using parents and joint consultations with the community, including students and young school leavers, it must 'start a shift' around the local area. It won't touch everybody at once and there are bound to be those who prefer to work from doubt rather than change, but it could make a start.

I was impressed recently to read a letter in *The Times* from a retired gentleman in which he outlined what his generation were doing in their locality. They were exploiting for positive good their 'right to be nosey', as retired persons. Often they had taken it upon themselves to speak to every stranger they saw, from their windows, or when out in gardens and walking their dogs or themselves. One of the results in their immediate vicinity is that no robberies, in an area of vulnerability, have taken place from the time they worked out their system. We are all familiar with the cry from social workers after the tragic death of some vulnerable person to pay attention to our neighbours.

One problem is of course that it takes will and energy and often has to reverse a trend which is long established. I myself was taught not to be nosey, so as a teacher of some age now, can I reverse that when I retire? Have I the energy and will to start a new 'career'? If selective noseyness might be a useful tool for society then it has to be inducted before society as a whole can appreciate it and that means teachers initiating now with parents. Doubters will immediately rush to remind me of all the dangers of this. And somehow doubt is always more convincing than hopeful caution.

We've got photocopiers, overhead projectors, video machines and films and books and typing courses in some of our schools. All the children learning to type could be collating information, working as secretaries to groups. Making demands on themselves to improve their skills because of the public nature and responsibility of their work contribution. We have teachers' centres, schools and homes to meet in, as well as local community centres and church halls. Teachers who can think in this way can be 'lent' to groups, or seconded. Teachers and parents could share the information they pick up about experiments; people could share their ideas. Groups could research specific interest areas with the help of research students in higher education or primary schools! And these research efforts could use local expertise or be just happy chance discoveries where people have to learn how to do it by themselves. My daughter did a useful bit of local research over a year long, when she was ten, as part of a project, and I am grateful to her school for an authentic rigorous piece of trusting and the support which was given to her, to which her father and I made our contributions.

Then it might be possible for staffs to take a close supportive look (using children as well, because they are the clients after all) at the different styles of teachers and their inclinations as performers in the classroom. For example, I'm quite a useful group teacher because I'm comfortable and imaginative in devising ways of either getting class consensus when necessary for the study, or tolerating a fair amount of variety of levels and speeds and types of work all in process at the same time. Some teachers are better at small group teaching, others as private tutors. The same applies to children. At some stages of study we all need private tutors. Student and teaching and parent power should be able to supply all the various kinds of help and it needn't continue this division in style between school and home. Recently at the Friend's Centre in Brighton after a day's teaching of children and teachers, I was very impressed with the work which started right after, on a reading programme for the community members who for various reasons need reading instruction and support. And there must be a lot of this kind of activity around which never gets discussed. We urgently need to think more globally about education in our culture, then all the people can share the responsibility for the future.

The teaching force could do a serious study of the different styles of teachers available, so that all types can be usefully employed in any school or small community. 'Enabling' teachers don't like using strict instructional methods if they can avoid it. But good instructors are unhappy employed in 'enabling', especially if they have to pretend they are natural enablers. Teachers with no projection, even when they try, are not helpful to themselves or the class if the numbers are too great. We need all kinds of teachers who can be authentic, because they don't do the damage which inauthentic teachers do. I don't think one is a 'failed teacher' because one can't handle the statutory size of classes. Local authority inspectors and head-teachers might do a good supportive service in helping staffs take a close look at their social skills in regard to style and group size. Vivienne Apple is probably not a failed teacher at all, and she needn't have been lost to our schooling system because of the experience she had in teaching.

I really think too that pupils can assist in this close look at teachers and styles. They have a sense of honesty about the teaching they experience, especially when they are given responsibility for their opinion. One of my ex-students, working in Washington DC with high school 'low achievers' taken from their classes for special studies in the basic subjects to work with her, gained their support by collaring all the school video equipment (it wasn't being used much at the time, but it is now) and planning projects with groups which made them responsible

189

for further outcomes. One of the questions discussed was 'why we fall a bit behind in lessons' and some of the videos were made upon the basis of different teaching styles. It needed tact to enable the students to learn to enter classrooms, and it needed trust and generosity on the part of some teachers. It also needed careful consideration from the children about good, bad, hopeful, productive teaching methods, so they had to be very discriminating and most careful of the 'poor' teachers when they convened meetings with individual staff members to discuss the lessons they had put on video. It was hard work, and some teachers wanted it stopped, but it had very helpful effects in practice both for some children and some teachers.

If pupils can use their capability to recognize authentic behaviour in teachers, and themselves, it seems to me that they can begin to discuss this matter of need-interest and object-interest for the good of all, because we need student energy in school. Often when I'm teaching a high school class, sometimes one showing difficult behaviour, I'm always interested that someone from the class will approach me and start talking about 'What's different about this, Miss?' and my heart lifts. This begins a process of real pleasure in learning and teaching together.

## Teaching for the future

When I consider the new examination system we may be getting, the cynic in me wonders if we are just once again going to paint the shop instead of examining and improving the goods. I heard the minister talking about the 'different levels' which will be available, but nothing said about the minute particulars of teacher skills and detailed pupil, teacher, society, interaction and responsibility. We can't take it for granted any more. There isn't an alchemy of teaching, there is a craft which in some people works like an art, but we can raise the numbers of high level achievers both in teaching and learning if we set our minds to it.

Vivienne Apple wrote that 'No amount of lessons in *discipline* [my emphasis] in college would have helped me with my problem (which is no doubt why they laughed when I mentioned it), for the problem was me'. This to me, typifies the way in which our profession is either unable or unwilling to share and name and specify skills of social action, practical knowledge–getting and social science. Most of the high level teaching skills are based on common sense – by that I mean the inner understanding we all have about 'what is going on here'. For example, we know that part of the problem of 'discipline' is that the students often have no context in which the work they do has any purpose other than some vague future possibility. But the future is *now* for people with need-interest dominated behaviour.

Also, long-term future goals as industrialized and social science people are telling us, may have to give way to more flexibility. I wonder if Norman Tebbit was misreported a little when he said 'Get on your bike'. It offends our sensibilities not because it's a stupid remark, but because at this time many of those who need work have not themselves had the chance to develop the attitudes to do that. Society shift and pressure is running ahead of behaviour patterns. People in the future will get on their bikes, when there's been time to turn around maybe, but not people of my generation, who have been taught to 'stick with it, and you'll get your reward'. I have to remember not to think like that with my seventeen-year-old. In her lifetime who knows how many bikes she may ride? So what in the new examination system is going to be dealing with that, Mr Tebbit? If you'll help me name the problem, and support me in doing so, I'll try to tackle it.

## Unauthentic schooling

This brings me to a further point of authenticity for society. The dead knowledge which is still being taught. I did not say *deadly* knowledge. I mean the ways in which the collected and useful knowledge which expands the world for us as we understand it, is still being served up as if we'd only got books and writing to learn from, and teacher telling-talk. This makes school seem unauthentic as soon as children stop being given 'play' environments because the work of school – the learning-getting – seems to bear no relationship to the learning-getting systems operating outside. The child laws passed to save children from exploitation in mines, sweat shops, and up chimneys, have reaped a whirlwind which any adolescent recognizes, at least by instinct if not by cognition, that we have successfully also 'protected' our young from influencing society in any way which seems to matter. We have made them toys of society when small, and exploited them shamelessly as consumers when large. We have not permitted them to produce, however, or to assist in the fabric of culture-making. In spite of this of course they do, but not in ways which can assist the necessary cross-fertilizations of young and old.

The final insult to their energy is of course to remove the last initiatory ceremony into adult life – a place to work, and work to do which is recognized as a contribution. Yet the world is crying out for tasks to be undertaken: dirt cleared to make way for imaginative development; the lonely visited; the helpless to be given inventive technical aids as well as love; the handicapped used in society by clever patient tutoring; the waste recycled; the tender and rare preserved for all, and the problems of this transitional age tackled with fresh minds. If that new examination system will do any of this, I'm all for it.

191

## The danger of the status quo

Alvin Toffler has twice now gone into print in *Future Shock* and *The Third Wave* with clear (and hopeful) warnings about dangerously preserving the status quo and refusing to harness the energy of the young because of fear of what might happen. Mary Goldring, in her brilliant and frightening (for the West) series on Radio 4 as to why countries like Japan, Taiwan, Australia and the West Coast of the USA are likely to show signs of recovery first, discussed their capacity to move into a future as yet unshaped in detail, which makes their people able to embrace new ideas, as yet untested, and take on new perspectives. It is an attitude of mind, not a special dispensation of information they have, so presumably it is available to others – teachers included.

Doris Lessing also reiterates this in many forms in her *Canopus in Argos: Archives* series. So we have the skills of novelist, business reporter and social analyst all concurring. Marge Piercy in her utopian novel *Woman on the Edge of Time*[8] has given us a model we might put to the test in school. My own despair at not being able to find ways in the classroom to make work feel 'real for society in action' led me to develop the system of drama which I call the *mantle of the expert*. I can't think of a more 'normal' name which expresses the ideas behind it, namely that a person will wear the mantle of their responsibility so that all may see it and recognize it, and learn the skills which make it possible for them to be given the gift label 'expert'. It enables me to create context for school work. The gift of drama is that it makes micro-societies and micro-skills and micro-behaviour and endeavours available to the teacher. I needed a structure for authentic learning, even in an unauthentic establishment situation.

This kind of testing behaviour can be used to create dynamic learning and cross the boundaries of subject divisions when it is necessary to do so. I am not suggesting that drama teaches everything. Drama teaches people by demonstrating interactive social behaviour, and encouraging critical spectatorship, because art releases the spectator/action possibility in people. Art can isolate one factor from another, reveal something of infrastructure and give people a no-penalty testing zone, so that contemplation in flux is possible. So we have this paradox that art could be a vehicle for changing the work of school to make reality-useable outcomes. The image I have here is that of the cart horse which must overcome the inertia of the vehicle before it can move.

Ten years ago I prepared a short paper for my colleagues on the teaching we were doing. They were patient enough to glance at it. I

[8] Published in paperback by The Women's Press.

likened the formal education system to 'a great cart of war whereon all the spoils of a nation were collected'. Things piled up and tenuously held together whilst the oxen were rushing towards the deep river. We rush with it, fastening bundles on as they fall off, and we don't seem to be able to go to the front and say 'stop'. Maybe it was a bit radical then, but ten years later I'm even more worried for I think with Toffler that the escalation is upon us.

Teacher power seems very small when we consider the power of cash and more tangible energies, and teachers as a breed are probably more often viewed as those with long holidays and not much responsibility and 'nothing much to see for it at the end'. But the product at the end is society in action – thinking, knowing, living – and affecting single human beings engaged with their culture. The teacher should be part of recognized cultural power to influence. In a vain attempt to be seen as such, an examination system has been evolved, which seeks to evaluate the milestones of information which have been passed. But they do not examine the relevant factors for our age. It's no use teachers telling me that they would like to work in the 'mantle of the expert' way if the examination system gave them time to do so.

Take the example of my daughter who is engaged in Geography A-level studies at present. She's doing a good job with the help of concerned teachers in learning the vocabulary related to the areas of the world and their different physical features, which permits her to gain important concepts about the structure of the earth. They also have a computer in school, and can learn to use it if they are prepared to do so.

But my daughter's geography remains dead knowledge so long as it is not taken to today's need. She doesn't know, for example, that a man called Jagdish Kapur in New Delhi has turned ten unproductive acres into a world-renowned model solar farm with a bio-gas plant, so that he feeds his family and employees by means of processing their own waste and sells food at a profit in the market place. Nor does she know that Korea has developed 29,450 such plants; India has 12,000 with plans for 400,000; and that China plans 255,000.

Put these three things together: one, the internationally agreed knowledge of vocabulary and skill to know and name the physical geographical parts of the world; two, the computer which can feed information because it can scan for her all the now experiments, failed, successful, in process of developments, and all the papers on such projects available to all, via libraries, video and films; three, her mind, applied to new possibilities. Place these together and the examination could then be to produce a well-thought out project developed over a period of time related to any patch of land, for which she will have had to consult people outside the school, in addition to all the other

193

knowledge available through the usual channels. The piece of land may not be distant, though it could be so. There is a patch of green grass below our house at this very moment she could consider, and an interesting churchyard adjacent, to say nothing of many presently unproductive senior citizens' gardens on a near-by estate.

Surely such a project measures and stretches her as a citizen, a potential world member? How can we say it takes more time? Whose time? It's my daughter's time. What changes will the teachers have to accept? Well, first they will have to make available, not in dribs and drabs, a total geographical vocabulary and detailed advanced maps. Second, some experiences of authenticity, some of which will be academic, some visits to sites, some role-play, some video or film experiences, some meetings with citizens designed to raise issues about people and land-use, and in all these a central issue – the questions and the responsibility of the student – would have to be stressed. They must behave, think and discuss as geographical enquirers, not pupils. This means that they will need at an earlier time to have learned the skills of observation, questioning, note-taking, organizing information, perceiving relationships in apparently unrelated areas. A task for the primary school?

Third, time for the browsing syndrome[9] during which ideas can crystallize and form the choices of possible projects, from which one may be selected after consultation with staff. Perhaps the primary school could also induct the browsing syndrome?

Fourth, teachers could, during these consultations, enable their students to meet with the people in the community likely to assist best, depending on the area chosen for the research and development. This stage, that of finding the form, requires very high level negotiation skills on the part of the teacher, for their task is not to change or fix but to enable the student to penetrate the problem and seek for solutions by placing at their disposal any necessary tools and by providing support for trial and error.

Finally the student needs a willing, thoughtful audience for the presentation of the ideas, one who can seriously challenge (not knock down) assumptions and open the doors for further consideration. Such a project can then be seen by the examiners who would also have available the comments of the citizens who had participated in the first public demonstration. Doris Lessing has said something which is relevant here, again in *Canopus in Argos: Archives*, '. . . the moment any child was left excluded from a full and feeling participation in the

---

[9] I am indebted to a colleague, Roger Barnes, who introduced this name to me for an experience I have long valued, and helped me to understand its part in the genesis of knowledge in myself.

governance of its city, then she or he must become a threat and soon there would be decay, and then a pulling down and a destruction'. Placed as that passage is, when Ambien II is reflecting upon why, whenever a social and adaptation experiment is tried upon Shikasta things degenerate and go wrong, we can suddenly realize that she means *our* world, and there is that power of analogy again which the writer can call upon to bring things close.

So, suppose my daughter completes her A-level and wishes to go to university, what will she do there? She now has a vocabulary, a formulated project, and a presentation exercise behind her. Suppose that she then takes courses in:

1   tactful enquiry methods;
2   advanced connection making;
3   seeing all round a problem;
4   skilled questioning and negotiation;
5   civic law related to land;
6   careful observation of how people use space and territory;
7   precision in writing proposals;
8   technical drawing and presentation.

Could she after these, join an innovative project related to geography for a year *where help is needed*, finding it with the assistance of the computer? Finally, supposing she could then be 'allocated' a square mile of somewhere – inner city, desert, wild country, it doesn't matter what or who is there – could she be asked to draw together all she understands at present of human geography, technology related to geographical study, citizen power available in that small space, knowledge of its past, and make an assessment as to the possible likely useful developments which might occur? This last is a theory exercise to employ abilities of projection for good purposes. At present it happens in business and for army purposes, so I can't see that it is impossible for it to be used as an exercise in benign research. This task demands of students a very high level of ability to relate many sides of their natures to their geographical knowledge. My daughter's square mile of geographical site contains a shopping area, a mosque and a shifting population to which she will relate the practical issues of supply, demand, transport and people's needs in regard to spiritual health. Is this active citizen geography? What might her degree qualify her for? Will she have more to offer the work market?

## The enormous potential of teachers

In this paper I am suggesting that teacher power has enormous potential for these changing times, and I believe that one of the keys is

195

authenticity. It can make connections in a realistic way between the present work of schools which is based on entirely laudable skill and information areas, and society which is creating new models, systems of work and behaviour and new exciting technology for work and study. Between these energies, the school curriculum and change in society, stand a collection of individuals called teachers, who are freed in the main from 'hewing of wood and drawing of water'. What a privilege and awesome responsibility. They could function at present (and are often expected to under difficult circumstances in some of our schools already when there is a crisis to function) as a kind of stabilizing or holding energy, for they are the older generation dedicated to the younger generation being developed into citizens of power, use and value. Nothing says they must preserve the present systems of teaching and we have more to fear as a society if we hang on to the lumbering ox cart.

A teacher may ask where does my subject-interest and knowledge fit? I say that the stored proven knowledge is never out of date and gives a basis for other more up-to-date information to be added. The future battle is to make active users, developed, in some part, in this no-penalty zone we made, called schools. To create active users and knowledge-in-action, needs the go-between function the teachers already have. Any teacher reading this is capable of projecting their subject area and interest into community use. A teacher's kit needs a perception lens anyway if they are going to work with classes of children, and be responsible to society for their output. I'll try to outline now what kinds of contribution my area, drama, might make.

## The contribution of drama

*Dramatic work is first of all a social art.* In which the interaction of people comes under scrutiny in a specific encounter or matter of concern in which they are trapped. It spans all time, race, social strata, faiths, behaviours and feelings. Thus it is a mirror of society. As a teacher I can use it to create a reflective element which can assist the young people to perceive modes and forms of communication and inter-action and the effects on private individuals and in groups: people's humanity to each other. This includes the development of processes of communication, private and public language, listening skills, avoidance of polarization in social encounters, respect for the quality in language choices in such encounters, toleration of other's ways of doing things, and, because it is an art, application of critical thought to them. No two teachers need agree on the outward forms they choose to achieve any of these skills for youngsters, and they have plenty of devices they can select from and employ. Art is rich in offering a variety of ways to do something. Some teachers are better when they work through scripts, some better in non-verbal modes as a start, and some prefer simulation work or improvisational approaches. The outer form can vary providing it is used to induct inner revelations and reflections about the human condition.

*Drama is a detailed art.* It precisely examines at any moment the minute particulars of a situation, using sign as its basic component of expression. It therefore permits participants to perceive the complexity of communication during the actual processes of its occurring. It can therefore enable the learners to transfer this understanding to their living community. It trains them to notice first what signs are being used. Are those signs intended to inform, illuminate, obscure, engage the feelings, or merely have an effect in a social situation? Are they being helpful to society in their use? Baby food manufacturers at one time became very clever in using sign in their films for the Third World, ostensibly to suggest the values of breast-feeding whilst carefully undermining that in favour of made-up feeds. Even doctors taking part did not at first spot what they were supporting. All those nice white-coated sincere people being seen around the production of such foods and talking about them to the viewer. We are, because we now have television, already very efficiently teaching children to read signs in the real world, but the real world does not always yield to us the power to recognize and employ the skills it develops in us.

*Drama is a progressing art.* As opposed to the frozen time of the painting, the photograph or the drawing, drama activity demands that each action or sign produces a result – some change in understanding, each sign processes and births outcomes from the past, and creates the future in the present. It does this in a no-penalty zone of agreed depiction. By using this truthful artificial environment students can face up to emotional, affective 'people' responses before finally having to practise in society. So again we see the paradox of the artificiality of drama and its potential for real accountability in society. We can see this clearly in the work of the theatre where the ideas of playwrights are forged into action in the real conditions of audience presentation. The work I am discussing requires an extra dimension to be placed in it – that of knowing we are all engaged in the making of any encounter as well as the in-built scrutiny of it, in order to be responsible for its outcomes.

*Drama engages the affective zone.* It deliberately engages and explores emotional field forces. Resistances, moods, power ploys, submissions, denigrations, heroic acts, tremulous and bold ventures, daring and dangerous exploits as well as tender and delicate situations come under

197

examination by definition and restriction of circumstances so that they can be explored in detail. Schools at present function as if they have no mandate for affective learning, the deliberate engagement of what John Fines has called 'the celebration of the affairs of mankind' with the cognitive and analytical thought which is also necessary. Teachers have great freedom in selecting their methods and their materials. They can have a mandate to make learning interesting and useful. They do *not* have a mandate to teach without reflective processes and responsible outcomes. I feel ashamed of the antiseptic teaching I see where the object-interest is demanded without sensitivity to the demands it makes on the unready.

*Drama uses the person to bring it into being.* Conversely, the person is brought into possible new being by the same process. The child enters the zone of circumstance permitted by the drama situation, and in shaping the circumstance's future, the child's future is shaped, ready to be available in the real society which at present seems cut off from school.

## In conclusion

Because of the above five aspects it seems to me that drama is a seminal force in our particularly fearsome developing social process. Teachers who choose authenticity cannot afford to ignore its specific potentialities for good. They could, they can start now if they will so choose. I leave you with Alvin Toffler's statement, and one of Thomas Jefferson's, both of whom speak more eloquently than I and their messages span many years. Toffler in *The Third Wave* says:

> The responsibility for change therefore lies with us. We must begin with ourselves, teaching ourselves not to close our minds prematurely to the novel, the surprising, the seemingly radical. This means fighting off the idea-assassins who rush forward to kill any new suggestions on grounds of its impracticality while defending whatever now exists as practical, no matter how absurd, oppressive or unworkable it may really be. It means fighting for freedom of expression . . . if we begin now, we and our children can take part in the exciting reconstitution not merely of our obsolete political structures but of civilization itself. Like the generation of the revolutionary dead we have a destiny to create.

Thomas Jefferson said:

> Some men look at constitutions with sanctimonious reverence and deem them like the ark of the covenant too sacred to be touched. They ascribe to the men of a preceding age a wisdom more than human, and suppose what

they did to be beyond amendment . . . I am certainly not an advocate for frequent and untried changes . . . but I also know that laws and institutions must go hand in hand with the progress of the human mind . . . as new discoveries are made, new truths disclosed and manners and opinions change with the change of circumstances, institutions must advance also, and keep pace with the times.

I salute any endeavour, however small it feels, and each day when I enter a classroom of adults or children I seek to use my art of teaching and the art of drama in the service of a process for change.

# Appendix

Extract from a letter to The *Guardian* by Vivienne Apple in May 1983

. . . as an ex-teacher (failed), I would like to put the case for a much more rigorous selection procedure in order to weed out unsuitable candidates with good intentions – an asset insufficient these days to control classes.

I entered college in 1971 full of good intentions and enthusiasm, and with the experience of three sons of my own to practise on. But a class of 35 is entirely different. I had difficulty with discipline on all three of my teaching practices, but when I mentioned the idea of lectures – or even tips – on class control in college I was just laughed at.

I obtained a job on leaving college, at a junior school in a 'poor' area of Nottingham. I loved the kids, and at times when things were going well I enjoyed my job. But I became conscious of the fact that no amount of lessons in discipline in college would have helped me with my problem (which was no doubt why they laughed when I mentioned it) – for the problem was me.

Looking at those of my colleagues who were the best teachers, I saw that although they didn't seem to work any harder than I did at organization, lesson preparation, marking, and talking to the children, etc., they had something extra that I didn't have: a kind of 'aura' – to do with quiet authority, confidence, strength, or what you will. This quality is so difficult to define and isolate that I have no idea how it could be tested in an interview, but one thing I am sure of: until it is recognized as an essential qualification for would-be teachers, we shall always have problems with kids who delight in playing up and spoiling the chances of those who want to learn, and teachers going round the bend trying to cope with it all. – Yours sincerely, **Vivienne Apple**

# Part Five

# Resources and references

# Dorothy Heathcote's notes

## What is drama?

Drama is the selective expression of human interaction in which codes and patterns of behaviour may be examined because:

1 The area can be selected for review, in life it cannot, for we are busy living.
2 The theatre has developed over many years the different styles and modes which can be employed to do such reviews of people's dilemmas and problems.
3 The actual moment in time can be isolated, tried again, turned around, replayed with different solutions, because we can accept the conventions.

The theatre does this constantly, it shows life in action, how people fill the spaces between themselves and others – it can do what is the *reality* of life but *seems* to be the opportunity of art, *distort the view productively*.

It can uphold the moral code or challenge it with equal facility.

We can learn through theatre because we can bring our own experiences up against others in an identifying way. We can identify our experiences with those selected ones we are shown.

Using a process of identification can we employ the 'looking at life' for teaching?

Can it change behaviour patterns?

Can we learn identification? If so what and how?

Can it make us examine ourselves? Our own codes? Our own patterns of thinking and behaving?

Is it being tried in learning establishments? What has to be present to make it succeed?

1 That there is no moralizer present in the room, only the circumstances, you do not change morality by telling and exhorting.
2 The old jaded view must be given a new look of shocking proportions.
3 Somehow prejudice must be by-passed to let in new light upon old matter.

202

So these elements must come into play:

| | | |
|---|---|---|
| A | A problem must be seen in action | Must be interesting for the participants. Must seem to employ their prejudice – 'interest'. |
| B | The new element | Old familiar matter in new form to 'shock' into awareness. |
| C | Decisions must be called for | The active area of commitment to action and the solving of problems. |
| D | Employing experience productively not passively | Relevant previous experience comes into action. |
| E | Getting feedback – not to be ducked! | No escape from the immediate outcome and results of decisions. |
| F | Conscious examination of changes if any | A standing back from the action to review present conceptualization. |

## Drama in education

The word drama seems to explain one kind of activity – it looks as if it is about the reconstruction of life. In this form it is familiar to us on TV and in theatre and film. When we see it we can recognize human behaviour, sometimes like our own and sometimes shockingly different. We are usually outside this drama, so we are in a position to predict to a certain extent what is going to happen. To a certain extent we can enjoy the agonies, joys and pseudo agonies of those whose 'lives' we eavesdrop on. We can anticipate also and this is an important part of the pleasure.

So when a teacher says they teach drama we tend to think that we know what is going to happen. But actually using that blanket term isn't much use to us in school, because blanket words are not much use to a teacher. The elements of an activity have to be discovered first before teachers can put activity meaningfully to use.

What are the elements in drama which make it a possible learning tool?

*How does drama work?*
1  People have to work out the lives they are pretending to live in a together way.
    *So drama demands co-operation.*

203

2 People have to employ what they already know, about the life they are trying to live.
*So drama puts life experience to use.*
*So drama makes factual experience* (information) *come into active employment.*

3 People have to be able to live in two worlds at once and not get them mixed up.
*So drama uses fiction and fantasy but makes people more aware of reality.*

4 People have to agree to sustain a common understanding of what they are making together no matter how separately they may appear to be thinking. Footballers have to do this too – they don't end up all playing different games either!
*So drama stresses agreeing to all trying to sustain mutual support for each other while allowing people a chance to work differently – to bring personal ideas to the whole.*

5 People have to express thinking, feeling, actions to each other. If they don't then no one in the group knows what is going on.
*So drama makes people find precision in communication.*

6 Drama uses objects but often in a symbolic way. Chairs have to become thrones, but also these 'thrones' become the symbol of the king when he is absent.
*So drama stresses the use of reflection. Symbols become ordinary, but the ordinary also is seen to be symbolic.*

7 People have to interpret the actions of others but often in unfamiliar circumstances. You don't meet dragons every day; you don't have to be skilled goldsmiths; you don't have to battle with kings – or hospital matrons! You don't have to argue with warlocks; you don't face the rigours of great journeys nor cope with enemies who seek to take your life.
*So drama introduces you to living out crises in a testing kind of way. It tests your attitudes and your present capacities.*

*What use are all these to teachers?* The least usable part of the picture is the 'making plays up' bit. That is for making plays – all the rest are about training the skills of being a person in a community. To make this work for us in teaching demands new forms to be used in school. New outward forms that is, where the play is not seen but the inner demands can be made on the class. Some of these forms we have been experimenting with.

1 One class teaching another one by the ways they simulate events and stress a certain problem perhaps to avoid the confusion which occurs when all the information is given at once.

2 Using one person in role to meet the class – Julius Caesar, Florence

Nightingale, a tramp. Know your class's need and devise the role to meet it.

3 Setting up 'working as' rather than 'learning about' situations in other subject areas. (A group of infants who collected antiques might then run a museum service in the school – it *isn't* crazy and they *can* do it.)

## Types of drama

You can approach learning through drama in various ways. Each way makes a different journey, a different kind of demand on your planning and a different kind of demand on your class. Each way makes a different kind of learning happen.

1 *Roles*: where a person is the challenge.
2 *Mantle of the expert*: where the class is set upon a task in such a way that they function as experts.
3 *Analogy*: where one problem, a real one, is revealed by an exact parallel to it.
4 *Text*: where interpretation of someone else's work is the means of learning.
5 *Dance forms*: where emphasis on non-verbal signals, experiences, and explanations are the means of discovery.
6 *Simulation*: where a simulation of life is made.
7 *Games*: where the rules lead and control the play.

All these outer modes are 'respectable'. What makes them 'shabby' is the quality of the interior experience which is planned into them. Good 'interior form' can never have a 'wrong' external pattern.

*Roles*. When you use a role you gain:

A person for the class to respond to.
A life-style which comes into the room.
A holding-device which lures interest.
Something to inquire into, which acts as a focus.
A specific example of emotional/intelligent life and attitudes to challenge.
A pressure exactly where you want it.

But you must decide:

What that pressure is to be.

205

Exactly how the role will exert the pressure on the class.
Which symbolic objects will be essential to communicate the life-style.
Exactly what you want your class to experience through meeting the role.

You can't get away with 'shabby' planning ever! Using a role can:

Teach facts.
Challenge attitudes.
Pose questions.
Demand understanding.
Help you question yourself.
Modify class behaviour.
Make you want to read the book/play again.

*Mantle of the expert*

'Mantle' meaning: I declare that I will uphold the life-style and standards of my calling.

'Expert' meaning: 'Furthermore I will undertake to take seriously the acquisition and using of those skills deemed necessary in that life-style I have entered because of my calling.'

When you use this approach to drama you gain:

1   A commitment from the children to learn the information and skills they will need, for example an expert mariner must function within a framework of the sea, journeys, and the tools and skills of the seafarer. Because of the need for information it allows the teacher to use drama directly to run alongside and feed off the curriculum.
2   A discipline for the class which provides a framework in which the attitudes are contained without the teacher imposing rules and demands. For example, a mariner must obey the laws of the sea; a mariner must obey the pressure of the oceans' ways; a mariner must obey the social hierarchy within the vessel; a mariner must learn the trade.
3   A task orientated situation where the job in hand must be done first. So, doing the job, fulfilling the task is the vehicle which starts creative ideas flowing. Children employ what they know and no information will be fed to them first. Which means that:
Teachers can diagnose what children already know.
Teachers can feed information as it is seen to be needed by the class.
Teachers are forced to demonstrate that they can differentiate

206

between 'force-feeding' facts and creating the climate where fact, skill and understanding can grow together. Teachers who 'know it all' can't teach well through the 'mantle of the expert'. They can't wait for real learning to happen. They can't recognize real learning when they see it.

*Analogy*. You can't use this mode if you won't decide:

Exactly what you want to teach about.
What aspect of your theme or concept you want to parallel.
How to make the connection ultimately between the real situation you need to open up for consideration and the analogous one.
Exactly how to parallel the *inner form* and not the story line.

Every theme or concept is capable of having an exact parallel if you understand that it is this inner form which is important. Analogy is the best way of making something fresh and worthy of consideration when it has become too cliché-ridden, too familiar, too full of prejudice because of memory and past weariness. It provides a new face for old material.

*Dance forms*. This mode can be used when you decide your statements are complete without the need for words. You have to be prepared to interest yourself in:

Which concepts and ideas truly do not need words.
Which statements are clearer because the dance/movement form is employed.
The labour of clarity and precision in thought and act.

*Simulation*. Simulation means holding the mirror up to nature. You gain:

An exploration of interaction, and a chance to see the results of your action on other people.
An opportunity to work with feeling and thought simultaneously.
A chance to form your ideas into some kind of order.

The problems are:

Everyone can bring in any idea they fancy – this may make it difficult for the inexperienced teacher.

207

All these ideas have to be sorted out into working patterns.
You have to be able to make the rules of theatre work immediately.
You have to be able to win belief in the big lie, the Art Form, the agreement to pretend.

*Games*. Every lesson needs a spine – the central idea to suggest the task and the actions flowing from the task. In using games:

Rules help the teacher out of being the arbiter of behaviour.
Rules allow the teacher to be an equal player.
The task is clear to be seen.
The goals are clear to be seen.
The method of doing the task is clear.
Rewards and punishments are formalized.
Status – at any point – is related to task, chance, and rules, not to individual stature in the group.
There is an end product to be seen.

Games formalize life interaction processes and can allow a problem to be clearly seen so that: another look can be possible because the game allows us to side-step.
    Thus temporary relief from emotion and muddle can reveal the spine of the problem.
    Out of this insight comes energy and clearer purpose.
    Like Analogy, games work best when the central spine of the game exactly opens up the central spine of the real problem.

Whatever mode of drama you use, the first central part of each lesson is the *focus*. Out of the *focus* the task can be found and set. Out of the task arises all the potential learnings on which the teacher can focus for further tasks. The task provides opportunity for assessment of needs which brings modification of the task. The teacher must decide how to use the focus and the task in terms of:

Social learning
Factual learning
Reflective learning
Curriculum pressures.

The progress of the drama lesson can be described metaphorically:

The ship = the teacher plans how to make the focus work.

208

The tidal currents = the class behaviour, knowledge and understanding dictate the teacher's ongoing function during the lesson.
The voyage and discovery = these are made according to the way the teacher steers within the tidal currents.
The map = the map is not the plan, it is the outcome.

In every drama lesson there will be:

A general idea which will lead to the focus, out of which must be brought the *Reflection* and the *Universal*, without which there is no learning from the experience.

It must be remembered that:

It is not the doing – it is the considerations underlying the doing.
It is not the saying – it is the effect of the saying.
It is not merely telling people what you want them to learn, it is the experience arising out of the action which enables them to learn.

## Aims in drama

During any first session my aim is threefold:

1   I want the children to recognize that I am putting the onus upon them to have ideas, that I am prepared to accept their ideas and to use them and make them work. This decision-making, where children watch their own choices worked out in action, seems to me to be one of the important services which drama renders to education where we are trying to encourage children to think for themselves.
2   I want the children to work from the very beginning within a true drama context, that is not a vitiated art form watered down for them but the real thing with the real disciplines which drama requires, for example group problems jointly worked out in the present. All too often drama presents children with a story form with the emphasis upon events – whereas in fact drama reveals events through the feelings and attitudes of people. We would not ask children to paint with wrongly mixed pigments, the same applies to other art forms too, so I am, whilst accepting the ideas of the children, also 'mixing' them so that they are usable by the children.
3   It is important from the earliest time that all the children's needs are respected as far as possible, and therefore I must give those, apparently without confidence, the opportunity to hide and be reserved, and those who are too confident, the necessary challenges

to make them work more thoughtfully. Some children learn most at this stage by being 'onlookers', rather than 'ideas people', that is responders rather than initiators and I must respect this.

Finally, I regard the *effort made* to be of more importance to me as a teacher than the resulting drama, but at the same time the children are working for *their* result which may be great personal pleasure, or the satisfaction of their play needs, or many other things including the achievement of having made something happen.

## Questions I consider

1  What *precisely* do I want the dramatic input to do for me, the children and the learning area? It cannot be a *general* answer. It can usually be quite clearly named as a skill, for example 'to enable children to realize that old-seeming documents are often about the same matters modern people are concerned about' or 'to realize that things like books are *still* written slow and hard'.
2  Am I aware of how I use my *voice* in teaching? Can I feed information while apparently asking for it? For example, 'I'm looking for some marble but I'm not certain if the Carrara quarries will be best – have you any Carrara in? They say the green is very good, but I like the rose myself'.
3  There is *no need* to think *I* must know everything about the subject in hand before I start the work!
4  Have I clarified the simplest starting point? And have I considered the stages in building belief in the *authenticity of the work task?*
5  Have I divided the task suitably?
6  Have I thought carefully about how symbolic material will be used? For example, *charts* of plans, designs, maps etc. No work can *actually* be done, but it needs authentic record keeping, for example a herbalist needs reference material, diagrams of a garden, ways of *recording* measurement, receipts, recipes, drawings of shelves and jars – all the last five will be made as the work progresses – plus lists of ailments and charts of the body, etc.
7  People must be given the opportunity to work in small groups – because *talk* about the work is most essential for development. And groups need to cross-refer as the work continues.
8  Can I tolerate *not* giving direct instructions and answers before people have a chance *not to be told*!

# Films

### Building belief (colour, 60 minutes)

Dorothy Heathcote takes a class of ten and eleven year olds in America and explores with them the concept of the strength of a nation. They become a nation in its first struggling days in a hostile land. They choose characters for themselves and have to make decisions. By living the experiences directly, they come to know in a deeper way what the concept really means.

### Dorothy Heathcote talks to teachers

*Part 1 (colour, 30 minutes)*. A lecture about teaching drama. Dorothy Heathcote starts by comparing the formal lesson, where the teacher starts from where she or he is, filters the information and sets the pace, with the informal approach of starting where the children are, drawing out their own ideas. But in the case of drama this can be helped by practical considerations of sound, light and movement of people, or the lack of these (USA 1974.)

*Part 2 (colour, 30 minutes)*. Dorothy Heathcote talks about how a teacher finds material, how material can be used to expand the children's experience of life and be related to universal concepts. Questions are important and can be used in many ways but must never suggest that the teacher already knows the answers. 'Teaching is the art of receiving signals and controlling the signals back so that there is meaningful progression.' (USA 1974.)

### Seeds of a new life (colour, 55 minutes)

The film shows two weeks of drama therapy in a hospital for the mentally handicapped. The drama course is led by a group of twenty-two secondary school teachers working under the supervision of Dorothy Heathcote. At the core of Dorothy Heathcote's philosophy is her belief that the mentally handicapped have a right to emotional experiences as well as cognitive ones. The film raises the question of

211

the difference between drama as therapy and drama as education. Is it merely a matter of labels? Whatever we call it, the film demonstrates the success of drama with the mentally handicapped. (1976.)

## Three looms waiting (black and white, 50 minutes)

When Dorothy Heathcote decided to go into the theatre, the mill owner she had been working for paid her fees at the acting school, and told her there would be three looms waiting for her if she ever decided to go back. Watching her at work in Tyneside with a variety of young people from an approved school, a junior school and a hospital for the mentally handicapped, it is clear Dorothy Heathcote will never go back to those waiting looms. (BBC *Omnibus* programme.)

Available for sale or hire from Concord Films Council Ltd, 201 Felixstowe Road, Ipswich, Suffolk, IP3 9BJ. Tel: Ipswich (0473) 76012.

# Bibliography

Many interviews with Dorothy Heathcote, articles and speeches by her, and transcripts of her work have been published in drama and education journals throughout the world. The following articles and pamphlets are readily available in the UK.

'Drama as Education' in *New Destinations: The Arts and Education*, published by the Greater London Association for the Arts in association with the Cockpit, 1976.

'Heathcote at the National', NATD's 1st Annual lecture edited by Tony Goode, published by the National Association for the Teaching of Drama in association with the Kemble Press Ltd, Banbury, Oxon, 1982.

'In context' edited by Myra Barrs, published by the National Association for the Teaching of English, 1980.

'Drama in the Education of Teachers', published by the Institute of Education, University of Newcastle upon Tyne, n.d.

'Of These Seeds Becoming', chapter by Dorothy Heathcote in *Educational Drama for Today's Schools*, edited by R. Baird Schuman, The Scarecrow Press, 1978.

'Drama as Education: an argument for placing drama at the centre of the curriculum', by Gavin Bolton, Longman, 1984.

Books dealing with her work:

*Dorothy Heathcote: Drama as a Learning Medium*, B. J. Wagner, first published by the National Education Association of the United States, 1976; published in Great Britain by Hutchinson, 1979.

*The Drama of History*, John Fines and Raymond Verrier, published by New University Education, 1974.

*Exploring Theatre and Education*, edited by Ken Robinson, Heinemann, 1980.

213

*Towards a Theory of Drama in Education*, Gavin Bolton, Longman, 1979.

'The Work of Dorothy Heathcote', an article by John Fines and Raymond Verrier in the magazine *Young Drama*, February 1976, vol. 4, No. 1.

*Drama in Education*, prepared by Dorothy Heathcote's students, published by the Institute of Education, the University of Newcastle upon Tyne, 1967.

# Index

215